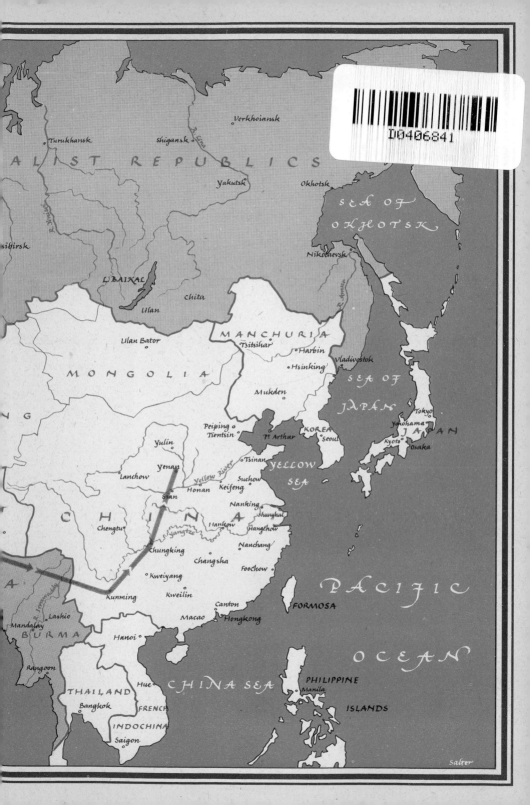

PEOPLE ON OUR SIDE

OTHER BOOKS BY EDGAR SNOW

The Battle for Asia

Red Star Over China

Far Eastern Front

Living China
(A COLLECTION OF
CHINESE SHORT STORIES)

PEOPLE ON OUR SIDE

by Edgar Snow

RANDOM HOUSE · NEW YORK

THIS IS A RANDOM HOUSE WARTIME BOOK
THE TEXT IS COMPLETE AND UNABRIDGED, BUT EVERY
EFFORT HAS BEEN MADE TO COMPLY WITH THE GOV-
ERNMENT'S REQUEST TO CONSERVE ESSENTIAL MATERIALS

Source material for maps, courtesy PM

*Published simultaneously in Canada by
Random House of Canada Limited*

PRINTED AND BOUND IN THE U. S. A. BY
KINGSPORT PRESS, INC., KINGSPORT, TENN.

TO LIEUTENANT-COLONEL EVANS FORDYCE CARLSON

So well thy words become thee

as thy wounds;

They smack of honour both . . . .

Contents

Maps and Illustrations

(Photographs in the Indian section by courtesy of D. G. Tendulkar, Bombay)

Book One

BROWN BONDAGE

IRAN

AFGHANISTAN
Kabul
Peshawar
Lahore
Kalat
Delhi
Jodhpur

Muscat
ARABIA

I N D I A

Benares

Bombay

Hyderabad

Goa

Madras
Mysore

ARABIAN

SEA

BAY OF

BENGAL

Colombo CEYLON

CHINA

Chungking

TIBET

Lhasa
Mt Everest

Darjeeling

MA ROAD
Kunming

Lashio
Mandalay

BURMA

Rangoon

THAILAND

Bang Kok

Sa

Calcutta

MALAY
STATES
Singapore

India

PART·I·JOURNEY AMONG INDIANS

I

Back to War

WHEN I came home to America in January, 1941, for the first time since leaving it in 1928, I had already seen about a dozen years of war, usually undeclared. I had traveled in Japan, the Philippines and the East Indies, but most of the time I had lived in China. I had covered rebellions in Indo-China and Burma and I had followed Mahatma Gandhi on his first great civil disobedience drive in India. I had reported the Manchurian incident and the Shanghai incident and I had been in Peking to watch Japan provoke the Lukouchiao incident which enlarged into the final ironic euphemism, the China "incident."

So I could scarcely remember a period in my years in the Far East when wars of some kind were not going on. Some of us out there saw a deep-going connection between all these acts of protest and aggression. We knew that Gandhi's spinning-wheel revolt was part of the same pattern inside which the Chinese savagely fought their civil war for a decade, and the Thakins rose in Burma, and the Japanese took Manchuria, and China finally united in resistance. They were all acts in a revolutionary upheaval which would eventually free Asia from feudalism and its institutions and overthrow imperialism. But of that more—quite a lot more—later.

It kept me fascinated for a rather serious decade of my life. I became a part of this history in a small way but enough to realize

3

in Washington, hard-working Wayne Coy, and as we were talking his telephone rang.

It turned out to concern me. I had hoped to see the President before leaving the capital, but I had not met him before and I had been wondering how to go about it. Now his secretary had located me at Wayne's, I never quite knew how, and in a few minutes I was on my way to the White House. When I got into the Oval Room and saw F.D.R. sitting there with a friendly grin I remembered what I had heard some Chinese far up in the interior say about "Lo Ssu-fu," as they call him. Suddenly there were many things I had wanted to tell him for a long time.

Forty minutes later I left the Commander-in-Chief with the conviction that he would, given the co-operation of Congress, lead us to victory and a wise peace. We had covered a lot of territory in that time and had even managed to settle the microcosmic dilemma of myself and the war. Outside, I felt a lot better about that job for the *Post*; it was worth doing. I went over to the War Department and signed on as a war correspondent.

Ben Robertson was going abroad for *PM*, too, but when I told him something about my experience he didn't seem properly impressed. "I never had any doubts about this job of ours, Ed," he said; "we're worth as much as a couple of generals."

"Brigadier, or four-star?" I asked. But Ben didn't like it when I called him General Robertson after that; he believed exactly what he said. I never knew anybody in the business, except Ray Clapper, who managed to keep his respect for the press so intact and so helped to restore my own. Ben's sense of mission and obligation were still as crusader-like as when I had first met him on the campus at Missouri, where we listened together to old Dean Walter Williams preaching his creed of journalism. Ben went on believing it and living up to it till the day a year later when he crashed in a clipper outside Lisbon on his last assignment.

It took us weeks to get away from Washington and we did not manage it till we did, after all, wangle generals' priorities. Only nine clippers were in service on both the Atlantic and Pacific then. It was long before the Air Transport Command, and over in Africa we found that Pan-American pilots were still ferrying most of our planes and personnel. There was no satisfactory communications system as yet and if a pilot got off the radio beam he had a hell of a time finding his way. Planes were carrying heavy overloads and there were some crashes. Once we almost added to the list when for four hours we flew into a black night searching for that elusive beam and got into it just in time to come over with five gallons of gas left in one tank. But that is strictly personal history.

Anyway it was still an adventure then and we got a pioneering thrill out of that flight over the Caribbean and across the incredibly broad mouths of the Amazon to Brazil and then one hop over the brine to Liberia. I would fly across Africa four times before I saw home again. The repeats were routine but that first sight of endless sand and rock, and then the green ribbon of the Nile laid down on the glistening waste into Egypt and finally Cairo: that was unforgettable.

In Cairo I called on Nahas Pasha, the Egyptian Premier, and I learned elsewhere how the British had put him into office after presenting King Fuad an ultimatum and surrounding his palace with troops and running a tank up the front steps. I learned a lot of other things there that are water over the dam now. Then I told Ben good-bye and went on by British plane across the Holy Land and Trans-Jordania and over barren Iraq down the lovely Shat-El-Arab to Sinbad the Sailor's home outside blistering Basra. And after a day's flight above the shimmering Persian Gulf, skirting Arabia, till we came into India at last, I could see what Karl Twitchell meant by a remark he had made back in Cairo.

Twitchell was leading an American "agricultural" mission into Saudi Arabia and he got the King to invite me to come into Ryad, his capital; and if I didn't get a scoop on the Big-Inch pipeline it was my own fault. One day in Cairo he showed me some of his excellent Kodachromes of the Arabs on a projector he was taking as a gift to Ibn Saud. He ended up with some pictures of New Hampshire in a glorious September.

"Ibn Saud ought to like that New Hampshire autumn!" I exclaimed.

"Good Lord," said Twitchell, "I wouldn't dream of showing those pictures to the King."

"Why not?"

"Up till now I've never told him anything that wasn't true and he believes in my integrity. If I showed the King those pictures and told him the colors of the leaves on the trees were real and not painted he would never trust my word again!"

Not only was Arabia a monochrome of barren sand and a

7

furnace of heat, but from the time I left Brazil till I hit Delhi it seemed to me there was practically nothing but wasteland below us. It explains a lot about the "backward" men and women in those big spaces that look so promising on our pretty colored maps. It's all One World, all right, and so is a coconut all one coconut. But an awful lot of both of them is husk. Several million young Americans are discovering during this war that the best slices of the meat and the sweetest milk of this earth are labeled U. S. A.—with very little of the husk.

II

Preface to India

UNBELIEVABLE India! India of the unforgettable peace of cool, shaded valleys and blue lakes mirroring the Himalayas, and of scorching heat and the choking dust of arid plains and deserts; India, the serene and obscure, the dazzlingly rich and the abysmally poor, the exquisitely tender and crassly inhumane, the sophisticated and the irresponsibly adolescent, the glorious and the despicable, the sensitive and the sordidly brutal, the generously brave and the craven; India, the mother of civilizations and the harborer of barbaric customs, the land of wooden plows and blast furnaces, of sacred cows and communal hatreds and prophets of brotherly love, of spinning-wheel saints and distinguished scientists; land of voluptuaries and ascetics, of the incredibly fat and the incredibly lean, of absolute feudalism coeval with modern capitalism, of naked fakirs who never heard of the rope trick and of political *detenus* whose jail record gives them social position; India, the giant of the future and the prisoner of the present, held in the now harsh, now gentle, hands of perplexed island-bred aliens who are in nearly every particular the antithesis of the people whose destiny they have shaped for nearly two centuries.

Indians are generally much darker than Chinese and other Mongoloids but they are considered by scientists to be Caucasians,

8

or the same racial type as Europeans. Nevertheless, Indian society seems to me more difficult than China for us to understand; far more complex, and cherishing more institutions with which the Occidental cannot easily find a point of sympathy. This is not simply because I have spent many years in China; every foreigner I know who has lived in both countries feels the same thing. Chinese themselves tell me it is easier for them to comprehend Western character than Hindu mentality. Unless you keep reminding yourself of the basic facts about India you may end up thinking that one-fifth of humanity is inhuman, which won't get you in anywhere but wrong.

What are some of the basic facts? To people who know India the next few pages will be elementary; yet to try to tell what the war has meant to the Indians, without recalling this background, is simply an impossible task. First of all we must remember the immensity of this country, with its 389,000,000 souls living in an area of 1,581,000 square miles: three times as many people as we have in the United States, crowded into half the space. Of this, "British India" consists of eleven provinces and accounts for 54% of the land area and three-fourths of the people. The rest of the Indians are divided among 562 Indian states sandwiched in between the provinces, and each sovereign unto itself under the paramount power, Great Britain.

All Indians may be Caucasians but there are many different peoples among them. They speak eleven principal languages and 225 minor dialects. Urdu and Hindustani are commonly understood over most of northern and central India, by over 150 million people. In the East over fifty million speak Bengali; in the South thirty million know Marathi and Gujerati; and living chiefly in the great cities are about six million Indians who know the English language in dialects all their own. But do not assume that language groups correspond to religions; they do not.

India has tropical climates and the highest snow peaks in the world, deserts without rainfall and the wettest spots on earth; yet nearly all the country is warm enough for thin cotton clothing. Most Indian men wear only a loin cloth and cotton turban and do not own a shirt; most women possess but one or two cotton saris. It is well that cotton is adequate because the great majority of Indians could not afford to buy anything else; their per capita income is less than $20 a year.

Over 90% of the population are peasants and the majority

9

are, in an economic sense, serfs or bondslaves working for a few million *zamindars*, or landlords. In the native states some of the peasants are in effect owned body and soul by the princes or landlords. Nearly 90% of all Indians are illiterate. They live in mud huts and for fuel for cooking they use cow dung which you see in the villages drying in flat cakes pasted on walls everywhere. In the cities the workers live crowded in tiny airless rooms or sleep on the streets; my own servant uncomplainingly slept on my doorstep. These people eat with their fingers and the diet of the poor consists of bits of rice, potatoes or unleavened bread. Twenty per cent of them are continuously in a state of semi-starvation and 40% live just over the edge of that condition. Only 39% get what could be called an "adequate" diet.

As great an influence as the rice bowl is a religion which stands above everything else as a social force and governs the lives of millions of people in a manner almost inconceivable to the Western mind. Not only what a man is, whom he marries and how he earns a living and when he takes a bath, with whom he dines and what he eats and wears, but his whole internal plumbing—how he copulates, even how he urinates or defecates and cleanses himself afterward and with which hand—are all events and functions which in theory and to a considerable extent in practice, are determined by his faith. Unless, of course, he is a Christian or a Sikh (they both believe in one God, and reject the caste system; and there are about six million each of Christians and Sikhs) or unless he is a Parsi (who does not burn his dead as the Hindu does, but feeds them to the vultures) or a Buddhist or one of the minor sects. But nine times out of ten an "Indian" will be either one of the 260,000,000 Hindus or one of the 90,000,000 Moslems.

Although Mohammed Ali Jinnah, as the Qaid-e-Azam, or leader of the Moslem Party, tries to prove that Indian Mussulmans belong to a different race, and are a separate people, his argument is no sounder than Hitler's myth of the pure Aryan German. Mohammedanism was introduced into India less than a thousand years ago by conquerors from the north. Most of them intermarried with the Hindus and were absorbed and today the vast majority are descendants of Hindu converts. But between the two religions there is a wide gulf in ideas.

Indian religious differences often are represented to be even broader than they are. As a result many have got the idea that all

10

Hindus are pacifists and believe in many gods, in contrast to the Mohammedans who accept the law of dynamic change and worship but one God. But there are many sects of Hindus and some of their teachings differ from each other more than they differ from Mohammedanism. Constant emphasis on the Indian Moslem as a warrior has also given most people abroad the impression that the Indian Army is virtually all Moslem. The fact is that the Hindus of all sects are a majority in it and outnumber Moslems almost two to one.

About 30% of all Hindus belong to the *Aryasamajists,* who believe in only one God. It is the *Sanathanists,* who are polytheists and cow-worshippers, with whom Mohammedanism disagrees most sharply. A basic conflict exists over the question of caste, which the Moslems do not recognize. Although caste orthodoxy is now rapidly deteriorating, it is still enforced to a considerable extent in all Hindu society. In contrast, Mohammedans teach that all men are equal before God and they practice democracy in the temple. Mohammedanism also respects the dignity of labor. While some Hindu philosophy may glorify labor, in practice Hinduism penalizes the hardest and lowliest toil by denying it even the status of caste. Again, it is a sin for a Moslem to lend money for interest. Hindus may engage in usury without loss of caste.

An important aspect of Hindu philosophy which has been given a special political meaning by Mahatma Gandhi is the teaching of *Ahimsa,* or non-injury. He has fashioned a weapon out of it, in the form of *Satyagraha,* or soul-force. In political practice this becomes "non-violent civil disobedience," a method of struggle peculiarly suited to Indian temperament because of the passivity engendered in the masses by centuries of subjugation. It has played a most important role in the attitude of the Indian National Congress toward the war. The Moslems don't take readily to *Ahimsa* and still more emphatically reject the Hindu doctrine of transmigration of souls and the idea of *Karma.* Undoubtedly these have been useful instruments in the preservation of Indian feudalism and absolutism and for enforcing docility in ignorant subjects.

Karma teaches that man's suffering in this world is punishment for sins committed in a previous incarnation. In the uncomplaining acceptance of life's misfortunes lies the sole hope of redemption: promise of a higher status in the next incarnation.

11

If you are an Untouchable today and behave yourself you may be reborn some generations hence as a rich merchant or a craftsman or even a prince. But if you misbehave or protest you may well end up at a later date in a lamentable shape as a pig or an ass: Hindus believe animals have souls too. All cows, which ideally symbolize resignation to fate, are considered sacred, and Hindus permit them to wander in and out of their temples, houses and streets, leaving their droppings behind them. A third of the world's cattle is in India, but 70% of the cows give no milk; like the people, they do not get enough to eat.

Nothing is more important to Hindus, except the few who have broken the taboos and are westernized, than caste. There are over 2,000 sub-castes but the main divisions are only four. Highest are the Brahmins (Jawarhalal Nehru is a Brahmin) who may be priests, lawyers, scientists, doctors, teachers and (a discerning note) journalists. Next come Kshatriyas, who provide soldiers and the governing class; (3) Vaisyas (Mahatma Gandhi is a Vaisya) who may be merchants and craftsmen; and (4) Shudras, or servants and serfs. You cannot change your caste, you cannot intermarry, you cannot mingle freely with any caste but your own. In short you cannot, if you are born in a lower caste, have very much fun, and it serves you right for the sins you committed in a previous existence.

Thus caste is a formidable barrier to understanding, fellowship, co-operation and the exchange of social graces not only between Hindus and Moslems but among Hindus themselves. It is also sometimes disconcerting for foreigners. Not long after I first reached India an ardent English-speaking nationalist, a young Brahmin disciple of Pandit Modan Malaviya, invited me to dine with him. He took me to his home, sat me down at a table, excused himself, sent in a servant with some food, and then to my astonishment reappeared and announced that he had already eaten. Later I learned that even as it was he would have to take a bath; had he eaten with me he would have had to call in a priest to go through a purifying ceremony. I took care not to cause a repetition of such embarrassment.

A foreigner is without caste, however, and thus not necessarily polluting, but the Untouchables pollute literally by their touch. Some fifty million Indians, or one-fifth of all Hindus, are Untouchables. They live in segregated areas, cannot use the utensils of others or draw water from the village wells, and are forbid-

12

den to worship in shrines or temples.* Ordinarily only heavy labor is open to them, or the dirtiest jobs such as street sweeping, collecting garbage and dung, or cleaning latrines.

In many cases even the shadow of an Untouchable is considered degrading. Dr. Bhimrao Ramji Ambedkar, the remarkable man largely responsible for giving the Untouchables a political status in India, told me that as a boy he had to audit his classes while sitting on the limb of a tree outside the village school. His teacher and the other students were afraid to be polluted by his shadow. Ambedkar went to Columbia University and later became one of the great lawyers of Bombay. In his career there he was never once invited to dine with a Brahmin colleague.

The origin of untouchability is vague, but whatever validity the institution once had it undoubtedly constitutes in practice today one of the cruellest forms of social and economic oppression inflicted by one group in a society upon another. It is one thing Indians cannot accuse the British of imposing on them. Nothing so endangers the future of Hinduism as Untouchability. Many Untouchables have become Mohammedans; even orthodox leaders of the Hindu Mahasabha, like Pandit Modan Malaviya, are beginning to worry about it. One of the planks in the nine-point platform of the Congress calls for the abolition of all forms of discrimination against Untouchables. So far this has not been realized, owing chiefly to the predominant influence of Hindu orthodoxy in the nationalist movement.

Gandhi himself has preached against the "abuses" of Untouchability, but he thinks the institution should be preserved in its "pure" form, as a division of labor. He himself called the Untouchables by the term *Harijan*, which means "elect of God." He named his little weekly paper after them. His own crusade for the betterment of the "Scheduled Classes," as the British call Untouchables, has done much to dramatize their predicament before the whole Hindu community. Dr. Ambedkar, in his post as labor member of the Executive Council (one of the wisest of Lord Linlithgow's appointments during his reign as Viceroy), has given political content to Gandhi's moral appeals on behalf of the *Harijan*.

Jawarhalal Nehru frequently dines conspicuously with Untouchables. Nehru personally campaigned to elect to office, on the

* In advanced communities there is some relaxation of these taboos; but not among orthodox Brahmins.

Congress ticket, an Untouchable who once worked as a servant in his own household. Another indication of Nehru's unorthodoxy: he approved the marriage of his daughter Indra to a Parsi named Teroz Gandhi—no relation to the Mahatma. Nehru's father, the famed Motilal, was one of the first Brahmin pandits to defy the orthodox law requiring a purification ceremony after traveling to a foreign country. His example was followed by many others. Machine-age civilization is now rendering some other taboos impracticable.

Considering some of the ways of Hinduism, it is not surprising that the followers of Islam in India increased from a few thousands in the fourteenth century to a religious nation of ninety millions today. Only in the last decade, however, have the Moslems found an astute political spokesman, in the person of Mohammed Ali Jinnah. And only since Jinnah formulated his scheme of "Pakistan" has he gathered enough followers to begin to give some semblance of reality to his boast that he speaks for all of them.

Pakistan envisages an independent Moslem nation, or a federation of states, to be carved out of India when and if the British leave. But although Jinnah planks for "complete independence" he does not appear to want the British to leave now or tomorrow or not until he has got much more Moslem support behind him. Perhaps what he really wants is for the British to partition India before they give anybody independence, and to give the Moslems —and Mr. Jinnah—control of a set of predominantly Moslem areas. This Pakistan might then make its own alliance or arrangements with the British raj. But Mr. Jinnah is not so foolish as to put all this so explicitly. He is as skilful a politician as Mr. Gandhi, but with all his be-monocled, impeccably (if flashily) tailored figure, and with all his fastidious soul, he is the antithesis of the Mahatma, whose wardrobe is not much larger than a fan dancer's. Jinnah used to play stock in a theatrical troupe in England; he is a wealthy lawyer and landowner and loves horse racing. We shall hear more of him later.

The Moslem League has become a serious political party only in the last decade but the Indian National Congress Party dates from 1885. It began its demand for independence when Gandhi assumed leadership after the First World War and made a success of non-violent civil disobedience. Although predominantly Hindu, Congress once numbered tens of thousands of Moslems

14

among its former nominal membership of 5,000,000. Its incumbent president, Maulana Kalam Azad, is a Moslem. Recently there has been some falling away of Moslem support for Congress, perhaps not so much because of Jinnah's haranguing as because of Congress leadership in the critical episodes described in later pages. That also explains to a major extent the growth of the Indian Communist Party, of which very little is heard in Britain and America. Today it controls the whole Indian Kisan Sabha, or peasants' union, which has well over a million members, as well as the All-India Trades Unions Council, with almost a million members. Of the Communists, who are inside the Congress, but have their own policy, more later.

All three organizations were allowed to function under a constitution which conferred limited rights of democratic self-government on the provinces of British India—but not on the states. In the Indian states there is no popular government, no political parties are allowed a legal existence, and feudal autocracy in most cases reigns absolute. It is necessary here to have a quick look at these islands of princely power, where over ninety million Hindus and Mohammedans live cut off from the rest of India.

III

About Princes

WHEREAS the average peasant lives, whether in an Indian state or a province of British India, on less than five cents a day, and the average industrial worker gets little more than fifteen cents a day for a 54-hour week, there are Indian princes and royal families who have literally never eaten on anything but gold plate and who are among the very wealthiest men in the world. The Nizam of Hyderabad is the richest. He has a fortune of $250,000,000 in gold bullion, besides two billion dollars in coin and precious stones.

In the far north of India, just south of Soviet Turkestan, lies the enchanting state of Kashmir, with revenues of over $50,000,000 annually. It is the sole property of a Hindu maharajah who rules a predominantly Moslem population. This is not liked by the Moslems. Many of them told me, during a visit there, that they considered their only hope of "freedom" lay in Jinnah's "Pakistan" scheme, which could eventually overthrow the "Hindu raj" now kept in power by the British. The present ruler's forebears bought the state, which is almost as large as Great Britain, for about $5,000,000. For once the British had no idea what they were selling. Kashmir and Hyderabad are together about the size of the Soviet Ukraine and are potentially almost as rich; but very little has been done to develop their abundant natural resources. Consequently Kashmiris are even poorer than "British" Indians.

All the 562 princes of India, ranging from the Nizam of Hyderabad down to the Bilbari in Gujerat (who "reigns" over twenty-seven people and less than two square miles) are protected in perpetuity by the British Crown. In many cases these states were already established under the waning Moghul power when the British came. Some helped the invaders to conquer India and their rulers were what we now call Quislings, or Fifth Columnists. Most states have treaties with Britain made after 1857, the year of the Great Mutiny. At that time the British, having already destroyed native rule in more than half the country, stopped annexing territory outright and instead established "alliances" with, in reality protectorates over, the domain of surviving nawabs and maharajahs.

It turned out to be a valuable device in maintaining British authority; so much so, in fact, that that authority would have collapsed long before now, without it. This fact has been fully recognized by every premier down to Churchill and no Cabinet has ever whispered any intention of abolishing the system of states. Few people outside India seem to realize that when the British speak of "granting popular government" to that country they are only referring to so-called "British India." All British concessions to Indian nationalism have always implicitly or explicitly reaffirmed the perpetuity of the Indian states. Indeed Lord Halifax told an American audience that to "scrap" the King-Emperor's treaties with the princes would be to abandon the very principles for which Britain went to war against the Nazis!*

* *Vide* Kate L. Mitchell's *Foundations of Modern India*. For a full text of Halifax's speech and an excellent study in general.

Professor Rushbrook Williams, an official apologist for the India Office and the "native states," has described very accurately the role of the princes in the system of *divide et impera*:

The situation of these feudatory states, checkerboarding all India as they do, is a great safeguard. It is like establishing a vast network of friendly fortresses in debatable territory. It would be difficult for a general rebellion against the British to sweep India because of this network of powerful loyal Native States.*

All these states are run as autocracies. Many are fantastic despotisms, with a populace living in an incredible social darkness full of squalor, filth, ignorance and disease, in the center of which are magnificent palaces where the prince and his courtiers enjoy the most dazzling pomp and luxury to be seen outside a Hollywood movie set. Only a few modern-minded princes have organized consultative bodies, appointed by themselves. But several states are more advanced than British India. Travancore has a higher proportion of literates, for instance; Mysore is ahead of many Indian provinces in education and industrialization. The late Gaekwar of Baroda introduced free compulsory primary education, which is not yet known in the British provinces. Some other good things might be said for a few of the states, but on the whole their rulers are backward and incompetent at best, and more often thoroughly corrupt and degenerate.

A fairly typical example of the average prince's attitude toward his subjects is that of the Maharajah of Dohlpur. Consider a fragment of our incredible conversation. I sat with him one afternoon on a spacious lawn where young men and women played tennis in the shade of great banyans. The dark little man was a picture of benevolence under his sky-blue silk turban; and his brown hands, glittering with diamonds, were a study in repose. How much at peace he looked with the world!

"Do you have a representative government of any kind in your state, Your Highness?" I asked idly. It was a social occasion and I had not really intended to talk shop. "I mean is there any kind of advisory council?"

"Oh, dear me, no; nothing like that, Mr. Snow," he responded in an Oxford accent. "We find here in India that if you once begin that sort of thing there is no end to it and the people

* Q. from R. Palme Dutt's *The Problem of India.* 1943. Dutt is the ablest Marxist writer on this subject.

always suffer. Lawyers get into office and begin to exploit the masses and the state becomes corrupt. It is much better to keep all the power in the hands of the sovereign."

"Quite so, Your Highness, I can see you aren't a Bolshevik. What is the percentage of literacy in Dohlpur? Higher than in British India, I suppose?"

"I'm afraid I can't tell you," he said, ruefully shaking his turban. "I don't carry such figures around in my head. But my policy is not to emphasize education. We find that here in India if the people once go to school they're not good farmers any more. Somehow it seems to soften them."

"Now that is odd. You take a country like the United States and you look at the average farmer and it's pretty hard to tell by his size or softness whether he can read or write, though you can tell it by looking at his farm. In Soviet Russia they educate all their farmers and it doesn't seem to make them a bit soft when it comes to fighting the Germans. How do you explain the softening influences of education over here, Your Highness?"

"I suppose it does sound strange to an American, but it isn't the same. When an Indian farmer learns to read and write he always becomes a lawyer. A state full of lawyers becomes corrupt and soft. No, we don't want to spoil the people that way."

I looked at him in astonishment and as far as I could see he was in dead earnest. In fact, this Maharajah of Dohlpur was a fairly good ruler of a relatively modest state and he dispensed justice, *sans* lawyers, with equity, in accordance with his feudal code. But he collected a tax from his subjects many times greater than the rate of bounty garnered by the King of England. So did the late Maharajah of Bikanir, a personal potentate who struck me as one of the best of the princes. He retained from his annual budget for the exclusive use of the royal purse, when I met him, 224,000 rupees, or more than he spent on education for all his subjects. The royal family, the royal weddings, the royal palaces and the royal retainers absorbed two-thirds of Bikanir's entire budget.

It is unnecessary here to prove that the total picture of princely India is an altogether anachronistic one in the modern world. Nobody knows that better than the princes themselves. I remember a stimulating conversation I had in Delhi with a certain Anglicized, bejeweled, bewitching princess whom I met at the ever-hospitable home of Ratan Nehru and his charming

18

and lovely wife, Rajan. "I can't stand this country," she startled me by remarking. "It is too stupid. It needs to be picked up and shaken and have its back turned on everything it has been. This terrible resignation to poverty, evil and dirt! And it's worst of all in our own states. If I had the power, do you know what I'd do? First thing, I'd wipe out all the princes."

"What do you mean wipe out, Princess? Liquidate? Sever the head from the body?"

"Exactly! I would like to make up the list myself. I know them all and I know enough about almost every one of them to prove they're rotten and corrupt! And they're all parasites. I may not know much else about India but I know its princes and they should all be wiped out!"

"You're not an Indian, Princess, you're a Russian!" I exclaimed. And so she was and there are not many like her, even in words. Certainly the princes themselves give no indication of abdicating voluntarily. That was made clear by the Jam Sahib of Nawanagar, chancellor of the Chamber of Princes, who invited us to a cocktail party to announce that he and his fellow sovereigns were determined upon "another century of rule." Unforgettable was the picture he made sitting there in the Imperial Hotel at Delhi, a huge hulk weighing as much as two Indian coolies. Jewels sparkled on his plump fingers and in his rich garments as he consumed Manhattan cocktails from which he plucked red cherries to hand graciously to the celebrated Burmese girl, Than É, who sat beside him taking notes for her radio broadcasts.

"No, the Indian states won't disappear. Land ownership will remain an internal problem of each state and so will education, judiciary, and all things necessary to sovereignty. We fought and sacrificed our blood (*sic!*) to win power and we mean to hold it. If Congress wants to rob us, if the British should let us down, we will fight! Have another cherry, Miss Burma?"

It should be noted that there was at least one exception to this "iron determination" to save the people from the lawyers. It was provided by the curious Maharajah of Indore. While I was in India he actually wrote out a promise of democracy for his not inconsiderable state and summoned a gathering of his people to hear him. Perhaps it was the influence of his American wife. But his own retainers twice prevented him from reading the proclamation and, reportedly backed by Delhi, succeeded in aborting the whole scheme.

19

Such is the broad, if all too inadequately illuminated, background against which decisive wartime events have taken place in India. Such was the state of the nation 300 years after the arrival of the British and nearly ninety years after Victoria incorporated the country into the Empire.

Many nationalists said that the worst indictment of this alien rule was not that it had fundamentally altered or interfered with Indian society, but that it had *not* done so itself and had prevented Indians from doing so. Britain merely kept the *status quo*, which meant preservation of a feudalism already disintegrating when she arrived. While British capital built railways and factories for very handsome profits, these were superimposed upon a top-heavy society without any attempt to achieve a balanced industrialization of India. That would have meant Indian competition with British industry in the internal and world markets, on the one hand, and a breakup of feudalism on the other.

One item which Indian engineers cite as in itself sufficient evidence of this: India has the largest high-grade iron ore deposits in the world, but under British rule here, which predates the American Revolution, the nation's annual industrial production is less than one per cent of that of the United States. In the Indian Army, officers complain of the same policy of retarded development. After generations of Indian fighting men provided for the King-Emperor, and with more than half a million Indian troops in service overseas in this war, not a single Indian officer even as high as a colonel has yet been given a combat command in the field.

The main "crime" of British rule, some critics said, was that it effectively "froze" Indian development and particularly class relationships. It efficiently maintained "law and order." It protected India from inner convulsions which in the normal course of events might have shaken and swept from the face of the earth much of the fantastic social structure still preserved today. Yet such reflections are now idle and profitless; no one can rewrite history.

It is pertinent here only in order to observe that it was the conservation of all such feudal anomalies which enabled the British, by manipulating them as backward and antagonistic forces within Indian society, to retain power with a minimum of brain power and brawn—until Japan appeared on the threshold with a new challenge from without.

20

IV

Politics at Allahabad

IT IS easier to state the terms of political struggle in India than to describe its social life. The former can be framed under three simple points. First, the majority of the politically-conscious population of British India wants independence and has wanted it for a long time. That was conclusively demonstrated in the provincial elections of 1937. They returned to power a large majority of the candidates proposed by the Indian National Congress Party, whose platform called for complete independence.

Second, no British Cabinet had ever recognized the foregoing fact by offering to yield power to an Indian national government at any exact date in the future.

Third, the Congress and other Indian parties, chiefly the Moslem League, have been unable to agree among themselves on the means by which they could compel the British to relinquish all power, quit India, and let Indians govern or misgovern themselves to their hearts' content or regret.

Basically, that is all there is to it. And yet what a fascinatingly complex stream of politics ebbs and flows round these rocks of solid truth, now obscuring them, now high-lighting them, now bringing to the Indians hopes of success by Gandhi's homespun methods of unarmed revolt, now encouraging the British to believe they can extend their lease on Empire here for many generations!

In September, 1939, the Congress Party was co-operating with Lord Linlithgow, the Viceroy, through their ministries in British India; but they had no power at all in the central government. What was this "central government"? Here a digression to explain.

For the most part the executive, administrative and even final legislative power in India are controlled at the center by the Viceroy, or Governor-General. He is appointed by the King, represents him personally, and is accountable to no one in India, but is responsible for his actions only to the Secretary of State for India, a member of the British Cabinet. He has an executive council, which he appoints himself. In the past it was made up chiefly of Europeans, but today a majority of its fourteen members are Indians. They do not, however, represent any Indian political parties, but serve as individuals; and they have no power except to advise the Viceroy.

There is also a Council of State, a kind of upper house; thirty-two of its members are elected and twenty-six are appointed by the Viceroy. The Legislative Assembly, or lower house, has 102 elected members and thirty-nine appointed ones. But only 32,000 people own enough property to vote for members of the Council of State and only 1,250,000 can vote for assemblymen. The Viceroy can veto any measure, and in wide fields of finance, defense, religion, foreign affairs and internal affairs the Council and Assembly cannot vote at all. The Viceroy can make any law himself, without their consent; they are largely puppet bodies.

In the provinces, however, the Government of India Act of 1935 provides for wider autonomy under elected governments for which 36,000,000 people could vote. The system here resembles the British Parliament, with each of the eleven provinces having a British governor appointed by the King, and responsible to the Viceroy, but assisted by a Cabinet of Ministers selected from members of the elected legislature, and headed by a prime minister. The provincial ministries actually control affairs of education, agriculture, public health and some other matters. The Governor retains the veto power, however; in time of emergency he can suspend the Constitution and govern alone, which is the case in most provinces today.

First elections under the Constitution of 1935 were held in 1937, when the Congress Party of Gandhi and Nehru won a large majority in eight of the eleven provinces. They formed ministries and worked fairly well for two years, until in September, 1939, the Viceroy unilaterally declared India a belligerent in the European war. Thereupon all the Congress ministries resigned, in protest against this denial of India's right to self-determination.

By the spring of 1940, accusing the British of carrying on the war without either referring their decisions to Indian opinion or guaranteeing India independence in accordance with the promises of the Atlantic Charter, the Congress Party had launched a partial

22

civil disobedience campaign under Gandhi. Thousands went to jail, many of them but lately officials in the government. Only at the outbreak of the Pacific war were they released by Churchill. He then sent out to India Sir Stafford Cripps, ex-Laborite and an old friend of Jawarhalal Nehru and Mohandas Koramchand (the Mahatma, or "Great Soul") Gandhi. As Lord Privy Seal in the Cabinet, Cripps was momentarily a powerful figure in England and, as an old advocate of Indian freedom, he was welcome in India.

But Sir Stafford had already left when I reached Delhi late in April. The balloon of independence raised by his flying visit now lay a deflated sack on which nationalist dreams had crashed again. Despondency was more widespread than before his arrival, especially among Congress followers led principally by Gandhi and Nehru.

Among some of the British bureaucrats, however, one divined a curious sense of relief, which uneasy people in Britain and America did not share. Had not Japan overrun Burma and already bombed the east coast of India? Was not a gigantic pincers about to close in from the northwest, where the Nazis were smashing at the Caucasus above Iran, while from the east the Japanese neared the frontiers of Bengal? If India fell to the Axis would not we lose our only supply route to China, our only military and industrial base of importance lying between Britain and Australia, and the manpower of 400 million people?

Allied countries were naturally distressed at the failure of the Cripps Mission to win the support of the Indian masses. What were the reasons for it? Those vouchsafed by the British, in a barrage of radio explanation beamed chiefly at America and with oblique thrusts toward China and Russia, left the general impression that the Indians had been offered post-war independence and immediate national self-government. They had rejected both because they could not agree among themselves and because Congress "did not want responsibility."

But it was more complex than that. What Churchill's Lord Privy Seal had brought out to India, "to be accepted as a whole or rejected as a whole" and in the time limit of two weeks, was not independence or even immediate dominion status. He brought instead a British Cabinet proposal which consisted of two parts. The first part provided for the election of a post-war convention, which would frame a Constitution to become the basis for a national government in British India. Each province would be permitted to vote itself into the union, or abstain from joining it, the electorate to consist of the enfranchised 36,000,000. Each Indian state, which, in effect, meant each Indian prince and his retainers, would also cast a vote on the new Constitution and either adhere to it or renew its pledges of allegiance to the British Crown.

The second part, a single paragraph, contained the only reference to the then current situation. "During the critical period which now faces India and until the new Constitution can be framed," read that paragraph, "His Majesty's government must inevitably bear the responsibility for, and retain control and direction of, the defense of India as part of their World War effort, but the task of organizing to the full the military, moral and material resources of India must be the responsibility of the Government of India, with the co-operation of the peoples of India."

Congress leaders were not satisfied with the methods proposed for calling a post-war constitutional convention. Obviously the powerful Indian princes, whose ninety million subjects had no vote, would exclude themselves. Millions of illiterates and propertyless Indians would cast no votes. In some predominantly Moslem states that might mean the difference between adherence or non-adherence to the union. What might emerge from this would be a patchwork of self-governing Indian provinces completely encompassed by "sovereign" states where the British would still retain real military, economic and political power. And yet what practical student of history could expect the British, or anyone else, voluntarily to abdicate from great areas in which the people had not yet organized power to overthrow them? Was it not the Congress' job to persuade the peoples of the Indian states to revolt, if they could?

In any case, it was not over the post-war paragraphs, but over the interpretation of Cripps' offer of an immediate share in the central government, it was over the defense of India, and who would organize it, that the Cripps Mission was wrecked. He himself told the House of Commons, in a statement accompanying his detailed White Paper, that the "final break" had come over "the form of the temporary government that might be in power until the end of the war, and the coming into operation of the new constitution (after the war)."

24

The day after he made his report I left Delhi for Allahabad, where the All-India Congress Committee had assembled to hear their leaders' explanation of the negotiations and the causes of failure and to find a policy to cope with the Japanese threat. The Indians put it somewhat differently, but their own White Paper made it clear enough that it was Churchill's refusal to concede what they called a "responsible national government" during the war that had caused them to reject the offer.

Congress President Maulana Azad said that at the outset Sir Stafford had told him definitely that the Viceroy's position in the new government would be no more important than that of the King in relation to the British Cabinet. But Cripps later modified this picture, according to Azad, until "We could by no stretch of the imagination even care to look at it."

Sir Stafford denied that to me when I saw him in London a year later. It seems from the wording itself that he was never authorized to interpret the paragraph so extravagantly. But in his remarks to me I also saw the ghost of an earlier optimism he must have carried with him to Delhi and which, in his interviews, might have given Nehru and Azad another impression.

"I told them all from the beginning," Sir Stafford said to me, "that no constitutional changes affecting the Viceroy's position could be made during the war. It would just have been literally impossible to move all the machinery involved. But I told them that though the present Constitution could not be changed there was no doubt in my mind that if they accepted the offer the Cabinet would have done as they wished about India. *It would have done as I said.*"

Other remarks which Cripps made to me helped to reveal the curious personality and psychological factors underlying this whole episode. Perhaps those factors more than everything else doomed the Mission to failure. They also explained a lot about why Congress finally allowed itself to be led by Mahatma Gandhi into a declaration of war against Britain instead of Japan. For behind all these negotiations there was of course the mighty influence of the Mahatma, fighting for vindication of his creed of non-violence.

"Gandhi was the real stumbling block," said Cripps. "For my proposals to have been accepted would have required the splitting away of Congress from Gandhi's control. It would have meant a revolt inside the party and a revolt requires a leader. I had counted on Nehru and I told him, 'Jawarhalal, if you will take up this offer, we two can decide the future of India. Your position in the Council here, backed by my position in the Cabinet, will give us such moral power that the Viceroy cannot dispute you here nor the Cabinet challenge me in England.' That was perfectly true, too, and there is no doubt in my mind that after the war Nehru and I could have got what we wanted. He seriously considered one night what it would mean and came to the conclusion that he could not fight Gandhi for control of the Congress. I told him that Gandhi might hold onto the Congress but that he could carry the country with him. It is a tragedy Nehru could not see it."

Thus it became clear to me that Cripps had staked everything on reaching an understanding with Nehru. "I told the Cabinet before I left that the offer was not what the Indians wanted and the odds were against it," he said. Then why had he risked his whole future—which at that moment was very brilliant, as he stood in England as the only man who could threaten Churchill's position as Prime Minister—on such a gamble? "I thought it was my duty," he told me crisply. "Indian support meant so much to the war effort that I could not justify refusing to make any attempt to secure it, however slight its chances of success."

At that moment I remembered being with a Tory British consular official in the Far East, a few years before, after he had received a telegram from his Ambassador requesting him to act as host to Cripps during his stay in the city. The poor man was aghast. "Why, the bounder is disloyal!" he exclaimed. "Don't you know Cripps has publicly preached revolution and abolition of the monarchy? I wouldn't have him cross my threshold if I hadn't received this order." Now it was war and in the supreme crisis Cripps had acted as English Knights of the Empire always act. He had thrown personal ambitions out the window on a lean hazard for the good of the realm. He had lost a great career but had satisfied his conscience. And it was the little Mahatma, who did not want to fight anybody but the British, who had defeated him, he admitted.

Not that Gandhi was pro-fascist; of course he was not. He did not know what fascism is. He had never seen it in action and he could not understand that its mission was specifically to wipe out kindly but obstinate people like himself. He thought he could exist in an Axis world as easily as the other one. All he saw was the British trying to drag him and his soul-force (satyagraha)

26

behind another one of their wars and he thought they were going to lose it anyway. He could not see anything in it for India except the chance of winning immediate independence in the time-space gap between victory for one side or the other.

The Cripps offer was to him "a post-dated check on a failing bank." It would not only be non-negotiable with the Japanese, but might do much harm if accepted as an honorarium for resisting the inevitable victors. Why go into business with a bankrupt raj and be held accountable for its failure? On the other hand, supposing the British won, after all, would they not be under obligation to re-write their check to the Indians anyway?

While Gandhi's information was incomplete, his judgment was not without moral logic when measured against India's past experiences. But it inexorably caused him to lead Congress away from its former policy of non-interference with the war effort to one of isolation from it, and finally into an abortive attack on the British. It was when I was at Allahabad that the old man began to gather his forces for that move.

V

Rajaji, Nehru and Gandhi

ON MAY 1st the All-India Congress Committee, meeting at Allahabad, passed a resolution which condemned the Cripps (in reality the Churchill) proposals, reasserted its stand that only a truly independent government could defend India, and called upon the people to oppose the Japanese by "non-violent non-co-operation" only, in the event of invasion. How that was to stop enemy bombers was not explained. Behind this curious declaration lay the story of Nehru's struggle against Gandhi's original resolution.

John Davies of the American Foreign Service had got off the train with me at Allahabad and we were the only two outsiders present at the final Congress session. Here we were especially interested in the position of Chakravarti Rajagopalacharia, brilliant lawyer and leader of the Congress Party in Madras, whose daughter Lakshmi is married to Gandhi's son Devadas.* Rajaji, or "C. R.," as he is happily abbreviated in the press, found himself out of sympathy with the Congress resolution. He pleaded instead for the passage of a measure calling for acceptance, in principle, of the Moslem League's demand for "Pakistan." Only after an agreement between the Congress and the Moslem League, he argued, could they organize a provisional government. And only after such an agreement existed could Congress hope to secure the withdrawal of the British power during the war.

"It is unnatural," he later told Gandhi, "for any government to withdraw without transferring power to a successor by consent, or without being forcibly replaced by another." Which was, of course, the whole point of *realpolitik* involved in all the subsequent episodes.

The Congress meeting was held in an old hall in Allahabad. Members of the Working Committee, the Congress "supreme command," reclined on the stage, while the delegates sat on the floor of the crowded theater. Some wore long close-fitting Indian coats and some the pajama-like *salvar* of the north, but the majority wore the *dhoti*—yards of white cloth wrapped round their loins. Nehru had on the white cotton *churidar* or breeches of his native Kashmir. The Mohammedan chairman, Maulana Azad, sat on his crossed bare feet on a chair.

"There is no use crying over spilled milk," Rajaji was saying. He was a dark, bony man above his white *dhoti*, but behind thick-lensed glasses there played an admonitory twinkling smile. "As the basis of action, we need Moslem support, otherwise we can do nothing but talk. Opponents of Pakistan say it is too vague a principle. Then let us make that its virtue. Concede the principle now, so that we can work together for independence, and argue about what it means later, when it must be referred to the people. ... Let us not just sit out the war. I say an agreement with the Moslem League would give a focus for men who have self-confidence and can act."

In a tense atmosphere the vote was taken, with only fifteen on Rajaji's side. He was heavily defeated and after this meeting resigned from the Congress general staff. But he came to sym-

* A violation of caste: Gandhi is a Vaisya, Lakshmi the daughter of a Brahmin.

bolize all over India the growing feeling that communal unity was the prerequisite of freedom.

John and I later met Rajaji, just before he left for Madras. He was philosophical about his personal defeat but worried about the future. Perhaps because he lived on the east coast, which had already been bombed, he felt the danger more keenly than others. The Congress resolution, he said, was entirely negative; it could not lead to effective organization of the people.

"The trouble with Congress is that it has been fighting the devil so long it doesn't know when he is licked. The British have become an obsession with us; we are like de Valera's Ireland. Congressmen will never work to win the war as long as it means helping a British government."

We found Nehru and Sarojinu Naidu, after dinner, over at Nehru's big sepia-colored mansion, left to him by his father, the great Motilal Nehru. Jawarhalal now used it chiefly as a rest house between long terms in jail. He too was feeling depressed and likewise sensed that the Congress resolution was weak and inadequate for a crisis demanding dynamic leadership. He looked tired and ill and still had the prison pallor about him; he had been out of jail only a few months. I had not seen him for about twelve years and though now he was fifty-three he was handsome as he had never been in his earlier middle age. In repose there was nobility in his face and I could not but agree with Clare Boothe that this was surely one of the finest human heads ever made.

Yet his bitterness had deepened with his sorrow and martyrdom. It seemed a grievous personal disappointment to him to find that Cripps was no different from any other Englishman when it came to negotiating India's freedom. When I asked him why the talks had failed he responded with unexpected acerbity:

"Cripps is a terrible diplomat, simply terrible! He has done enormous harm to Britain in the eyes of Indians. He amazed me after all these years. Apparently he never believed me when I said in the past that we wanted complete independence. Now when it came down to it and he saw we were in earnest he was hurt and surprised when I spoke of matters formerly taken for granted between us. 'You don't mean you really want to break away from us entirely, do you?' he asked me. Think of it! After all I've said and written and after all Cripps himself has written!"

"Was the real break because Cripps could not give you a

29

national government with responsible powers of a Cabinet?" I asked.

"At first he said we were to have a national government and the Viceroy would have powers similar to those of the King and naturally we took that to mean a responsible Cabinet. At last he admitted that all he could give us were positions in the Executive Council, with the Viceroy retaining the final veto power on all decisions. In other words, we would be mere puppets."

"Even so," I said, "wasn't it the first time the British had offered to form a central government council on party lines? Couldn't you have used the threat of unanimous resignation to bring such pressure on the Viceroy that he would have been obliged to respect your wishes?"

Nehru: "That's what Cripps kept saying. But India is more complicated than that. The Council would have represented all kinds of people, the Moslem League and the Princes and so on, people who owe their position to the British. Even so, we would have accepted a minority position, if they had offered the Council real power. We explained to Cripps what we wanted clearly enough—real control of the ministries with the exception of defense. We were willing to leave defense in British hands, but we wanted enough to say about it to be able to control some scandalous practices in the army, and to carry issues over the Viceroy's head to the British Cabinet, if necessary. Cripps finally said it wasn't in his power to give it to us.

"In final analysis it wasn't Cripps' fault. I don't know whether they withdrew promises made to him in London, but Churchill was much too smart for him. You know this combination of Churchill, Amery and Linlithgow is the worst we've had to face for many years. Amery* was the man who sided with the Japanese in Manchuria, you may remember. He said Britain could not logically oppose the conquest because the Japanese were doing just what Britain herself had done in India. And that's perfectly true, you know."

But at this time I did not yet know how much Cripps had counted on his personal influence with Nehru to "put over" his plan. Another thing I did not know then was how determinedly Gandhi had all along fought behind the scenes against any commitment to wage war on Japan. This became evident only in

* Leopold S. Amery, Secretary of State for India.

August, when the British published minutes* of the Working Committee meeting at Allahabad.

Sitting in his little mud-walled hut down in Sevagram, near Wardha, Gandhi had drawn up a draft which consisted of a demand for the British to leave forthwith and asserted that Japan had no quarrel with India. It declared that only the presence of the British might provoke her to attack; India bore no enmity against Japan and had no need of foreign help. She could defend herself non-violently. Gandhi declared that Congress opposed the scorched-earth policy and desired the removal of foreign troops, including Americans, presumably so as not to provoke the Japanese.

To these points Nehru took strenuous exception, according to the minutes. The Japanese were an imperialist country and "conquest of India is in their plan," he said. "If Bapu's (Gandhi's) approach is accepted, we become passive partners of the Axis.... The whole thought and background of the draft is one favoring Japan. It may not be conscious. Three factors influence our decisions: 1) Indian freedom; 2) sympathy for certain larger causes; 3) probable outcome of the war. It is Gandhiji's feeling that Japan and Germany will win. This feeling unconsciously governs his decisions. . . . The approach is a variation from the attitude of sympathy we have taken up about the Allies. It would be dishonorable for me to resign from that position."

Long and hot debate ensued, with Sardar Vallahbhai Patel and Rajendra Prasad staunchly backing Gandhi on every point. Nehru's own draft was rejected. In the end the compromise was worked out as already reported, but it did not satisfy either side and satisfied the old gentleman of Wardha least of all. Working indefatigably through a "new approach" he would, by July, once more win Jawarhalal round to support his principal purpose.

But before visiting Gandhi in his ashram let us have a look at the scene in which Indians believed the British raj was "a failing bank."

* Seized in a police raid on Congress headquarters. Nehru and Gandhi condemned such British methods—but never denied the authenticity of the documents.

VI

Invitation to Invasion

N<small>EXT</small> day at Allahabad while waiting for the train to Calcutta John and I found one of those Englishmen you meet, in the pages of the books we ignorant Americans write about India, along with the pukka sahibs from Poona and the red-faced colonels who think the Empire was sold down the river the day they disbanded the camel corps in favor of horse cavalry. He was managing the station restaurant. The Indians run the English a close second as the world's worst cooks, a congenital indifference to palatable food being one of the few sympathies they have in common, and when you get an English menu *à la Hindustan*, indigestion holds all the aces.

"Mark Twain complained because they didn't serve him his flies and lizards on separate plates in India but always in his soup," remarked John. "My experience is that since they've taken out the lizards you can't get the soup down at all."

"What else can you expect?" demanded the still faintly cockney voice of the weary maître d'hôtel. "You can't get a thing out of these buggars any more. The country's going from bad to worse. You Americans are responsible, too. We used to get a good cook for ten chips a month and glad to have it they were, but now they want twenty-five; your people are already paying them forty and before long it'll be fifty or sixty. They won't move hand or foot any more without baksheesh.* It all began when Curzon married that American woman Leita, she was the one! Wanted to buy over India for her own and give it back to the Indians, she did; wouldn't have a soldier in India today if she'd had her way! Twenty years ago a young fellow could come out and live pretty well, four or five polo ponies and his pegs every night at the club, not too much work and none of your sass from natives getting too big for themselves. Your missionaries spoiled the country by

* Tip.

32

telling every bloody Indian he's as good as we are. And now here's this fellow Nehru right here in Allahabad planning a revolution against us! Good Lord, no wonder the soup's bad!"

But there were other reasons, besides American interference, why after centuries of living together the Indians and the British still could not concoct a potable soup in the realm of politics. The accumulation of prewar plus wartime frustrations among Indians had by now produced an almost hopeless pathological state of mind. It manifested itself in the most profound distrust and suspicion of anything British, or anyone who might be doing a good turn for them.

The Indians are like most of us in that they can hate only one enemy at a time. For them the Axis remained a remote menace, compared with the source of all evil long installed on the throne. In a kind of masochistic way many were resigned to submit to anybody who would give the British a good licking.

In its more extreme forms Indian distrust was directed against the United States, Russia and China, as well as Britain. When Henry Grady came out with his economic mission to investigate possibilities of improving war production and to make recommendations (which everybody knew in advance the British would simply file away to collect dust), the Indian industrialists saw in it an imperialist scheme for acquiring new concessions. When Russia signed the Anglo-Soviet Treaty some Indians denounced it as a betrayal; it meant Russia would not free India from Britain. Nehru himself had had to stop talking about the importance of helping China. "People said, 'Jawarhalal has lost himself, he has lost his perspective,'" he told me. "I had to drop China."

Even what had happened to their own countrymen in Malaya and Burma at the hands of the Japs was blamed on the British. In the disasters suffered in those countries the Indians saw only British lack of vision and mismanagement, which delighted as much as it disgusted emotional nationalists. Perhaps nothing did more harm in this period than the policy of Sir Reginald Dorman-Smith's government, in Burma, of segregating white refugees from brown when the exodus was under way. Some 400,000 Indians started back from the occupied territories and those who got home had gruesome tales of discrimination to relate. Thousands of Indians had died of thirst, starvation and disease on the so-called "black road," owing to inadequate government preparations, while the Europeans were mostly safely evacuated by steamer or by air.

The debacle was a revelation of incompetence which shocked many Indians and even frightened the princes, some of whom were suspected of secret dickering with the enemy. Under the circumstances the nationalists' doubts of British ability to defend the country and their demands for a government in which they could have responsibility for mobilizing the popular forces for war, were quite understandable.

Indian industrialists and capitalists were among the most suspicious and worried groups. Would not "scorched earth" ruin their factories? It was a British plot to put India still further back industrially! For years the raj had pursued a policy which had prevented, by acts of omission and commission, the balanced industrialization of India. Lack of heavy industry in a country with the world's richest iron deposits was at least partly attributable to practices which consciously sought to keep the Indian market dependent on British production. Before and after the outbreak of the European war the little group of Englishmen (it was really an astoundingly little group which made policy affecting nearly 400 million men) repeatedly prevented Indian capitalists from setting up automobile and aircraft plants. And the same colonial policy was responsible for the backwardness in equipment and training of the Indian army.

In India there was never any real planning for war production. Fundamentally it was just as "impossible" for the British to conscript industry as it was to conscript men for the army or to organize the village population, educate them in the tasks of patriotism, and mobilize them to perform useful duties in national defense. There had never been any planning of production in time of peace; an untrained and hostile population would not accept it in time of war. Actually Delhi just gave out orders on a competitive basis.

If the jobber preferred to make fancy hats or bedpans instead of gas masks or shell casings he could get his material on the market by bidding against the fellow who might be trying to fill army orders. I found that after three years of war the government still had not established effective control of iron and steel. Bicycles and even steel ashtrays and waste-baskets were being produced for the civilian market and you could get any order filled in brass. Whether Europeans or Indians, manufacturers sold to the government for one reason only—profits. If they could have had access to Japan and made more money the Indians would doubtless have preferred to sell there. The Viceroy told me it was "impossible" to try to control these profits. "Industrialists here are the greediest in the whole world," he said.

On the train going to Calcutta I met an Indian steel expert who knew the industry of his country inside out. Before the war India produced a maximum of 867,000 tons of steel annually, or somewhat less than one-seventh the production of Japan, a country about one-seventh its size and with miserable resources. By 1942 Indian production had risen to 1,200,000 tons and it was hoped it might actually reach 1,500,000 tons before the war was over. But of this only about 20,000 tons was machine and tool steel.

"Most of what tool steel we do produce is going to Persia and our armament output is painfully small," the Indian expert told me. "We make about 125,000 rifles a year, 300 armored cars a month, maybe a dozen heavy guns, and a few other odds and ends and that's about the size of it. The rest of the story of India's 'enormous war production' is what you Americans call the bunk —it's propaganda."

"What's the reason for this low production?"

"That's simple. The government has no plan but it can hold up other people's plans. For example, in March, 1941, I requested authorization for new installations to increase steel production by 100,000 tons. We didn't want a subsidy, only government permission. It finally came through marked 'no objection'—after six months!"

"Six months! France was lost in two months," I exclaimed.

"They haven't heard about that out here yet," said Mr. X, in this case an Indian who was doing one of the most important jobs in the country. "The basic trouble is that all the machinery here belongs to the nineteenth century, including the Viceroy. They still write their chits in longhand, from the Viceroy down. I'll wager there isn't a dictaphone in the whole secretariat. You know how they file their letters? They thread them on a piece of string; I've seen Ministers spending their time threading and re-threading letters! Or look in one of the British banks here, you likely won't find an adding machine in the place, they still write out everything in longhand in big ledgers."

Calcutta, when we reached it, was filled with refugees streaming in from Burma. Over 200,000 had already arrived and thousands were still on the streets. Sarojinu Naidu took me around for a couple of days to visit the improvised shelters put up for them by the Congress people and the Mariwari Relief Society. The city government had made no adequate provision to care for them; many arrived half-starved and ill and died without getting food or medical attention. Cholera was spreading rapidly. In one camp I visited, twenty people had died and the director had been unable to get the bodies removed. Sanitary conditions were medieval in these camps.

Thousands of essential workers had already fled after the Japs tentatively bombed the east coast and succeeded in sinking over fifty of our ships. The rest of Calcutta's population was ready to panic at the first air raids, yet little had been done to accommodate hundreds who might have been wounded. Dr. John Grant of the Rockefeller Foundation had set up a blood bank but after many appeals still had less than enough blood to meet expectable needs of one big raid. It was already evident there would be a food shortage. Hoarding and speculation were the chief occupation of merchants and usurers. This was a full year before the outbreak of the famine which eventually would take a toll that the complacent Leopold S. Amery would, in 1944, underestimate for the House of Commons at "not over a million lives."

The whole Calcutta area, which contained roughly 75% of India's munitions industry, had only forty-eight anti-aircraft guns and there were spare parts for only eight of them. About 80% of India's oil imports had come from Burma; now it was discovered that reserves amounted to only a three months' supply. We had just one squadron of American planes here and no spares or adequate servicing facilities. The British had only a few Spitfires and Hurricanes, hastily flown in from Egypt, and a few old Blenheim bombers. India's own best divisions were still in Africa and along a vast frontier the British had less than two divisions of but partly mechanized troops. Locally some Europeans were enlisted in a volunteer corps and marched around puffing and panting once a day. But patriotic Indians were not permitted to enlist or bear arms; the British did not trust them.

There were amusing sidelights. An Indian merchant who had evacuated Rangoon by steamer bitterly assailed the British because many Indian women and children had been left behind, including his own. Yet he did not think it odd that he himself should be

36

sitting in Calcutta telling me about it. He was also indignant because the evacuation ship had not provided separate utensils for the "Scheduled Classes." Then there was the Viceroy's message, after he had inspected the civil defense organizations of Calcutta. It ended with the assurance that "Nothing could be better than the work that has been done here."

An Episcopal minister told his congregation that in view of the unusual times it would be well to have fewer garden parties and less dressing for dinner. He was roundly denounced in letters to the *Statesman* which insisted that appearances must be maintained; the stiff upper lip, one mustn't panic the natives, be a stout fellow. But the Chamber of Commerce unbent so far as to circulate to its members a suggestion that under the circumstances a certain relaxation in business dress was permissible; employees might wear shorts in the offices, since many were now riding bicycles which "entails a certain amount of physical exertion." But under no circumstances should they appear with an open collar when interviewing managers.

Thus it was clear after a brief survey of Bengal Province, which was the key to India, that the region was both physically and psychologically unprepared to repel an invasion, and that if one came the Indian population would offer no resistance, that Subhas Bose's* well-organized fifth column would aid the enemy, that workers would flee from the railways, munitions industries and public utilities, and that the whole administration would disintegrate, as it had in Rangoon. The only question was whether the Japanese had the forces, the shipping and the air power to mount an attack, or whether they would concentrate everything in the Pacific. The British had no choice but to gamble against an invasion. Fate was kind.

All that was true but it seemed a poor time for Americans to carp and criticize. Some hard-working British soldiers were now trying to organize a defense out of the chaos which confronted them and they needed all our help—real help. It was up to us to reinforce them if we could; so far we had sent little but staff officers who were big talkers without forces. I agreed absolutely with Clayton Lane, our brilliant consul in Calcutta, who said, "It isn't economic or military missions we need here but planes, infantry divisions, guns, tanks, a few shiploads of machinery, a

* See p. 311

few hundred locomotives, two or three railway operations men and plenty of the grenadiers with hairy ears."

It was a relief to leave the heat and defeatism of Bengal behind me when Major Richardson, one of General Stilwell's pilots, offered me a lift up the Brahmaputra Valley, to the eaves of the world in Assam. Before I saw the province of Bengal again, millions of people would perish there, not as a result of Japanese cannon fire, but as victims of a famine promoted by war and imperial incompetence, and its old pal, *laissez-faire*.

PART-II-''OPEN   REBELLION''

I

Enough Rope

FROM Assam I flew across "the Hump" and over the hills of northern Burma, on one of the dozen transports then opening up our only supply line to China. I flew back with Colonel Robert Scott and we picked up a Jap fighter near Myitkyina, shook him off with the help of the Himalayan clouds, then got lost in the soup, and finally came in with ceiling zero, landing perfect. But that is author Bob (*God Is My Co-Pilot*) Scott's story, and dog does not eat dog.

All I can say is I'm glad Scott had along his usual help that day, although at the time I only saw a cool young flyer named Jake Sartz, who actually held the controls. A few weeks earlier Lieutenant Sartz had set up a record when he ferried seventy-five evacuees out of Burma and to safety, in one trip of a twin-engined DC-3 made to carry twenty people.

It was my third visit to Chungking since the war began and I found out that nothing much would happen in China till the arrival of promised Lend-Lease aid. And this negative story need not here be told at all; I shall be going to China again before this book is done.

In June I came back from Assam with Brigadier-General Caleb V. Haynes, the man who pioneered our miraculous airline over the Hump, and as we let down over Delhi there was a dust ceiling of about 500 feet. After we landed on the dark field we stood for a moment under the wing of the plane and put our hands in our pockets to cool them off. The mercury stood at 135°. It goes up still another dozen degrees here before the rains come, and that too is one of the things to remember when trying to understand Indians.

It did not take much nosing about in Delhi to sense that the British were more absorbed with getting Congress out of the way than they were about any immediate Japanese threat to Bengal. Marshal Lord (then General Sir) Archibald Wavell told me he did not expect an invasion—not from Japan, at least. But I was then more interested in his explanation of why things had gone wrong in Burma and Malaya. Wavell had been the goat, although it was obvious he was not primarily responsible, any more than General Sir Harold Alexander* was, for the debacle in Burma. They had both been pulled into positions of command only at the eleventh hour.

It was now considered a mistake to have put Burma under Wavell's Singapore command; it should have been regarded as part of India's defense perimeter, so that reinforcements could have been drawn from there. Yet the one general who knew India and Burma best (Sir Claude Auchinleck) had been yanked out of his job and sent to Egypt, because Churchill was not expecting the Japs to attack in the East. Thus the man with twenty-three years of military experience in India was in Africa, where he later took the blame for the lost battle of Tobruk, while the experts on desert warfare were floundering about in the jungles of Southeast Asia with troops equipped and trained to fight in the open.

Wavell simply told me that they had failed because they were not ready. "We were not ready because we had not had time to recover in Europe. You can't be strong on all fronts simultaneously and the East was sacrificed. Our troops had not been properly trained for jungle fighting; we didn't have the air power we needed; we were just not ready. I suppose that means we didn't

* Who was, incidentally, Jawarhalal Nehru's classmate at Harrow.

39

really believe the Japanese would invade us, at least our people in Burma and Malaya did not think so."

Sabotage, guerrilla activity and fifth columnism, he thought, had played a minor role in Britain's defeat. "Its importance has been exaggerated." He was tired and troubled enough as it was; he did not want to tax himself with new-fangled ideas of political warfare. He believed only in the big battalions. "In the final analysis only military power wins wars." But politics was not then Wavell's job, and I went to another source, farther "up the hill," to find out how British officials were going to try to prevent Indians from stabbing them in the back, as the Burmese had. I went to see the Viceroy who for seven years held the reins of British power in India.

Lord Linlithgow was a lonely, aloof, austere and no doubt much misunderstood man when I visited him out in the viceregal mansion in New Delhi. He was temperamentally unsuited to adjust himself to Indian personality and I think he knew it. But even an extraordinarily imaginative man would have found it hard to see India from that big red sandstone mausoleum, surrounded by gardens where the stink of the excrement carts never penetrated from the streets of the lower castes.

The Viceroy's Palace cost five and a half million dollars and contains some six miles of corridors and probably twice as many miles of marble balustrades. It is altogether more imposing than Buckingham and has everything in it, including the world's largest throne room; everything but life. Some day it may make an excellent museum or public recreation hall, though the ventilation will have to be improved. Inside its solid masonry, which promises to outlast any of the other "seven cities" of ancient Delhi, dwelt a man who was paid more than the President of the United States—24,000 pounds annually. The little "study" where he received me would embrace two Oval Rooms.

Six feet four of stoutly built Presbyterian Scot, and with a long stubborn spade of a jaw. Linlithgow was wearing tennis clothes and a white woolen muffler in the air-chilled room. A ponderous man and a methodical one, but energetic and profoundly conscientious, "with firmness in the right," as he saw it, he was, with me personally, both helpful and patient. For over two hours he gave me a lecture on India until by the end I knew the country was ruled by an obstinate, discouraged, and honest man.

40

The trouble was entirely with the Indians, as he saw it. They couldn't get together among themselves. The Moslems didn't really want the British to leave India and the Congress would rather have them stay than seek an agreement with the Moslem League. Whenever these two groups would agree and come and ask him for the powers of a Cabinet he would welcome them and form that Cabinet.

But Linlithgow was sure nothing of the sort would happen. Meanwhile he wanted me to believe that his Executive Council was already a Cabinet. It was true he had the veto power, but had he ever used it? Not once. And that was perfectly correct, as I learned from talking to Indian members of the Council later on. They pointed out, however, that most decisions were made in advance by the Viceroy and his British secretaries. Of course if they disagreed with those decisions they could always resign. But as none of them represented any organized following, and the pay was good and the quarters magnificent, why be romantic?

As for Congress, the Viceroy saw no possibility of lining it up in support of the war. Congress was nothing but Gandhi, and Gandhi had shown, by rejecting the Cripps offer, that he did not want responsibility. The Viceroy had known in advance, he said, that the Indians "were not ready for it," and he had told Cripps so when he arrived.

"Democracy? This country will break up when we leave. There won't be a united democratic India for another hundred years."

That was the Viceroy. He made it clear enough that the British were not going to leave as yet. And they were going to come down hard on Congress. The day of "appeasement" was over. He did not see any way of bringing the Indian masses into or behind the war, beyond his Executive Council and his official "national war front" which was backed mainly by the princes. It was not up to him to bend a knee before Congress.

Outside the palace, chiseled in stone, is an inscription: "Liberty will not descend to a people, a people must raise themselves to liberty." It was a fitting last touch to the Viceroy's upholstery; he was waiting for the Indians to raise themselves to him. And from an American point of view, which is the only one I can give you, that seemed to me the whole trouble with British rule in India.

In my mind I contrasted what I saw here with what I knew

41

of the Philippines. When the Americans arrived in the islands they found a population fully as backward as India's and with nothing like the unity of historic civilization. It was a land of many peoples, speaking eighty different dialects—Mohammedans, Igorot head-hunters, pygmies, pagans, Aglipayans and Catholics, divided by centuries-old feuds. But in one generation 55% of these former illiterates learned to read and write. Twenty thousand American teachers went in and taught them the rudiments of science and democracy. Americans helped them to raise themselves to liberty, encouraged them to forget their sectarian quarrels and to unite to build a nation—which they did.

I could never forget the national demonstration I witnessed on the fortieth anniversary of the American occupation. Millions of humble Filipinos marched out under banners of the infant republic to pay tribute to the United States "for the boundless blessings bestowed upon us," the first time in history any people ever spontaneously offered thanksgiving to its own conquerors.

The Philippine Commonwealth is only about one-eighth the size of British India, but it is half as big as Burma and larger than Malaya and it contains just as varied religious and racial elements. Filipinos fought for their flag and for America when the Japs came because they were fighting for themselves, and because they believed Americans had tried to give them a square deal. All this may be in bad taste and impress Englishmen as more vulgar American boasting, but I mention it here merely as a reminder that the Philippines did prove that in a single generation you can raise a colonial people to unity and statehood, if you want to do so. The Americans did so for complex reasons and not entirely unselfish ones. Congress wanted "to turn 'em loose" because most Americans wanted them freed as soon as possible. But what really pushed the Independence Act through were the pressure groups who opposed the competition of duty-free Philippine agricultural products in the American market. Over in the U.S.S.R., however, where Stalin did not want to turn the former Tsarist colonies loose, the Russians proved in their own way—as we shall see—that "Asiatic peoples" can learn as quickly as white men.

But there was no denying the fact that the average Indian felt that this government was neither genuinely interested in his personal welfare nor that of the country, but only in profits and holding onto power. After so many years there was still no common ground between the rulers on high and the average wretched subject who owned little more than the g-string he stood in. The British hated the Brahmin mentality and the brutality of the caste system but liked the simple peasants and workers. They claimed to be necessary to India because only they could protect the interests of the minorities. Yet admittedly British rule tolerated some of the worst abuses of minorities in the world: the ostracism of fifty million Untouchables, the disfranchisement of ninety million subjects in the Indian states, the denial of a vote to 260 million Indians. Nor was there any adequate plan for the salvation of some eighty million people constantly in a state of semi-starvation. They too must "raise themselves to liberty."

The whole business was *laissez-faire* in its utmost anarchy.

One of the reasons I went to see the Viceroy was to urge him to launch a production campaign by establishing a national industrial co-operation administration. I argued that such a movement could rise above politics, train skilled workers and technicians for the nation, help rehabilitate the villages, provide work for the refugees pouring in from Burma, put native goods on the shelves of the stores being emptied of foreign commodities which could no longer be imported and help keep prices down. By mobilizing labor power in this way, production could be maintained, commodity shortages overcome, and hoarding and speculation controlled. Ultimate famine would be averted.

I had already talked to Nehru about such a scheme and he had told me he would support it. Even Gandhi, as the champion of village industry, could not readily have opposed it. Why not make a beginning by calling in the militant youths who were clamoring for "mass mobilization" and ask them to go to work on this program? Even if it failed it would at least pose some kind of positive thesis of government leadership.

The Viceroy was very kind and tolerant. He had heard all about "Indusco" and our attempts in China from Sir Archibald Clark-Kerr. But Archie and I didn't know India. The Indians "weren't ready for that" either.

There was no mutual trust here, no mutual confidence or respect as a basis for anything constructive. There was only mutual frustration. There was too little contact between the top-heavy government apparatus and the human microcosm for the benefit of which it presumably functioned. There was no warmth in this rule, not the love of the master for his dog nor of the teacher for his student nor of brother for brother.

43

Yet curiously there was not the atmosphere of the last days of the Tsar here either. In this period Indians had an amazing amount of freedom of press, speech and organization. It was amusing when Generalissimo Chiang Kai-shek came down to Delhi and issued a high-sounding statement urging the British to grant "real political power" to the Indians. Chiang knew very well that in no part of his China did the people have freedom of the press. Nowhere had his party ever permitted the election of even one municipal or county government. By contrast, Congress officials in India were still free to resume control of affairs in the provincial governments to which they had been constitutionally elected; and the Congress press freely railed against the British in a way nobody in Chungking would have dared criticize the Kuomintang. In Calcutta, Delhi and Bombay I saw Communist demonstrators carrying the Red flag and shouting *inqilab zindi-bad** at the top of their lungs. In Chungking they would have been shot.

The British also did nothing whatever to prevent Gandhi from calling a meeting down in Wardha to prepare for the "open rebellion" which he had been advocating now for weeks in *Harijan.* They gave him all the rope he needed. Up on the hill they simply quietly waited for the old man to issue the call for this hopeless revolt, so that he could be put out of the way for the duration.

II

God or Anarchy

No POLITICAL party carrying such enormous national responsibility was ever afflicted with a spokesman given to utterances so likely to bewilder and antagonize the world as was Congress under Gandhi the Mahatma, at this time. In everybody's mind there are conflicting wills and purposes but most politicians are

* "Long live revolution!"

astute enough to reveal their mental struggles to the public only in the form of a finished thesis. Gandhi exhibited the vagaries of his own efforts to make up his mind as candidly as a housewife hangs out her weekly wash.

After rejecting Cripps' proposals Gandhi announced that India could not attain independence till the Hindus and Moslems solved the communal question. Then he changed his mind and said these differences could only be settled when the British had left. He wrote in *Harijan* that the first thing India should do when independent was to seek negotiations with the Axis. Japan had no quarrel with Indians but only with the British and he demanded a complete withdrawal of all foreign forces. Then he reversed this stand and said he wanted British troops to remain, only they would have to support themselves, of course. British officials were to leave, but Gandhi had nothing concrete to replace them with except "God, or, in modern parlance, anarchy."

And yet, there was no questioning this, Gandhi still personified and articulated, more than any one individual, the leadership of India to the masses. His contradictions did not bother them. A lot of the incomprehensible things he said were addressed to the mystical Indian soul which intuitively understood him. And when he spoke "logically" he was talking for the Indian bourgeoisie, which supported him both morally and financially. Nobody else in India could play this dual role of saint for the masses and champion of big business, which was the secret of Gandhi's power. With all his vacillation he never deviated from his fundamental objective, which was to keep Indian attention focussed on the British as their main enemy. He did not want the movement to be side-tracked by the red herring of fascism versus democracy.

To try to understand Indian nationalism without seeing Gandhi, and especially in his native habitat in the heart of the Central Provinces, was to make life unnecessarily complicated. So I went down to Wardha in July, 1942, when the Congress Working Committee met for over a week to frame the called-for revolt. Wardha had few charms. The water was polluted and you had to drink it purpled with permanganate; there was a cholera epidemic, malaria was widespread, and the sticky, oppressive heat killed many people annually. The soil was sandy, the landscape flat and uninteresting. The chief difference between Wardha and a hair shirt is that the latter is removable, all of which probably

45

explained why India's No. 1 living saint chose to set up his "model village" of Sevagram, as it was called, outside this town of 30,000 souls. Perhaps I am prejudiced against Wardha; it was there that I caught dengue fever.

At night after the Working Committee met I would go over and drink coffee with some of the small group: Jawarhalal Nehru, Khan Abdul Gaffar Khan (the huge Pathan from the Northwest Provinces, adjoining Afghanistan, who was proud of his sobriquet, the Frontier Gandhi), Mr. and Mrs. Asaf Ali (a brave and energetic pair of rebels), Mrs. Sarojinu Naidu (a sensitive soul, full of courage and genius) and one or two others. We sat on the floor and leaned against huge hard pillows and talked freely on every subject. Gandhi was never there; he did not drink coffee and he was not a member of the Working Committee. But every day the Committee would talk and then a delegate would go out to Sevagram to consult with the old man. It seemed a democratic procedure; Gandhi apparently brought them to serve his will by sheer personal magnetism and enormous self-confidence. But of course he had big financial interests on his side too, which the Working Committee could not ignore.

It was hard to believe that revolt could be organized in such an atmosphere. The house was small and quiet. Horse-drawn carts were the only conveyance, and there were no telephones at Wardha and Sevagram. The British did not bother these Congress leaders; but neither did they send anyone down to talk things over with Gandhi and Nehru who, the Viceroy frankly admitted, "could lead Indian opinion overnight to our support." Fundamentally, I doubted that. I do not believe in the great-man theory of history, and I think in this case, as in others, Gandhi and Nehru merely personified the synthesis of a tangled web of very complex forces which they could influence only minutely. But the point is that the British believed otherwise and yet followed a do-nothing policy. The only foreign contacts Congress had at this time were with a few foreign newspapermen. As far as I remember, we were all Americans with the single exception of Guy Emeny, of the *News-Chronicle*, one Englishman who sincerely tried to understand Gandhi's position. (Emeny was to be killed a couple of years later in a plane crash with Major-General Orde Wingate, over in the Burma jungle.) It seemed incredible to all of us in Wardha that things would just be allowed to drift to a smash-up without any attempt at compromise for the common need.

In this period I had several long talks with Nehru about the wisdom of revolt. It was hard to question the Indians' right to act for what they thought their own best interests, but I argued that the move would be misunderstood abroad because objectively it would help the Axis. It was still possible for Congress to participate in the government. By assuming limited power at the center they could organize the people, get men into the army and train them, and prepare in a practical way to strike for full freedom at the right moment, regardless of who won the war. But the strongest argument against a civil-disobedience campaign was that it was certain to fail.

To my surprise Nehru agreed that they could not make the British give up power. It became clear to me that he had been won around to support the idea because he believed it was the only way of keeping the Congress united; it was simply easier to unite on an anti-British program than either an anti-Axis or a pro-Ally basis. Gandhi had again convinced Nehru that he was "in touch with the masses." "He has an intuitive understanding of the people that I lack," Nehru told me. "Even if I went into the government I could not deliver the goods." The people thought as Gandhi did.

"A nation can go down either supinely or fighting," he said. "If we go down now fighting we shall not be permanently suppressed. The only way to build up a spirit of resistance in this country is to organize the people against the British, and then these organizations can be quickly turned against the Japanese when they arrive." Nehru also did not believe any of the specious promises of Churchill and his mouthpiece Amery. He figured that Indians had to make a show of strength because if they could not force concessions out of the British in this crisis they would never get freedom. "I have the strongest feeling," he told me, "that the British mean to hang on here and we shall never get rid of them if we do not strike now."

The truth was that Nehru had restrained Gandhi as long as possible, hoping for some change in the British attitude and a new approach to Congress. Maulana Abad Azad had also been reluctant to act while still hoping for American intervention. Both of them had made their position perfectly clear to Colonel Louis Johnson, the President's special representative in Delhi, and before he returned to Washington he had given them strong reason to suppose Roosevelt might put pressure on Churchill to reopen negotiations. They believed the threat of rebellion might even yet bring that result. And in my own mind there was at this time no doubt that if Nehru and Azad had been given the slightest help they could still have pulled the Congress around to support of the United Nations.

Isolated as he was, however, Nehru had no choice but to resign or support the Mahatma's policy, and he preferred unity. He did succeed, however, in giving to the final resolution the character of a last-minute appeal for American intervention. While demanding immediate freedom and the right to form a provisional government, that resolution in return promised co-operation with Allied troops in India, aid to China, and resistance to the Axis. With publication of the resolution on July 14th, and its call for action under Gandhi's leadership, the Congress machine began to organize on a nation-wide scale. It was certain in advance that the All-India Congress Committee, which met three weeks later in Bombay, would fully endorse the directive.

That day I went to Sevagram to visit the Little Generalissimo himself. Arch Steele (the *Chicago Daily News*) and I bumped out on the back of that instrument of primitive torture, the Indian *tonga*, or two-wheeled cart. Gandhi had a very special one, I noticed, pulled by a fine beast which stamped and noisily stirred the bells around its neck. On its sides were painted portraits of the Congress leaders. Gandhi's own face was on the front, right behind the horse's tail.

Sevagram was a cross between a third-rate dude ranch and a refugee camp, a colony of mud huts with thatched roofs set in a cactus-sprinkled countryside. A dirt path led through the cluster to a hut that looked like the rest, except that it was surrounded with a fence of sticks and there was a *charka*, or spinning-wheel, adorning the wall in crude bas-relief. A cow wandered by morosely (cows in India are rude and insolent as camels) and scrawny chickens strutted about the yard. Inside, squatting barefoot on the matted floor, sat the toothless seventy-four-year-old messiah whom all India was waiting to hear speak the word of command.

Amidst this collection of simple buildings, chickens and cows, in a place infested by scorpions and poisonous snakes, and kindly spinners and toilers carrying out his creed, the Mahatma had, between sessions at prayers, spinning, and administering purgatives to relieve the aches and pains of patients in his own hospital, thought up his last headache for Churchill. Gandhi hated science almost as much as he hated machines and he especially welcomed anyone who came to get his own personal mud-pack cure for high-blood pressure. Here also he edited *Harijan*. A combined Dorothy Dix and Dorothy Thompson, he offered everything from advice to young maidens on how to avoid being raped to recommendations to Churchill, Stalin and Tojo on how to win the war.

And now, as he spoke to us out of this background, his words were so incongruous you could hardly take in their meaning. He sat there leaning against a big white pillow, his brown body naked except for a few yards of cheesecloth round his middle (and how we envied him in that withering heat) and over his big gold-rimmed glasses he peered down at us now kindly, now a bit petulant. He was going to lead a mass movement, he explained, on the broadest scale. It would be the biggest of his life, his "last struggle," but it would be non-violent, in so far as he could make it so.

"And do you really expect the British to withdraw in answer to your threat?" I asked.

"Of course," he said, "if the British wish to withdraw that would be a feather in their caps. But I want to stress this point. There is no room left in the proposal for negotiations." He wagged his bald pate determinedly. "Either they recognize the independence of India or they do not. After that many things could happen. Once independence is recognized the British would have altered the face of the whole landscape."

But he did not, he emphasized, mean any statement on paper; he wanted a physical withdrawal now. "Next it would be a question of who would take over India, God or anarchy." In one breath he said that Free India would make common cause with the Allies. In the next he said, "If I can possibly turn India toward non-violence then I would do so. If I could succeed in making 400 million people fight with non-violence it would be a great gain."

What a stubborn and honorable old saint he was! Not even now would he personally endorse that part of the resolution promising to fight Japan. Yet if he had influence enough to bring Congress into line behind him here, was there not every possibility that he would later be able to bring a Free Indian govern-

49

ment round to withdrawal from the war? But he denied to me that he would ever use soul-force against his "own" government to get it to obey his will. Absently pulling on his big toe and looking down at us in his childlike, innocent way, the old man touched off his heavy artillery.

"This time it isn't a question of (giving the British) one more chance," he said. "*It is open rebellion!*"

And that was that. Gandhi certainly intended his remark to be taken literally, as he later repeated it several times. With the rope the British had given to him he now surely hung the Congress for the rest of the war. He played the game of the men "on the hill" just as they had foreseen he would.

As I left I had a feeling that he was right about one thing, anyway. Whatever happened, it would indeed be the "last struggle" in which Gandhi would lead a great nationalist struggle. It was the biggest gamble of his life and the old man knew it. You may not agree with a lot of things about Gandhi, but no one could deny the honesty of his convictions, nor his fighting courage in defense of them. And these too are qualities of his greatness.

As Gandhi said elsewhere, he had not much time left and he wanted to see India free before he died.

III

The End of Non-Violence

ON AUGUST 9, 1942, the day after the Bombay meeting of the All-India Congress Committee adopted a long resolution which incorporated the Wardha directive, the British arrested the Little Spinner and Jawarhalal Nehru and several hundred other Congress leaders. Eventually they were to cram the jails with about 48,000 prisoners.

The suddenness of the action, taken without waiting for Gandhi to make any preliminary move to negotiate, surprised the

Indians. They had expected a few more days in which to prepare; but preliminary instructions had already gone out through all the provinces and retaliatory action commenced at once. Protest meetings and demonstrations took place everywhere and were met with ruthless armed suppression in which hundreds lost their lives. In Delhi we saw British Tommies open fire on unarmed crowds and here alone there were hundreds of casualties. Thereafter began an extensive revolt news of which was largely suppressed in the outside world. It took the British six months fully to suppress it.

This rebellion failed and was futile first of all because under Gandhi's leadership it could have succeeded only if Indians had been prepared to martyr themselves wholesale. The event proved that there were not four hundred million, nor even four million, people ready to die to vindicate Gandhi's *satyagraha.*

Actually, Gandhi had compromised a good deal on his definitions of "non-violence" in this revolt and many methods sanctioned were certain to result in tragedy. It is doubtful anyway whether such a thing as *ahimsa* or non-injury could ever be reconciled with mass political action of any kind, because that involves the mobilization of force, and no real distinction can be drawn between coercion or force and violence. Other Indian leaders frankly recognized this fact. As soon as Gandhi was put away they adopted violence in nearly all its forms. But their means were insufficient and poorly organized, by men who were amateurs at armed insurrection.

No revolt could succeed in India without the participation of the Army, from which Gandhi had completely isolated himself. The various Moslem political parties remained almost entirely aloof, the Sikh community gave little support, and the negative attitude of the young Communist Party split away large segments of the working class.

Thus it turned out that the action which Nehru thought necessary to preserve unity in the nationalist movement actually rived it on class, communal and party lines. Congress in the past had commanded elements from the extreme left to extreme right united on the single demand of independence. On the right wing belonged the pro-Japanese Gujerat merchants and Bombay mill-owners, the Hindu capitalists like Birla, and Parsi industrialists like Tata, who, although not active in Congress, contributed large sums to Gandhi's "war" chest. This Indian bourgeoisie had as its Congress spokesman Vallahbhai Patel, the sixty-eight-year-old "uncrowned king of Gujerat," a blunt and ruthless character who was Gandhi's number-one organizer.

In the Right Wing also belonged the Fascist-inclined followers of Subhas Chandra Bose, the escaped Congress leader who later became "marshal" of an independent Indian Army organized by the Japanese at Singapore—of whom more toward the end of this book. Mostly Bengalis, who favor terrorist methods, Bose's disciples are known as the "Forward Bloc" of Congress. The British had declared it illegal after unearthing terrorist plots and connections with the Axis, but the Forward Bloc still had connections inside the Congress. It seems scarcely likely that Patel, Gandhi and Nehru were unaware of that.

On the left wing were Congress socialists, with their membership drawn chiefly from middle-class intellectuals in the cities. Some of them claimed Nehru as their leader but he disclaimed the honor. Although he is avowedly a socialist, and in fact helped draw up the socialist program of reconstruction, Nehru wished to be above factions, as future leader of what he hoped would remain a Congress Party uniting all nationalist groups. Congress socialists did not believe in *ahimsa* and frankly advocated other means of overthrowing the British. In Bombay, where they were fairly strong, some leading socialists told me candidly that they could see no difference between Japanese imperialism and British, except that one was brown and under it at least Indians would not suffer from color discrimination. Such men were often called fascists and followed what was, objectively, a policy favoring Axis collaboration. But I felt the great majority of them were simply so blinded by their emotional frustrations that they would have made an alliance with the devil himself to get rid of the British.

The chief rivals of the Congress socialists were the Communists, who were also an intra-Congress organization. They were again legalized as a party in India only in the spring of 1942, after many years of underground operation. In Bombay in July I heard P. C. Joshi, the general secretary of the Party, deliver what he said was the first public speech he had dared to make for seven years. In spite of their illegality, however, these Indian Reds had maintained an influential following and once their leaders were let out of jail they quickly built up a large membership of zealous, hard-working youths.

Incidentally, it is interesting to note that the Indian Communist Party evidently was completely cut off from the Comintern some years prior to its dissolution in 1943. This was evident in the curious "deviation" of the Indian Party on the question of the war. Most national Communist Parties immediately abandoned whatever qualifications they had attached to their support for the war when Hitler invaded Russia, but a full six months later the Indian Party was still opposing Indian participation in it. The Communist Party of Burma, which was affiliated with the Burmese counterpart of the Indian Congress, the Dobamma Aisyone, or the Thakins, likewise continued to oppose the war as "imperialistic," until shortly before the Japanese invasion. When they came out for "anti-Japanese resistance" they were the only part of the Thakin nationalist movement which wanted to help the United Nations. Unconvinced of that, the British put most of them in jail all the same.

It was just before Pearl Harbor that the Indian Communists changed their party line to combine demands for independence and for all-out war against fascism. Even then, it was the only important group in Congress which unreservedly supported the war. For that reason the Viceroy removed the ban on the party and permitted the Red flag to fly again all over India. The Communist Party is now much the most powerful left-wing organization in India, and because of the stand it took against Gandhi's call for rebellion it is the only part of the Indian Congress which still remains legal. Its prestige and following are now such that it is certain to play a much more decisive role in the future of the Indian nationalist movement than heretofore, despite the intense distaste with which it is regarded by Congress conservatives.

At the Bombay Conference the Communists in the Congress Committee energetically attacked Gandhi's call for "open rebellion." They declared that it could only end in beheading Indian nationalism for the rest of the war, and in extensive bloodshed without hope of victory. Only Japan would benefit. The vote of the eleven Communist delegates was smothered in the Committee itself, but throughout the country they proved to be stronger than was then generally supposed. For the first time they were able to hold large working-class groups loyal to an independent discipline. This was especially true in the two largest Indian labor movements, the National Trade Unions Council and the All-India Kisan Sabha, which the Communists "captured" from Congress socialists.

The Communists refused to support Congress' call for civil disobedience. They opposed strikes, riots and sabotage as harmful to the war effort and encouraged the workers to remain at their jobs. They appealed for national unity to support the war against fascism. They backed Rajagopalachari's demand for Hindu-Moslem co-operation, through "acceptance in principle" of the Moslem League's demand for Pakistan as the necessary preliminary to a successful fight for independence.

As a result of these cleavages the "insurrection" got relatively far less mass support than it got from the extremely anti-British bourgeoisie and from middle-class radicals and intellectuals. Thus in Bombay few mill workers went on strike but the mill-owners themselves, led by Patel's friends such as Mafatlal Gagalbhoy, in many cases staged lockouts. Foremen and managers simply told the workers to go home and promised to see that they got their wages. But when owners saw that the revolt had failed they quickly reopened the factories.

A curious thing happened in the case of the big stoppage of work at the Tata Iron and Steel Company in Jemshedpur, which cost the British 300,000 tons of lost steel production. The Tata Company has the most enlightened labor policy in India and its workers had no serious grievances. But just before Gandhi was arrested the owners inexplicably distributed a three-months' "Bonus" to all employees, who then promptly went on protest strike, led by their foremen! In contrast, practically none of the miserably paid workers in state-owned enterprises—and none whatever on the railways, most important of all—made any serious move to back Gandhi.

All the same, if the Japanese had attacked India at that time it would have been a different story. For the revolt revealed the existence of a very extensive fifth column in India. The most effective sabotage to railways, industries and government property centered in Bengal and Bihar, which were for weeks virtually isolated from the rest of India. Beyond doubt, fifth columnism would have assumed grave proportions had pressure by the Japs drawn off any of the military and police power which the British concentrated against it.

One thing that impressed me at this time about the hatred of many upper-class Indians for the British was the big role played in it by resentment against racial and color discrimination and against the English colonial's manifestations of superiority. I don't know what it is that makes the average middle-class Englishman, well-behaved and unassuming and likeable enough at home, begin to take on these patronizing and gauche airs very often as soon as he finds himself among "natives" anywhere, but it is a disease which permeates the entire colonial bureaucracy and poisons relations between the British and their subjects in many lands.

It is all very well to feel superior to other people if you can dissimulate it as skilfully as the Chinese do, but neither the English nor the Americans are as highly civilized as that. Admittedly there is nothing in the British attitude in India which is as bad as the treatment of Negroes in our Southern States. There is also nothing worse than the Brahmins' discrimination against their own Untouchables, and there is no doubt that one reason the Brahmin caste is so sensitive about British discrimination is either its own bad conscience, or a feeling of frustration at being unable to invoke its social superiority. But the Brahmins are not foreigners and the British are.

The humble Indian peasant is used to being treated as a slave, but the educated Indian, from prince to army officer, deeply resents things like exclusion from white society and membership in the clubs, and being barred from some hotels and restaurants in England and America. Even in Bombay I was refused access to the Restaurant Breach Kandy when I tried to take an Indian friend in to eat with me. The management actually had a sign on the door, "For Europeans and their European guests only"—a standing affront to thousands of Asiatics who saw it.

Sir Dinshaw Pettit was an Indian who had received all the honors one could get out of the British system. One day when I was visiting Kay and Bob Stimson in their Bombay home (a friendly place of wit, wisdom and generosity) I walked down the shore to see Sir Dinshaw in his villa amidst fragrant gardens which stood green above the sparkling bay. The Baronet asked me, "Why did the Burmese help the Japs drive out the British?" I gave various reasons: because they were misled into thinking the Japs intended giving them freedom, because the Japs played on the common adherence to Buddhism and they didn't know the Zen Buddhism of Japan is a very different order from the carefree Burmese religion, and so on.

"No, you've missed the most important point!" exclaimed Sir Dinshaw. "It is because they hate the British for their color

55

prejudice and superior ways. All Orientals hate the British because of this stupid bias. It's done more harm than anything else; it is at the bottom of all the trouble."

So here was my friend with his fifty million rupees, his villas in Europe, his baronetcy in England, and his palaces in India, but still an unhappy man. There were still places where merely the brown of his skin would bar him. I could not have taken him into the Breach Kandy, either, though I could probably have taken my dog there—if my dog had not been in Connecticut.

Even the Tata family resented patronage and condescension in the British and told me so. And I remember especially vividly an interview I had with Wolchand Hirachand, the big Indian shipping magnate and business entrepreneur in Bombay. At Nehru's suggestion I went to call on him in his large suite of air-conditioned offices. He told me of his vast interests worth millions of dollars and how he had fought for Gandhi—financed him and sat in the street to stop traffic. It must have been quite a roadblock at that; he had an enormous fanny. As for choice between the British and Japanese, he said frankly he preferred to take his chance with the latter. In Japan they had received him as an equal and had given him the best suite in the Imperial Hotel and banqueted him everywhere. In England the hotels were always "full" and big business men would not invite him to their homes; and in America they told him that they could not register a black man in the hotels.

"But the Japanese would ruin you, you know," I said. "You could never operate this profitably under their control."

"What do I care about losing my property?" This outsize Indian sitting on top of a huge fortune said to me with tears in his voice. "Look at me now, am I a free man? No, I am just a slave!" It was a terrifying experience.

Such feelings blinded hundreds like Wolchand to whatever virtues British rule otherwise possessed. I thought of encounters like this very often when in Russia I saw Asiatics living under the Soviet system, with none of the rights to amass private wealth that the British allowed the Indian bourgeoisie. They had few of the "civil liberties" Indians had, either. But the bolsheviks had done one thing which made up for a lot. They had abolished the rights of "private enterprise"—or "private privilege," if you prefer—but with it they had also abolished racial and color discrimination.

I have gone into this whole episode in some detail because abroad not much is realized of its significance. For one thing, the British here probably lost their last chance to reconcile the forces of Indian nationalism to continued membership in the Empire. Henceforth nothing short of amputation will satisfy the decisive elements in Indian society. It was also perhaps Gandhi's last act as generalissimo of Indian nationalism. Vigorous younger forces will no longer be dominated by him nor his quasi-religious political theories—though they will continue to be an influence. Nehru realized that when I last saw him.

"India has had its back straightened by Gandhi; he has taught us the value of unity in political action and during this period probably no other method could have succeeded," he told me. "But I do not believe now that we will ever get power by non-violent means. This is our last attempt."

A new leadership based on militant organization of working-class power combined with support from the Indian industrial bourgeoisie, and tied in closely with trends in China and with other Asiatic revolutionary movements, and not afraid to penetrate and use the Indian Army, may emerge after the war. Sooner or later it will adopt violence on a major scale unless there is a fundamental change in policies pursued by the British Cabinet, to take cognizance of the proverbial handwriting on the wall.

But what was going on at this very moment, up in the mountains of the Caucasus beyond India's northwest frontier, was in a real sense deciding the future of these unfortunate people in a far more conclusive manner than anything they did about it themselves.

In September I flew out of India and over Iraq, bound for Russia at last, where, after all, man's fate was indeed decided by soul-force—articulated in the only language that fascist imperialism could understand, the language of cannon.

IV

The Teheran Gateway

IRAN is as exciting and romantic as its name until you get close to the filth and disease that kill eight out of ten children before they are five. But you can't smell it from the air and at 5,000 feet the long sands and rivers look weirdly beautiful. Even on the ground it is still nearer the Arabian Nights than anything outside Hollywood. The greatest battle in history was being waged beyond its frontier on the Caspian Sea when I first saw old Persia, but the country seemed far removed from war.

When I flew into the mountain-rimmed capital, Teheran, I was trailing Wendell Willkie's *Gulliver* and comfortably ahead of three other gentlemen who foregathered there to decide the fate of Hitler in December, 1943. I rode up from Basra with Brigadier-General Don Shingler of our Persian Gulf Service Command, a one-man coalition of engineer, diplomat and commander who did one of the great jobs of this war when he opened up our south gate into Russia. As we crossed the bands of yellow and green sand and the earth which cradled a half dozen buried civilizations tracing back to centuries before Christendom, I realized Shingler could turn to writing guide books any day the army stopped appreciating him.

Not long after we left the ruined fortresses where Sindbad is supposed to have lived, outside Basra, he consulted his map and the landscape and then leaned over and plucked my sleeve.

"There's Al Qurna down there." He pointed out a town of sun-baked brick set among palms and gardens, a thin ruffle of vegetation beside the Euphrates, black under the desert sun. "Somewhere near Al Qurna, Adam ate the apple that started all the trouble, or so they say. This is where Eve used to run around in the altogether. Probably it was once the confluence of the Tigris and Euphrates."

Sindbad's successors hereabouts claimed the original apple

tree was still alive as recently as the First World War. It seems it had disappeared during a celebrated international incident when some Tommies, slightly overheated with beer and midday sun, went on an unauthorized souvenir hunt one day and broke off several of its branches. The inhabitants were Moslems, but they had a civic pride in public property and revered the sacred tree as the apple of their eye. They chose some Tommies and, when the fighting was over, nothing was left either of Adam's apple tree or the sinners. I hasten to relieve Don Shingler of responsibility for the story, which can be blamed strictly on the traditions of Sindbad.

Beyond Al Qurna lay the city of Ur of the Chaldees, where Abraham was born, and farther along our course Shingler pointed out the ruins of Babylon. Outside Baghdad we swooped low over Ctesiphon and the great arch of the meeting hall built by the Sassanids more than 1,000 years ago. It still holds out against the elements and the laws of gravity, and since Hitler isn't coming that way now it has a good chance of lasting another thousand. We left Baghdad—an excellent thing to do to that pestilential hole—and climbed 15,000 feet. To get to Teheran you step over the rim of those biblical mountains which rise in the distant Caucasus and end in the wastes of the Baluchistan.

Americans did not visit Teheran much oftener than Lhasa before the war, but thousands of them came in soon after I did. Iran meant more to us, and we meant more to Iran, than most people faintly realized that September of 1942. Nearly every government ministry had one or more American experts serving in an advisory capacity. Iran had appealed to Washington for these knowledgeable gentlemen, through our popular minister at Teheran, Louis Dreyfus, and at the same time had coyly asked for Lend-Lease aid. We supplied the advisers first; then lend-leasemen Winant and Kidd arrived to talk over what Iran might be wanting in exchange for the precious oil she was pouring out to the Allies.

Aside from oil, why should we take so much interest in this obscure little country halfway around the world? Well, it isn't so little; it would make half a dozen Britains. And it wasn't so obscure any more, either, not when it formed our only land bridge to Southern Russia. It had become to the Soviet Union what the Burma Road had been to the Chinese, only far more so; it ultimately proved our most important line of supply.

59

On paper, Iran had been an ally of Britain and Russia since January, 1942, though an odd arrangement specifically relieved her of fighting Germans, even in self-defense. Earlier the British and Russians had moved in troops to depose the old King, Riza Shah Pahlavi, and to put his son on the throne instead. We were not party to that operation, done in the interest of Allied security, for Pahlavi was allegedly pro-Nazi. But we had our own treaty of alliance with Iran, not on paper but in the hearts of many Iranians, who liked Uncle Sugar a little better right then than most foreign powers.

Teheran, which a few years ago saw nothing in its streets but camel traffic from the desert, had become a focal point where hopes for a Soviet victory converged in the form of the first concrete Allied help. A thousand and one items, from trucks to thermometers, were flowing in to fight Hitler. Goods entered on four different railways and roads, one of which started in far-off India, and met in the capital on the way to their destination.

American engineers were constructing docks, harbors, roads and bridges for Iran, and would soon begin a new railway. Technicians had arrived to man repair and assembly depots and the large plants recently erected for General Motors and Douglas Aircraft. Great new oil refineries at Abadan, which alone produced enough high-octane gasoline to supply Allied needs in this part of the world, were being developed chiefly with American materials and partly by American technicians.

For the Americans South Persia was no bed of Rubaiyats. They baked in desert heat ten months a year and dreamed of home the whole twelve. In Basra I was solemnly assured the thermometer reached 147 in the shade at the airport, while Abadan claimed a record three degrees higher.

Iran is full of dysentery, malaria, trachoma, typhoid, typhus, cholera and smallpox, and there is a delightful punishment known as Baghdad boil, or Oriental sore. But the place does grow the loveliest roses of the East and it produces excellent wines and caviar. Teheran itself is set amongst the white petals of a flower of mountains—a jewel in the lotus. If Russia had had the same rate of mortality as Iran, more newborn babes and children under five would have died there from preventable diseases in 1942 than on the battlefields. Yet Teheran, now a city of more than half a million, has a healthful climate, and many call it the best in the Middle East. A little more than a decade ago it was

60

a noisome spot like Baghdad or worse, a mere hazard in the desert, a collection of narrow, canopied streets winding between mud-brick walls, hiding a few places of gardens and cool beauty, but full of hovels of darkness and filth. Old Riza Shah Pahlavi changed it. Rome was not built in a day, but Pahlavi rebuilt Teheran in a decade.

As a starter, he made himself a new palace with a fifty-car garage. Houses and shops were torn down ruthlessly to make way for the wide streets and paved arterial roads with the tree-lined walks you see today. The plazas and squares were laid out and filled with statuary and fountains. Electric lighting and power were introduced. Impressive government edifices and several streets of modern shops were erected and a number of schools, hospitals and other public buildings appeared. Even the British got the idea. They put up a magnificent structure, finished to resemble a mosque, to house the Imperial Bank of Iran. As a climax, the Shah ordered a streamlined railway station. The result of this burst of energy is that Iran's capital became one of the most attractive cities in Asia.

"It looks clean enough. What's wrong with it?" I asked when one of the few American residents complained about the health hazard soon after my arrival.

"What is the most important thing about a city? Its water supply! The people who rebuilt Teheran forgot about that. Look at the water in the drainage channels in the street. See that man over there washing his feet? See that woman near by washing her baby? Down below, somebody else is filling a bucket of drinking water. That's all the water Teheran has. When you turn on the tap in your hotel room, that's what comes out of the spout— billions of germs."

"You're just pampered," I said. "You should live in Wardha, where you have to drink your water in the purple."

But the city has its compensations. They might be summarized by saying it reminds you of old Harbin. It is semi-Asiatic, semi-European and with a brisk, invigorating climate, a mixture of seemingly every race, from flaxen-haired Czech and Polish refugees to impoverished Mongoloid tribesmen in from the hills and the debt-ridden peasant serfs and dark Arab camel-pullers and hooded women clothed all in black.

The shops were crammed with goods, more than I had seen in any stores from Cairo to Chungking, but at fantastic prices

61

for anything imported. Inflation was already rampant. Fine Persian silver work, miniature paintings and soft carpets which formerly were cheap, now cost more than in America, but that did not stop American soldiers from investing heavily, just as in India they were cheerfully victimized on all sides by fake jewels made in Japan. On the other hand, caviar, vodka and Persian wine were plentiful and still relatively cheap. You could buy caviar fresh from the Caspian at five American dollars a pound, and a dozen gorgeous roses for a dollar. But whisky was twelve dollars a quart and an empty vacuum bottle cost twenty.

Fruit stalls were crammed with luscious pears, apples, pomegranates and grapes, and there was a seemingly inexhaustible supply of meats, nuts, confections and pastry. At least inexhaustible for that 5% of the population, including Poles lately released from Russia, and then living on Anglo-American funds, who could afford to buy them. It may seem a trivial subject to you, but the discovery of all this milk and honey after the scant markets of China and India was something for me to wire home about. And I did.

Only Cairo presented as brilliant a display and variety of uniforms. At dusk Teheran's main street was a manikin parade. Polish, British, French, Persian, Indian, Egyptian, Russian and American costumes were among the throng, which was definitely a male show, women providing only a somber background. Persians themselves sported a variety ranging from the powder-blue garb of the *gendarmerie* to the soft mustard color of the army, and they easily took first honors. The Russian influence dominated, from the high-crowned hat to leather boots, but there were some touches of genius in Teheran tailors. The same figures who, when you passed them in laymen's clothes, made no impression except to arouse the subconscious thought that there goes another fellow who probably washes his feet in your drinking water, were, in uniform, all Robert Taylors and Cesar Romeros.

The new Shah, Mohammed Riza, was Commander-in-Chief of all in uniform. Though still very young, he had so far been a well-regulated king, abiding strictly by the Constitution and Treaty. Unlike his wastrel brothers, he was sober and earnest and obviously devoted to his strikingly beautiful Egyptian-born queen, Fawzia. A trained soldier, his first love was the army, over which he had established his direct control; and he was eager to modernize it with tanks and airplanes. After Wendell Willkie patted him on the back and took him for a ride in a U. S. Army Liberator, the Shah began to believe he would supply him; but to date he had only got General Rigley as adviser to his Quartermaster Corps.

Second to the Shah in power was Ahmed Ghoram, Prime Minister, and some said the Shah was second to him. Ghoram bossed the parliament, whose members were entirely appointed by Mohammed's father. European-educated and vocally strongly pro-Ally, he looked like Sven Hedin and wore gold-rimmed spectacles, giving him a professional air. His fluent French made him seem continental, so that it was incongruous to see him finger a string of yellow Islamic prayer beads throughout our talk, beneath the gilded candelabra and statuary which festooned the whole palace.

The Prime Minister explained that royalties on oil had made Iran rich in sterling. Large credits had accumulated in London. She was one country ready to pay us cash for any help authorized by Lend-Lease. Ghoram himself wanted machine shops and arsenal equipment. "If we had a good arsenal, we could be a greater help to Russia." He shrugged his round shoulders. "Naturally the arsenal would also help make our army self-sufficient, too. We think, because of our geographical position," the Prime Minister went on rather wistfully, "we ought to have closer economic ties and relationships of every kind with America." For this reason, Iran chose Americans rather than Russians as advisers. America is far away, Russia sits on the northern frontier. His meaning was perfectly clear.

The same idea guided the old Shah when he handed out contracts for construction of the Trans-Iranian Railway, which runs from the Persian Gulf almost to the Russian frontier across mountain passes 7,000 feet high. Germans built one section, Americans another, and the British were assigned the most difficult, while various oddments were contributed by Italians, Belgians, Swedes and Czechs. Steel and rails came from Soviet Russia, sleepers from Australia, locomotives from Sweden, and further supplies from Japan and Yugoslavia, while the Teheran station was built by the Swiss. Today no foreigners have a financial interest in the railway which is owned entirely in Iran. But the American Army operates it as far as Teheran—which pleases the young Shah immensely. Americans, he figures, will go home after the war.

There was in Iran the same expectation one found everywhere from Egypt to China—that somehow America would protect everybody's independence and in addition put a car in every garage. One thing our troops and engineers had done, anyway: they had brought the land of Haroun-al-Raschid and of old Omar out of its isolationism. It had become one of the main crossroads of the world and we were there as traffic policemen.

Judging from the declaration at Teheran in December, 1943, by Roosevelt, Stalin and Churchill, the earlier fears that this land would be swallowed up by its Russian neighbor have now been put to rest. If any international guarantee is worth anything, the one made to Iran should assure it a brilliant independent future. It was given the most explicit promise of international economic aid and right to participate in world affairs on a basis of equality yet made to any small nation.

Book Two

DAYS OF VICTORY

U. S. S. R.

PART - I - ACROSS THE STEPPE

I

Into Russia

•๑⟦⟧๑•

"THEY change their clime, not their disposition, who run beyond the sea," observed the smug Horace, and he was quite right; you cannot get much more out of a country than you take to it. This is especially true of Russia, I think; a man's previous environment and experience almost invariably determine the impressions he gets of that country. That is why you hear such vastly different answers to the same questions from people who ought to know.

The night before I flew into Russia out of Teheran I had dinner with Bill Chaplin, and with Jim Brown whom Bill was relieving as *International News* correspondent in Moscow, and with Edmund Stevens of the *Christian Science Monitor*. Brown and Stevens had seen much the same things in Russia; they had had somewhat similar experiences, and they agreed about certain basic facts. But they were as far apart on interpretations as William Henry Chamberlain, for example, and Walter Duranty. The latest crop of correspondents was evidently repeating the history of the earlier ones.

Later on in Moscow I got together with a colleague one night and drew up a list of the special equipment a foreign student ought to take with him to Russia. We decided this should include, besides general familiarity with history and geography, the following: 1) a knowledge of Russian history, language and culture; 2) a knowledge of the history and culture of Eastern Europe and some residence in that area; 3) knowledge of some history, culture and language of Eastern Asia; and 4) knowledge of the history and theory of Marxism and social revolution in both East and West. We made up a score board for the correspondents and diplomats then in Russia and gave them ratings. There was not one with all those qualifications.

In addition to such positive assets an observer in Russia ought to be dispossessed of as many negative factors of approach as possible; he should be as objective as a good juror. It must be recognized, for instance, that a strong believer in clerical or Church authority in temporal affairs would not be able to examine Soviet Russia without bias. An individual familiar only with strictly Anglo-Saxon parliamentary processes in government would also be under some handicap; such a limited background is not likely to enable one to understand means and ends in Russia. And it goes without saying that racial antagonism, class prejudices, congenital pacifism, or hatred of the whole idea of socialist society, are all barriers to a correct judgment of forces inside Russia.

As far as the prejudices were concerned, at least, I felt little encumbered when I entered the country. It was true I had been reared as a Catholic; but I knew the history of the Orthodox Church in Russia too and reasons for the bolshevik attitude toward it. Long residence in China had divested me of racial or religious prejudices and perhaps made me more of a Taoist than anything else. And in fact I was to find that my Asiatic background gave me an insight into some things about Russia that perplexed or astonished other people. The Far East was the practical school in which I had studied Marxism and its influence; and it was in Manchuria that I had first met Russian culture and power.

It is only the habit of an old cartography, in many ways as outdated as the early concept of a flat world, that prevents us from thinking of the Soviet Union as the continent of Eurasia, rather than as part of Europe. It is of course an amalgam of East and West and a synthesis of the historic influences of both cultures, as overlaid upon the Slavic peoples struggling up toward socialism from the depths of centuries of Mongolian despotism and Tsarist absolutism. Tatar blood flows freely all through Russia and there is a strong flavor of Asiatic habit, method and philosophy behind the practice of socialism in Soviet society even today. Many things the casual foreign observer sees here and imagines to be peculiar to socialism are in fact simply a mixture of Slav and Tatar.

But there is danger in assuming that because the U.S.S.R. is Eurasia its inhabitants have anything in common with so-called Eurasians of the colonial world. Incredible as it may seem, some visitors in Russia even during the war tried to treat them as a colonial people or to take a paternalistic or patronizing attitude toward them. Nobody senses condescension more quickly than a Russian nor resents it more. He simply considers such people fools and uses them accordingly.

It was hard for me to see how anyone could feel "patronizing" toward Russia at the moment I flew across the border early in October, 1942. After what I had seen of India, Iraq, Iran and North Africa I knew we and the British did not have enough forces in this region to stop the Nazis if they broke through to the lower Caspian Sea. The battle for Stalingrad was already two months old and the Germans' right wing had penetrated deep into the Caucasus. We flew very low into Baku and tree-hopped all the way to Kuibyshev. The Germans came quite close to Baku, exactly how close I do not know, but later on the mayor of the town was reported as stating that Baku's own guns had "saved the city." If it had gone to the Germans, if Stalingrad had not held, all the Middle East and India would have been exposed to Axis penetration.

It was then widely believed outside Russia that Stalingrad was already doomed. I did not agree with this and I was heartily sick of hearing people say, "Of course we were all wrong about Russia." We were not all wrong and I am glad to have it on record* that I believed from the outset that Hitler had embarked on catastrophe by invading Russia. But even at this time people in India and Iran quite seriously commiserated me and warned that I would have to leave Russia by way of Siberia. There were rumors that Russia was seeking peace. (Actually the first concrete peace offer was made shortly afterward and it came from Germany, not Russia.) It was expected in Allied councils that Japan would invade in the East.

Hitler had, it must be remembered, occupied an area about the size of our Eastern and Southern American states, including Texas, which contained some sixty to seventy million people, or a population half the size of our own. The conquest covered only a tenth of the U.S.S.R., but it was the most developed tenth in every respect. It held half the working coal mines, produced

* In *The New Republic*, July, 1941.

three-fifths of the iron ore and pig iron, about half the steel and machinery, and about a third of the harvest. More than half the electric power was lost and 30% of all Russia's railway mileage. The finest cities and the capitals of the richest provinces had fallen; Leningrad was blockaded and Moscow was still an embattled city.

Was it possible that Russia could yet find the strength within herself to throw back the German colossus, or even to hold it further? It was a test for all time of two ways of life. It was a test of whether a society organized on socialist lines, and led by workers and peasants, could survive a maximum threat to its existence. Those convinced that it could not, those who had predicted speedy Red Army disaster, or internal political break-up, or economic collapse, or wholesale desertion to the Nazis, had yet to be proved fully wrong. Even to many sympathetic onlookers it seemed that this nation of peasants could not possibly defeat the mighty Wehrmacht; all it could give us was a little more time. I was glad, therefore, to be reassured when I reached Kuibyshev and went to see Solomon Lozovsky, assistant Commissar for Foreign Affairs, who said, "I do not speak English, I only suffer English," but nevertheless managed to make himself quite clear.

"Why do the Russians fight so hard and how can they go on fighting today, that is what Americans want to know, is it so? Listen, Americans did not understand us in the past. Some were influenced by lies about us; they would not believe the truth. That is why they judged wrong about us. Now they see how our people fight and they realize there is something here in Russia which keeps them going. Do you want to know what it is? The answer is that the revolution has created here a new social consciousness and that men and women in this country have something to fight for, to die for or to live for, as the case may be, but to *fight* for!"

As Russia unfolded beneath my eyes during the succeeding six months, as Red victories mounted and slowly the world breathed more easily, I was able to look for this "new consciousness" among men and women and children laboring in the fields from dawn to dark, and by the light of the moon, and in the factories day and night, and in battle, tireless and fearless in their valor.

I did not find the answer all in one place or all at once, and I do not claim to have all the answers now. On the whole I never saw another great country where relations with the foreign press were more inexpertly handled, where there was so little understanding of the needs of individual correspondents of good will, and where, as a result of repeated frustration and bafflement in one's efforts to secure the minimum degree of co-operation required to collect one's material, so magnificent an epic of anguish and glory was more inadequately presented to the world. Nevertheless, day by day I saw a little here and little there until finally I came to some conclusions of my own about the "secret" of Russia's fighting spirit, and toward the end of this book I shall try to sum them up as best I can.

Lozovsky was right about something else, I should point out. Before I left for Moscow I asked him if he thought the Japanese would attack Siberia. He hesitated for a moment and then smiled above his beard, which is like Kalinin's. "No," he answered emphatically, "we do not think Japan will attack." Which was quite a statement to get from a commissar in Russia in that dark October of 1942.

II

Southward from Moscow

NOT long after I reached Moscow I heard Josef Stalin, in his role as Peoples Commissar of Defense and Supreme Commander-in-Chief, deliver his famous speech on the 25th anniversary of the October Revolution. All Russia was silent as he spoke and even in the front lines men clapped on earphones to cut out the noise of cannon and listen in. In Moscow the giant amplifiers that keep the squares echoing with voices all day long now lifted this soft, slow, confident Georgian accent high to the heavens. It boomed into Red Square and turned the corner into Revolutionary Square, opposite the Metropole Hotel, where we sat listening. When Stalin paused to drink a glass of water (once he apologized for this, saying he had eaten too many herring that morning and

Russia roared with laughter) the gurgle sounded in the square like the rush of Victoria Falls.

He had been "instructed," Stalin said, to review the work of the government and the party organs since the preceding November, and his report covered the "peaceful construction and organization of a strong rear for our front on the one hand, and the conducting of defensive and offensive operations, on the other." He described the complex work of evacuating industry and workers and setting up new plants, of meeting new demands on production despite the war, and of organizing the railways. "It must be admitted," he concluded, "that never before has our country had such a strong and well-organized rear."

But the main part of his speech was devoted to examining the position at the front, which then looked so critical to the outside world. And the bulk of his remarks emphasized that Russia's reverses till then were due to the tremendous weight of power which Hitler was enabled to concentrate on Russia owing to the absence of a second front.

"According to authentic information which is beyond all doubt," he said, "of the 256 divisions which Germany now has, no fewer than 179 are on our front. If to this we add twenty-two Rumanian divisions, fourteen Finnish divisions, one Slovak division, and one Spanish division, we get a total of 240 divisions (over 3,000,000 men) fighting on our front. . . . You can now imagine how grave and extraordinary are the difficulties that confront the Red Army and how great is the heroism displayed."

One could also imagine at this time how important it was for Stalin to assure his people, as he did, that "sooner or later there will be a second front." Looking back, it seems incredible that millions of Russians were then expecting a second front in 1942, as I soon discovered when everywhere I went men and women anxiously asked why our "promise" had not been kept. They were to go on expecting it, month after month. But what an appalling effect it might have had on morale, if these people had known definitely that not in 1942 nor in 1943, nor even during the Red Army's offensive in April, 1944, would the Anglo-American coalition open a major front in Western Europe!

Fully realizing the need for reassurances, Stalin denied the defeatists who were then suggesting, inside Russia as well as outside, that because of "the existence of different ideologies and social systems," the Allied coalition could not organize joint action

72

against the enemy. *"The logic of facts,"* he asserted, *"is stronger than any other logic"*; it is stronger than ideologies as such; there would be a second front "because our Allies need it no less than we."

But Stalin never intended to wait for deliverance by Britain and America. On the same day he made a promise all his own. "The day is not far distant," he said, "when the enemy will feel the weight of the Red Army's blows. Our turn will come!" And before the month was over the Red Army began to fulfill that pledge. From Leningrad to the Caucasus, the entire front was transformed, as the Russians seized the initiative, halting the Germans in the tracks of their own offensive.

For days the correspondents clamored for permission to visit the front, but the Press Department gave us only the assurance that Stalin had made about Allied help—"sooner or later." Nobody went, except Henry Shapiro, of the United Press and it was hard to complain much about that. Obviously Stalin had to do something to cheer up Shapiro, after having given the rival Henry (Cassidy, of the A.P.) a celebrated scoop by answering one of his letters. When finally a trip was organized for some of us, late in December, we knew the issue was already decided at Stalingrad—though the Germans would not surrender for another month.

We started southward in some style, in a Wagons-Lits sleeping car bound for Saratov. It was the same kind of car I used to see on the old Blue Express in China and, for all I know, might have been one I had ridden in years ago. The same samovar steamed in the same little galley and the same white-haired Russian poked charcoal into a glow and smiled as we filed in. There was the same profusion of brass and mirrors and the same red carpeting down the aisles. But the resemblance to good old days ended with the Wagons-Lits car. The rest of the rolling stock was ancient and unpainted and in the high-floored, large-wheeled, wide-gauge Russian style: some third-class carriages crowded with soldiers and peasants bundled in dark shabby overcoats, fur hats and the knee-high felt boots called *valenki*.

"We're locked in," Eddy Gilmore of the A.P. announced, as he tried the door leading to the car behind us. "The front one's locked too. I thought we'd get a chance to talk to some Russians on the train but we're strictly segregated."

"They've heard about your fifth-column work in the Metropole, Eddy, and they're taking no chances."

"You can talk to me," grinned our pink-cheeked conducting officer, Lieutenant Colonel Anatole Vladimirivich Tarantzev, who had been loaned by the Red Signal Corps for the trip. The Colonel was studying English; I was trying to learn Russian. I took him up on his offer and invited him into my compartment to kill a bottle of vodka.

Tarantzev was thirty-two, unmarried, and a graduate engineer from the Ukraine. He had been studying electrical science when the Nazis struck and the army called him into service. Then he was wounded in the knee. While convalescing he was sent to work with the staff in Moscow. In this way he had ended up as shepherd to some foreign correspondents adrift on the steppe.

"A sad fate for a fighting man," I remarked.

"*Nichevo*, I can improve my English," said the little Colonel.

He showed me a camera I had never seen before. It was a late-model Leica with a built-in light meter synchronized with the shutter speed, and Tarantzev said he had taken it from a German officer.

"What happened to the officer?"

He opened his eyes very wide and drew the back of his hand across his white throat. Somehow the gesture was incongruous in this cherry-cheeked youth looking so lovely in his gray astrakhan cap and his fine greatcoat with its pretty blue-tipped lapels of gray worsted.

"Do you treat all prisoners that way, Anatole?"

"*Nyet!* You don't understand. This officer was killed in battle. If a man is not killed in half an hour after capture he will not be killed. If he gets behind our troops at the front then he is safe. We treat prisoners good, *very* good."

"But what if the prisoner claims to be a Communist, what then? Does he get any special consideration?"

"They all claim that. As soon as we capture them they cry, '*Kamerad!* Down with Hitler!' But always they fire the last bullet and always they fight till we are around them. We don't trust them! 'Why do you shoot at us till the end?' we ask. They look surprised. 'We have to shoot at you as long as we have ammunition, don't you understand? That's orders!' "

Anatole massaged his injured knee and grunted with disgust.

At Kusinov the weather was clear and the air dry and sharp,

with only twenty degrees of frost. Women laborers unloaded and loaded freight in the yards and looked like animated mounds of earth in their piles of shapeless rags. Their breath condensed in spirals that rose high above their heads. We saw a dozen boys clamber into the unheated cars and each one carried from three to six rifles strapped across his back.

"They take them to the front," explained Vladimir Kazhiamakov, our escort from the Foreign Office, who was to be killed on a later trip like this one. "They repair them in the shops here and then they bear them to the sharpshooters at the front. It is for them a great honor."

The train creaked on across a white landscape broken here and there by black bands of birch standing tall and thick and straight. Many times we were side-tracked as high-priority military trains passed on and it was not till late the next day that we came into semi-Asiatic Saratov. Outside the station we were delayed for an hour and I walked with Sam Gurievitch, of Reuters, between the steaming trains drawn up beside ours. We came upon a group of Red soldiers and I noticed several Asiatics among them. One had all the features of a Mongol but with a very white skin.

He was a Daghestanian, he explained, when we spoke to him. Daghestan is an autonomous republic lying on the eastern side of the Caspian Sea, between Azerbaijan and the Kalmuck Republic, toward which we were headed on this journey. Both Daghestanians and Kalmucks are related to the Mongols, who ruled this part of the world for centuries until the Russian boyars and the Cossacks raised their heads a few centuries ago and broke their power in a great battle fought near the present city of Stalingrad.

But Georgi, our Daghestanian, apparently had little interest in the ancient glory of his people. He was twenty-two and had been in the army five years and had risen to the rank of sergeant. The army had taught him to speak and read Russian and Ukrainian; he had tasted the big life and wanted more. Now he aspired to become an officer, to return to the Ukraine, and to marry the girl he hoped might still be there.

"Do you call yourself an Asiatic or a European?" I asked.

"I am an Asiatic. But I like Russian culture—the music, the dancing, the theater. Ah!" He shook his head enthusiastically. "It's wonderful!"

"And you really think they will let you become an officer?"

"Why not? Look at me: I'm strong, that's because I fed at

my mother's breast till I was seven years old. Why not be an officer? My head isn't so hard. Anybody with my ability can be an officer in the Red Army, if he's willing to study."

Georgi confided that he was taking a couple of German officers to Moscow for questioning. It was his fourteenth trip of the kind, he said. He was about to let us see his charges when his own commander shouted an order and he moved off to his car.

"We've got Fritz* on the run now, the worst is over," he yelled over his shoulder at us. "We'll be back in the Ukraine before the year is over!"

In Saratov we dined copiously at the Railwaymen's Club, and in the morning I ate the most expensive breakfast of my life. It cost us 220 rubles each, which worked out at over eighteen American dollars. There was borscht, sausage of different varieties, cold fish, chocolate, caviar, red wine and quantities of vodka. We were to have no warm food again for thirty-six hours so we ate and drank like Russians; that is to say, as Russians would have liked to eat and drink. By the time we stepped out into the sparkling streets again the party was hilarious. Even late that evening, as our train pulled slowly over the wide bridge at the Volga to enter the former German Republic, big Ronnie Matthews, *Daily Herald* correspondent, was still living in a world of his own.

"Gentlemen, you are now crossing the most famous Russian river," he announced. "You are crossing the Vodka."

"And what happened to the Germans, after the Volga Republic was dissolved?" I asked Tarantzev.

He pointed eastward. "Karaganda," he said.

"But there must have been some good Soviet citizens among them?"

"Yes, maybe there was a good one. But in war we cannot take chances. The Volga Germans held a knife on our backs and never could we tell when they would use it. They had to go. Maybe they will come back after the war."

"We have crossed the Vodka!" echoed Matthews.

In the morning we were in Kazakhstan, and Asia proper, and rode all next day down the camel steppe. Here and there were groups of charred buildings destroyed by bombing, and I realized for the first time that the Germans had actually penetrated Asiatic Russia. Along the track were trains loaded with guns and equipment in clumsy-looking four-wheeled wagons moving toward the

* The Russian equivalent of Jerry and Kraut.

76

front. Other trains with captured and damaged weapons rolled slowly to the rear and now and then smoke-grimed faces, some of them young girls, peered out curiously at us.

On either side stretched endless, barren steppe, where the simple elevation of a train seat enabled you to see for miles. Not that there was anything to see. But here and there a village arose out of nowhere, or a tiny group of men was outlined on the sky. Alec Werth, the *Sunday Times* correspondent, sat gazing thoughtfully at the monotonous scenery. He looked up and smiled in his half-apologetic, small-boy manner. Alec loved Russia, where he was born, but he liked puns almost as well.

"Do you know what Ribbentrop said to Molotov when he was kissing him good-bye on his last trip to Moscow?" he asked.

"So what did he say?"

"Watch your steppe!"

We let it pass; Alec had his good points too.

On the whole, one did not see the signs of intense activity one had expected to find along a main line of supply behind a great offensive. Late in the afternoon we came upon a demolished settlement where several trains had been bombed and shattered. It was Basunchak, and here an east-west line came unheralded out of the salt marshes of Kazakhstan. No map showed a railway running into the Saratov-Astrakhan line from Central Asia. We had stumbled onto something.

It must have been unknown to the Germans till the Stalingrad campaign began. Perhaps it explained a lot about the surprising amounts of goods the Russians had been able to bring up to the eastern bank of the Volga, where they prepared their massive counter-blow. It was a new railway completed in secrecy after the war began and it reached eastward as far as the Ural River, where it doubtless tapped the output of the great industrial centers of Soviet Asia.

III

War and Space

THE weather was softer when we left our train near the Leninisky airfield and the air sleds scattered about were useless where great patches of plain had been blown bare. At midday the sun was warm and bright in contrast to the twilight Moscow calls its winter day.

We had come out upon the lower Volga valley and the old homeland of the Torguts, who, 300 years ago, wandered here from Mongolia. For a century they pastured their cattle along the Volga, until the Russian nobles, advancing from the north, threatened to exterminate them. Nearly the whole tribe, several hundred thousand strong, began a great trek back to Eastern Asia and on the way had to fight all the armies of the Russians. Only a small portion of the original party ever reached Mongolia. But part of the nation voted to remain in Russia; it moved southward, to settle on the right bank of the Volga, in what is today the Kalmuck Republic. And there it was that the Germans had begun their last counter-attack to save Stalingrad and relieve the twenty-two divisions trapped in the Red Army encirclement.

Since August 23, 1942, the Nazis had thrown wave upon wave of Storm Troops against Stalingrad, which the Reds had chosen to defend as a fortress. In the first fifty days of fighting alone the enemy lost about 180,000 killed, and sacrificed 1,300 planes. It wasn't enough; the Reds had kept their toes dug into the right bank of the river, thwarting Hitler's grandiose plan. That plan had been to sweep up the river toward Kuibyshev, to Kazan and to Gorki, according to Stalin, in co-ordination with another pincer which was intended to close in from north of Moscow. The giant forceps was supposed to meet before the Urals, and Hitler had hoped he could then pull all European Russia away from its Asiatic hinterland.

But the key crossing of the lower Volga, and the gateway to

the Urals, had held. Around Stalingrad the Russians organized the great counter-offensive, which opened on November 19th, to impose the first major defeat suffered by the forces of Nazidom after years of unbroken triumph.

The counter-offensive developed in three stages. In the first, the Red Army drove deep wedges close into the German flanks on both sides of Stalingrad, thrusting in from the northwest and southwest. These drives met fifty miles beyond the city on November 23rd, and began to draw together in a circle of death around the Germans. The second stage was the offensive near Voronezh, launched northwest of Stalingrad. And now the Reds were moving rapidly ahead with the third phase, as they struck far south of Stalingrad, down from the Volga to the Manych Canal and the Don Bend leading into Rostov and the Sea of Azov. This drive would eventually free all the sunny slopes of the Caucasus and cut off the hand which Hitler had almost closed over the oil of Baku.

Before the southern wing had developed its power, however, the Germans made a last desperate counter-attack to threaten the Soviet flank below Stalingrad. Planes dropped leaflets over the city, promising the beleaguered Sixth Army "liberation before Christmas." The optimism was short-lived. Hitting the Germans at the Aksai River, the Russians got under way with their delayed southward offensive in mid-December. And it was behind this Red force, striking in the direction of Rostov, in co-ordination with another Red column cleaning up along the Caspian seaboard, that we moved now into the Kalmuck steppe and toward the Don Valley.

What was already abundantly clear was that the Germans had made two primary errors at the beginning of this campaign. They had underestimated their enemy's capacity to resist; in spite of the lessons of Moscow in 1941, they had counted on taking the key points months earlier than even the outer defenses actually fell to them. Secondly, they had gravely underestimated Russian reserves and had poorly guessed the ability of the Red Army to mount an offensive so far away from its new industrial bases. Both these miscalculations had led them to attempt a stupendous task with insufficient means.

Why had they made those mistakes?

"I cannot answer you that," said Tarantzev. "But I can tell

79

one reason. We know how to fight on the steppe and in the winter and the Germans do not."

It was as good a single reason as any I heard.

We were now in the hands of the Red Army and at Stalingrad had our first breakfast with Red officers. For days afterward I never managed to eat a breakfast without a glass of vodka, several times a full tumbler of the stuff. I was finding it a novel way to begin the day and trying to like it. Next to me sat a young lieutenant-colonel, an army surgeon named Alexandrovich Osipov, who must have been taking the morning off, judging by his assimilation of vodka. He wore on his blouse the Red Star medal.

"Oh, that? I got it for flying in behind the German lines to operate on some wounded men. Now, as I was saying, the proportion of heavily wounded is increasing in this campaign. About 40%; it used to be only 30%. We call any case curable under twenty days a light wound."

"Have you seen any American medical supplies hereabouts, Colonel?"

"We are getting some now. Very excellent too."

"In what categories are shortages especially acute?"

Osipov looked at me blankly. Vodka notwithstanding, he was giving out no unauthorized information.

"Shortages in medical supplies? Not at all, not at all. We have everything we need, thank you."

We drove on from the small hut to a local army hostel where some women service troops met us and invited us to "rest." A small phonograph was cranked up and while most of us lay about on the cots which filled the big room a few hardier colleagues like Eddy Gilmore and Robert Magidoff tried dancing with the girls who looked after the place. Suddenly we realized they were dancing to German and Italian music.

"Of course," laughed Katya, the big blonde. "Presents from Fritz!"

I went downstairs and crossed the street to a leaning-over statue of Lenin and, while I was idly looking at it, a man in officer's uniform came up. "Excuse me," he said in English, "you are an American, yes? My name is Brown. Maybe you could tell me about a friend of mine in Galveston, Texas? He went to America some years ago but we wrote to each other every month, before the war."

It turned out this fellow was a Jew from the Ukraine, who

edited a newspaper in German for distribution at the front and among the prisoners. He claimed results were good. Germans who surrendered with his paper on them received special treatment and, he said, hundreds of captives were found in possession of copies.

"It is a happy thing to have America and Britain as allies," the editor was saying. "So many things to ask you. Tell my friend in Galveston . . ." But the colonel came up and, looking sourly at Brown, told him to buzz off. We were leaving.

Does anyone in Galveston know somebody named Brown who lived in the Ukraine? He sends his greetings.

IV

Paradise and Beyond

WE DROVE off in battered Russian cars across the treeless plain, wrinkled with ravines as we neared the Volga. There were few towns or even villages; only now and then one saw the crude huts of collective farms or cattle ranches. Suddenly there was a frozen stream, with timber lining its banks and exactly in the center of a temporary wooden bridge a stalled tractor was holding up two lines of traffic on each side of the bridge. The driver clambered over the tractor with a torch, trying to thaw out the feed pipes.

From nowhere in particular a couple of hundred Red soldiers materialized and crowded around the stalled machine. Somehow a steel tow cable was produced, the longest one I ever saw, and one end was tucked into the tractor frame. In five minutes the soldiers had pulled the tractor out of the way and then had disappeared again in the steppe and we were moving into the dusk.

Long after dark we reached the Volga. In the distance we could just hear the rumble of cannon and the sky was faintly flushed over Stalingrad. Our head-lamps, one of them blacked out with a gas mask, only dimly revealed the surface of the river for which so many youths had perished since last August. We crossed on a wooden bridge laid on long logs strung together caterpillar fashion, and resting on pontoons sitting above the ice. Over it rolled an endless traffic of night: trucks, cars, camel carts, sleds and sleighs.

Late at night we reached Ryegorod, which means Paradise, and was just the kind of dump you find called Paradise in our own western states. Quarters were assigned to us in a townsman's frame hut, where there were pallets of straw laid out behind the big Russian tile stove. Major-General Nikolai Constantinovich Popov, who had been expecting us since early morning, dropped in before he retired. He wore a greatcoat and chinchilla hat, adorned with a red star, and he had fine gray eyes set in a swarthy face. When he spoke his name Popov no longer seemed funny.

Popov had probably done more than anybody else to organize victory in these parts. As deputy chief of the rear services, co-ordinating supply and transport, he had somehow brought enough across the Volga before it had frozen, and while it was under the fire of German artillery ten miles away, to enable the Red forces to meet the enemy offensive, repulse it, and launch a victorious counter-attack of their own.

"How did you cover all your preparations, General, with the Germans in your front yard and the river at your back?"

Popov removed his hat and rubbed a hairy, muscular hand over his shaved head. "We developed night sight," he explained. "We learned to see at night as well as you can see in the daylight. While it was light the enemy could see nothing unusual but at night the roads and the river swarmed with life. Our drivers learned to go anywhere without lights. They learned the secrets of the steppe."

"You mean to tell us, General, that you supplied your whole army here by way of that little bridge we crossed back on the Volga?"

"The bridge you crossed was built only a few days before our offensive began. Until then we ferried supplies across the river in the arms of men or on their backs. We used barges and boats, too, but they were easier targets for the enemy. The surest way was to send men over at night. They still came over after the river began to fill with ice. They jumped from one piece of ice to another, one minute on their bellies and the next on their toes. Sometimes they fell in and their comrades hauled them out still

82

hanging on to their guns and ammunition. Enough got across to supply and reinforce our troops on the south bank and to enable us to open the attack."

Once General Wavell said that the maintenance of a steady flow of supply is almost the whole art of modern warfare, a task which air power has enormously complicated. Certainly in desert warfare supply is everything and in warfare on the winter steppe it is everything too. Yet I was struck by a singular fact next day, as we followed in the wake of this fast-moving army. It was that we rarely saw a supply train or even a column of reinforcements. No doubt they were near, as we had seen when they appeared to tow the stalled tractor, but by day they concealed themselves in the brush and off the main roads. The moment darkness fell the roads filled up with a mysterious traffic debouching out of an apparent void.

Moving along the windy expanse I thought of Chekhov's pictures of the steppe and how well they gave you the terrifying loneliness of it. It was more like Inner Mongolia near Kueihua or like the Ninghsia grasslands west of the Yellow River, only there were more miles and miles of it without a tree or a ripple in the bleak, brown earth. To lose one's way here was like losing it on the desert and the road was lined with straw-tufted standards to guide the traveler through sudden blizzards.

When infrequently we came upon settlements they were huts made of unbaked clay bricks, surrounded by fences of thatch overlaid with mud, and again it was like China. The cantilever wells with their huge arms stood out like warning sentinels on the horizon. Sometimes you saw against the gold and blue of the wide sky a solitary windmill in silhouette, untouched by the war, its great cross turning like a Tibetan prayer wheel.

How could treachery be organized in this candid landscape, serene as the face of a child? White-robed scouts crept back and forth across the land, blurred by night, and spied out enemy troops. Then came the great armies. If one of the battles fought here had been lost it might have changed the history of the war.

At Zhutova and along the Aksai River and between Kotelnikovo and the Don River we saw how such a decisive battle was fought. Till then I had thought of major tank battles as matters decided in a few hours or at most a few days. Here one went on for two weeks. The Germans began it with 600 tanks, supported by the Luftwaffe, and for four days the Russians fought rearguard actions as they retreated toward the Volga. Then for eight days they defended a line of their own choosing, preparing to counter-attack while Popov's men floundered in the icy Volga and swarms of peasants hauled shells on their backs across the snowdrifts. On the twelfth day the Red Army hit back with 500 tanks and began the chase which had now brought it within striking distance of Rostov.

I visited part of this battlefield on foot and later saw it from the air. Along the Aksai, which was a negligible stream but with a high right bank, the Germans had built a series of tank barriers made of steel rails and girders, and had dug in their artillery beyond them. But after silencing the firing points the Russians had simply outflanked the defense system—which extended for miles—and forced the battle to the enemy tanks. Wrecked equipment was strung out everywhere and near Abganerova I saw a hundred German tanks, struck dead in their tracks.

Aside from such remains here and there, which in themselves told little more than the booty of time you might see in any peaceful junkyard at home, war in the steppe left few tales behind. It is only in the cities, where bombs and shells furrow through whole acres of homes and obliterate old growths, just as a plough buries last year's stubble, that the tragedy hangs on long after the event. In the steppe nothing remains after a few days to show that a couple of hundred thousand men fought here—except the torn letters, the frayed photographs, the broken shoes, the empty brandy bottles brought all the way from Paris, and the soon-buried corpses.

The steppe is a dream battleground for tankists, where infantry without armor is quite as helpless as in the desert. One evidence of German overconfidence was that Marshal von Mannstein here deployed tens of infantry divisions of Rumanians and Hungarians to hold static lines of defense, on the assumption that the Russians had lost the means of mobility south of the river and could not recover it. There are no natural barriers except rivers and ravines in this country and battle develops so swiftly that an infantry position can be rendered hopeless in a few minutes. Here the front moved as much as 200 kilometers in forty-eight hours; once begun, a retreat could go on unchecked for scores of miles. Thus, when the Reds did attack with success they caught virtually the whole Rumanian Army behind a pincers used successfully against the Nazi tank forces. The Germans fled to avoid encirclement and left their allies high and dry. Division after division surrendered.

At Zhutova, where thousands of men had been killed a few days earlier, we met two old, head-shaking, tongue-clucking women carrying babes in their arms, wandering through the wrecked village. They talked excitedly about the battle, which they had witnessed in part. On the very next day, while the Red Army was still gathering up its dead and wounded, they had come back to what was left of their home. It happened to be Christmas Day.

One of the young children was wearing new Rumanian boots several sizes too large for him and a Rumanian hat. He took us into his back yard and showed us a solitary corpse. I have seen hundreds of bodies on battlefields around the world, but it is odd how individuals stay in your memory long after you have forgotten masses of corpses which you could not distinguish one from another. This Rumanian at Zhutova was a sturdy and handsome youth, with a neat mustache. His trousers had been yanked down hastily and the lower part of his body was naked. Under a covering of light snow you could see that his sexual organs had been removed. *Sic transit gloria mundi.*

PART - II - LIBERATING THE DON

I

The Cossacks

THE Blue Danube is not blue and the Black Sea is not black, but quiet flows the quiet Don. It was a delight to come upon the long, dark banner of it curling among the purple hills, after a whole week in the unbroken steppe. We first saw the lower Don near the elbow where it turns westward to meet the Donetz and Sal Rivers above Rostov and when it was just being cleared of enemy troops.

The German radio had been explaining Marshal Erich von Mannstein's retreat here, blaming the weather which favored the Reds by freezing the Don so that Russian tanks could cross to the right bank. The fact was, only narrow strips of ice fringed its shores. The Don had frozen a month late and held up the Red Army until bridges could be thrown over by night and the very difficult crossings forced in time to break up the organization of a new Nazi counter-thrust to our rear. But it had been done, and now the Red Army rolled on toward the sea.

The Don country was coming back to Russia and in the vanguard of its redemption proudly rode the Cossacks. There was color even in winter hills here and in the wooded fields. Under the crisp snow you sensed the special warmth of this rich earth. Cossack villages were lively in contrast with the monotony of the steppe: substantial two-storied houses, with bright green or red-tiled roofs and pale yellow walls, broken by blue-shuttered windows which opened into hot kitchens where big-bosomed women baked the nourishing black bread of the land.

Not far away corpses still lay stiff in the Russian frost, but a window of life had been opened again and light streamed into the Cossack settlements. While I interviewed Red Army men in a schoolhouse I saw red-cheeked children glide past the windows on their small skis. They were running errands for the army and happy to see their own again. And on the road I passed more of those boys carrying bundles of rifles to the front, rifles as big as themselves.

Here were the hills and valleys of double defeat for Hitler, political as well as military. In the Donbas and in the Kuban, farther south, anti-Soviet revolt had first flared into civil war in 1918. It was in this country that the former Cossack land-owners, deprived of their holdings and special rights enjoyed under Tsarism, had resisted collectivization till the last. Among them the Nazis therefore had hoped to win sympathizers, and though the idea now seems strange there were plenty of experts then who used to say the Cossacks "would rise as one man" to help the Germans.

"We have not come to stay," the Germans told the Cossacks. "We only want to dissolve the collectives, redistribute the land, get rid of the atheists and Jews and drive the communists into Asia. When that is done there will be peace and every man can work for himself."

They did dissolve the collectives. They even gave land and a few cows to the puppets who helped them. They did kill all Jews who could not get away. They closed schools and made it an offense punishable by a thousand-ruble fine not to attend church. Then they smeared the towns with pictures of Hitler and appeals to people to emigrate to the paradise of the New Order in Europe, full of milk and honey for all. Their posters depicted Russia as completely blockaded from Anglo-American help, with Japan cutting off the whole Far East. The Germans told the Cossacks that the Red Army was in flight, Baku had been occupied and Moscow surrounded. And until a few days ago the people here had had no proof it was not so.

But the word Cossack means "free man," and these people evidently knew quite well the difference between freemen and serfs. Since the time of Ivan the Terrible the Cossacks had always defended the Ukraine, the Volga and the Don against every invader. And though it was the Cossacks who began the civil war it was the Cossack General Budyenny whose troops defeated the White Armies.

The Cossacks were no longer the restive peasants of civil-war days. A new generation had now grown up, glad of its heritage but educated in the Soviet idea, too. Collectivization had come to stay and even many of the older folk had been reconciled. The Red Army had wisely restored some Cossack privileges. Again they rode their horses and wore the black square-shouldered astrakhan cloaks and the jaunty hats they loved. Again they sat upon their own saddles and used their own bridles and designed their own uniforms, each unit with its own dazzling markings. And again they sang their ancient songs of battle.

"It seems there is still plenty of need for cavalry in this country," a Ukrainian officer told me, "and there is no better horseman on earth than the Cossack. He loves his horse better than he loves himself. The Cossack will go without bread to feed his horse. After a long march he waters the horse before taking a drop himself. On a cold night he sleeps on the ground beside his horse with his own blanket and greatcoat thrown over both of them."

General Seliavonov, Commander in the north Caucasus, here made bright again the traditions of his people. His Cossack scouts were everywhere during the offensive, feeling their way through the dark bush of the steppe at night and returning with enemy "tongues" plucked from the very doors of Nazi headquarters. The dry, hard-bitten cavalryman Seliavanov was imperturbable and calm like the great Kutuzov with whose medal he had just been decorated. He was called by his men "the proud one."

Near Vladikavkas, a Russian told me, enemy tanks were counter-attacking, when Seliavanov's frightened men began to run. He dismounted and started walking slowly toward the Nazis, carrying a small whip in his hand. "Where are you going, Cossack?" he shouted above the confusion of battle to each man he met on the run, "These tanks are only machines made by men. What man has made man can destroy!"

Seeing him unafraid his troops shamefacedly turned back and a rout was avoided. Now they marched on triumphantly with the vision of Kuban inspiring them: the memory of the white houses and green valleys filled with orchards and vineyards before them, the crowded shade of trees, the valleys of the Cossacks.

The Germans made other attempts to conciliate the Cossacks. Few people were executed and comparatively little property was wantonly destroyed. I mentally compared Vyazma and Mozhaisk, for example, west of Moscow, where I had found as much as 80% of the homes burned in some villages. People there were shot for the simplest infractions of rules and both men and women brutally tortured for trivial offenses. The Nazis helped themselves to everything and drove thousands of civilians back to Germany.

While we were near the Don Front we made our headquarters at Kotelnikovo, which the Russians had retaken a few days before we arrived, and there we learned that the Germans had been relatively considerate of people. Normally the town had had a population of about 18,000, mostly Don Cossacks, but 1,500 refugees had entered just before its capture. Some 15,000 people stayed on during the five months of German occupation.

I talked to the mayor, Andre Povich Terekhov, who had led the evacuees down the steppe, driving before them thousands of cattle herded together from the neighboring collectives, some of which were very prosperous. They had, he regretted to state, been obliged to leave too swiftly and could not drive the swine with them as well. It had been a major error, he conceded.

"As we drew near the Volga some German planes spotted us and began to shoot at us with machine guns," Terekhov recounted. "Our entire herd was wiped out, but for some reason no people were hit." Even so you could tell he felt it was better for the animals to die like good bolsheviks than fall into the hands of the enemy.

When they were forced out the Germans took about 300 people with them, mostly railway workers and technicians. As for "volunteers" to work for the New Order in Europe? About thirty Russians who had served as policemen followed their masters, into exile. Such was the "mass response" of the Cossacks to Nazi propaganda.

--------‹›⟦⟧‹›--------

II

The Pushnestikovs

--------‹›⟦⟧‹›--------

ALEC WERTH and I stayed several days with a Cossack family in Kotelnikovo, who lived in a tiny kitchen and bedroom. There was Guy, a precocious youth of thirteen, for whom we quickly developed a warm regard; his mother, Mme. Pushnestikov, who adored her son so much that she forebore interrupting when he was speaking, which was the supreme concession; and Babushka, her own mother. Babushka was a withered leaf of eighty who had picked up a piece of shrapnel in her leg. She rarely materialized much beyond the cough that kept coming from the shelf in the kitchen, where she lay convalescing.

Guy's mother was born in the Don Bend and her family once owned a large farm, she said. During the critical days before collectivization they sold out to kulaks for four sacks of flour, as lots of Cossacks did in those days, and left the land. Then she married a penniless worker and they migrated to Kazakhstan, where they lived for ten years. It was in this period that she acquired a mouthful of dazzling gold teeth.

"No, my own teeth weren't bad," she explained, "but we thought the gold ones very handsome." She looked sideways at Guy, who smiled at her indulgently.

"Motka's gold teeth aren't fashionable any more," he put in. "People like stainless-steel teeth much better nowadays."

89

"My God," I said to Alec, "I wish I had the Weinstein brothers here to see this. They spent three solid weeks working on me before I left New York. They had the theory that the purpose of dentistry is to save your own enamel."

The Pushnestikovs couldn't stay away from the Don country, however, and when a new brewery in Stalingrad offered work for the husband they had moved back. Later Mr. P. became a railwayman and now he was somewhere in the Red Army, still alive, they hoped. He had not had all the educational advantages, it seemed. But he was a strong young man (a yellowed photograph showed him handsome and looking younger than his wife) and "very steady," Motka said. She herself was a teacher in the primary grades and had supported Guy and her mother, till the Germans came.

"What were they like?"

"Five of them lived on us," said Motka, "all German tankists. They seldom spoke to me except to give orders. I had to do their cooking and all their work. Food? We got half a loaf of bread a day, that's all. They ate very well: tinned meat, butter and vodka, but they never gave us a morsel. We made a thin soup from what we scraped from their plates. Once I washed their dirty linen and it took me two whole days. I thought they might give us something but only the youngest thought of it; he gave me one bun."

Even so, they ate almost as well as the Rumanians, Motka said. "The Germans wouldn't have Rumanians in the same house with them and wouldn't let them walk on certain streets. The Rumanians used to come to the kitchen door and beg. Sometimes out of pity we let them have a little of our soup and they ate it greedily."

They were a broad-minded family, we thought, being so moved by pity for one set of one's own persecutors as to give them soup made from the leavings of the other set. But the Pushnestikovs were oddly objective in all their discussions of the enemy, and there seemed little bitterness in them. Though they were atheists it seemed to us they put lots of Christians to shame.

"The Germans didn't behave like gentlemen, there's no doubt about that," admitted Motka. "At the same time this is war, you have to remember that. How do we know they aren't quite decent people in peacetime?"

Alec repeated that to me and said in amazement, "Think of being fair enough to say that about men you've watched stuffing

90

themselves with food for months in your own home, while you starve!"

"No, they never beat us," Motka declared. "But just before the Red Army came back I had a feeling that they were getting ready to leave. One of them asked me to do some washing for him and I refused. He turned red in the face and pulled out his gun but I still refused. Then he shot a hole through the roof. See, it's still there. That's when Babushka fainted"—and she pointed to the ailing old lady—"and I cried out to the German, 'You've killed her.' He was frightened and put away his gun and said nothing more about the washing."

Babushka moaned from her shelf: "Mercy, what a war! In the old days it wasn't so bad. If you weren't a soldier they didn't shoot at you. Nowadays anybody is fair game; you can't even cross the street without being hit. Shooting at women, think of it!"

The old lady was pretty deaf. During the fighting around Kotelnikovo she had gone into the yard to hang up some washing. Shells were bursting in the vicinity but Babushka couldn't be bothered. Suddenly, to her indignation, a shell landed near by and left her in a heap and with a fragment of steel in her leg. It was a minor wound but serious enough for a lady of eighty. So Babushka was simply disgusted with this kind of war and could not understand why grown men would not leave her alone to die in peace.

Guy was a clever boy but a poor advertisement for five months of German occupation. Hunger hadn't dimmed his bright blue eyes nor his lively surprising mind, but he was fragile as a moth and when I felt for his muscle my fingers closed round an arm like a stick. He never once complained about his troubles, and he evidently had plenty. He never asked for food. His mind was busy with the future. He said he was going to Moscow to attend school and he hoped one day to go to America. He was a Pioneer and would soon be a Young Communist; and for a Communist he believed anything was possible.

"Did people here believe the promises of the Germans?" we asked him.

"How could we believe them? They didn't consider us cultured or their equals or even people at all, everybody could see that. We were just slaves in their eyes. They only used us boys to look after their cows and pigs and made the girls keep house and clean up their dirt. They made us do all the work but gave us nothing."

"Didn't they feed you?"

"We got enough to keep alive. Everyone was rationed 250 grams of bread a day but no more. Some people had hidden food but we didn't. Women who would sleep with the Germans got better food, but they were not many. We used to have plenty to eat before the war. The collectives sent in wagons full of fresh vegetables and meat every day. People here were eating and dressing well. We had dances and movies every week."

"Did you ever see American films?"

"We had many in Kotelnikovo. Chaplin was our favorite; I saw *City Lights* three times. Everybody was becoming cultured, too. My friends were all planning to become scientists, doctors, engineers or teachers. But the Germans closed all the schools. They don't want Russians educated and whether you are cultured or not, they simply don't care, they treat you just the same."

"Your friends will be scientists and engineers—what about you, Guy?"

"I want to navigate and command a ship. I have never been to sea but I have read a lot about it. I'm pretty good at geography, too."

"You are? Could you find my home town on a map of America—Kansas City, Missouri?"

"Oh, yes, I know Kansas City. The Missouri River is there. I read about Missouri in *Tom Sawyer* and *Huck Finn*."

"What other authors do you like?"

"Oh, Pushkin, Gogol, Turgenev, Chekhov, Tolstoy, they're all good."

"And Marx, Engels, Lenin and Stalin, I suppose?"

He nodded; and wondering what kind of impression this literary miscellany had left with him I asked whom he considered the greatest man alive.

"That depends on what standard you judge by," answered this cool little Cossack cucumber. "Everybody is great for somebody and somebody considers nobody great. If you are a scientist or an engineer you would say one thing, if you're a politician you would say another. Some years from now people will have opinions about living men quite different from our own. If you were a German you would think Hitler is a great man, but here in Russia we think Stalin is the greatest man."

These pearls of wisdom were delivered in a modest little

voice but with the greatest cheerfulness and aplomb. Five months of German domination hadn't in the least shaken Guy's magnificent self-confidence.

"And you take America, now, you Americans think your richest man is the greatest."

"Is that so? And who is our richest man?"

"Morgan first, then Ford."

"Suppose I told you most Americans would probably answer that Franklin Delano Roosevelt is the greatest living American. He isn't very rich."

"But when you say that you are judging on the basis of politics. America worships capitalists, not politicians."

Alec and I decided you had to get up earlier than we did to be ahead of Guy Pushnestikov. "He's the most objective little man I ever met," Alec said.

It was impossible to buy anything to eat in Kotelnikovo; not a store was open yet. We discovered our hosts were living on a meager ration of flour furnished by the Red Army. But the table where Alec and I ate, run by the Red Army too, was plentiful with vodka, sugar, chocolate, bread, butter, potatoes and even a few apples; it was far better food than we ate in Moscow. We surreptitiously carried away something from each meal, altogether too little, it seems to me in retrospect, and gave the loot to the Pushnestikovs. They took it under protest and I hope they had a good meal or two. But you could not be sure about that family. Guy may have decided that, objectively, they had no right to it, and should turn it over to the Red Army. And Motka would certainly have obeyed him.

III

General Malinovsky

TWO Russian generals who perhaps made the strongest impression on most foreign correspondents during the winter and spring of 1943 were General Rodimstev, whom some of us met later in

Stalingrad, and General Malinovsky, who commanded the Third Ukrainian Army that marched into Rostov-on-the-Don.

Rodian Yakonovich Malinovsky was a Ukrainian, forty-four, and when he came into the room of the little schoolhouse where we interviewed him, in a village near the Don, he was freshly shaved and smelling of eau de cologne, so that I thought of Tolstoy's description of Napoleon. Like Napoleon, too, he was short; but unlike Bonaparte he had a hard muscular figure without any belly and he was handsome in his well-tailored uniform. Like nearly all the others, Malinovsky was of peasant origin, and he rose from the ranks; but you had the feeling, which some of the others did not give you, that he would have been a general in any army Russia ever had.

Malinovsky sat down at the teacher's desk and helped himself to a German cigar and passed some around to us. Then he explained his position in a few swift sentences.

"The enemy tried to forestall our offensive here by throwing a striking force of three tank divisions against us, one of which he brought all the way from France. Their objective was to relieve the encircled garrison at Stalingrad. Our task was to bleed this group white and then to take the offensive. After twelve days of defensive fighting we counter-attacked and the enemy fought fiercely. The right wing of my army advanced along the Don, the left wing struck toward Kotelnikovo. We had great success. Feeling the threat to his whole position in the Caucasus, the enemy has hastily brought up reserves and is hitting back at us around Zimovniki. But there is no doubt that these forces will also be routed. . . ."

So they were attacking around Zimovniki. I was not filing spot news and I was not going to quote the General at length. Now, as he talked, I kept thinking of Zimovniki and wondering whether the bodies I had seen would get a burial before the place changed hands.

We had visited Zimovniki the day before; it was not far from the Russian artillery positions, so that the dark gloomy sky was a little noisy with cannon. ILS and Stormoviks raced overhead; dispatch riders came in and out of the town. There was a feeling of near-by battle, but just a feeling; it was as close as the Russians would let us get. Only a couple of days earlier the place had been in German hands. Not far away was an airfield where there had been a skirmish; a few half-destroyed German planes stood forlorn in the snow and we had come upon the remains of a wrecked enemy anti-aircraft gun, with its crew blown in four directions. There was a long list of conquests painted on the ruined gun mount: so many anti-tank guns, so many field pieces, so many tanks, and one Soviet naval vessel. And now in turn this gun was doubtless listed among its victims by some Red battery.

Where the main battle had taken place, over a strategic ravine, the usual evidence was strewn around. The field was still mined; little triangular yellow flags marked with skulls and bones still stood among the heaped-up debris of battle. At one point we saw an enormous munitions dump, a stack ten feet wide and as high as a man, stretching for nearly a mile, full of small arms and mortar ammunition. "Gifts from the Rumanians," the Russians said.

Inside the dreary town of Zimovniki a few civilians already were back exploring the ruins, which included the usual armless and headless statue of Lenin. German signs still marked all the roads; in a cemetery on one street some German dead lay under swastikas; their comrades had evidently been surprised and had fled, leaving the bodies naked and exposed. While the others inspected a school which the Germans had turned into a stable, I crossed the street to walk in a little park beyond the town hall. In the exact center I came upon some Russians digging an enormous pit, some forty or fifty feet wide and quite deep. Around it the Russian dead heaped in piles were like marble, caught in just the attitudes in which they had been killed.

The frozen corpses looked so freshly made I felt ashamed to stare at them; it seemed indecent. They were men of all ages, with wounds of every description, and in the strong realism of their postures you could see just how each man had died, whether in horrible pain or blissfully instantaneous. I noticed that the Russians had left the uniforms on their dead, whereas the Germans apparently had stripped theirs. They were always trying to find a little more warmth in Russia.

It had been a slow business, digging in that rocklike earth. And now I wondered, irrelevantly, if the pit had been finished, if those Russian bodies had received a covering of earth.

I had had a dream that night which I had confessed to no one, wherein I walked into a white valley and drawing closer saw

95

that it was white with crowded corpses, millions of them reaching
farther than I could see. Then a storm arose, a storm of a curious
sort, with a falling of huge flakes, and as it swelled above me I saw
that the flakes were leaflets, each crying out, "Dig! Dig! Dig for
Victory!" and as they fell the figures rose up and began to dig.
From afar came dispatch riders with orders and the diggers
listened and obeyed and kept changing the path of their digging
and increasing the tempo. They were well-bodied young men with
splendid muscled limbs and softly curling hair and they all showed
fine parts and strong white teeth and there was grace and rhythm
in the pattern they made and they seemed to be singing something
from Bach. I saw long-forgotten faces among them, some were
brother Betas from Missouri, but when I shouted none of them
heard but kept on intently digging, till they were hidden to their
loins. Then a swarm of women appeared in scarlet robes and
wove between the pits and beckoned to them but they paid no
heed, they kept on digging, until only their soft hair waved in the
storm, a sea of grass, and then the valley was empty again, and it
was green and the storm was gone . . .

"For the first time since the war began," Malinovsky was
saying, "the Germans are showing signs of confusion in their
command. They are turning troops from one sector to another
frantically and rather aimlessly. They are leaving behind too
much equipment. And their officers, when captured, now begin
to express bitter disappointment with the strategic directions of
their higher command."

"What new factors explain this weakening of the enemy and
your success?" we asked.

"The new factors are, first, that Soviet troops have gained
valuable experience in fighting the German Army, and second,
our spirit has been strengthened by an enormous hatred accumulated in the heart of every man and every officer. Third, our
growing strength in arms is such that even our infantrymen can
now stop up to 150 tanks with their weapons. Our resistance
prevents the enemy from developing his attack with lightning-
like speed; he cannot gather momentum. Most of all, the reorganization of the Red Army has greatly improved the quality of our
command . . ."

Malinovsky did not elucidate his last point, but it was clear
he referred to such matters as the abolition of the political com-

missar system, or the so-called "dual command." Formerly the military commander had been in effect but half a commander; his political commissar could overrule him and conflicts of will and opinion often hindered operations. The system traced back to the early days when the Reds had found it necessary to make use of the technical skill of Tsarist officers, whom they could not fully trust, and whose leadership they had checked by means of Communist commissars appointed with equal powers of command. But in October Stalin had announced the end of the political commissars. It was explained that since all higher officers were now Communists, while many former commissars themselves had become trained commanders, it was feasible and desirable to unite both military and political authority in one man.

Few outsiders then realized the far-reaching significance of that decision. Its popularity with the field command was obviously immense. Some of the ablest generals in the Red Army now for the first time got a chance to demonstrate their prowess. It is a fact that from this time the Red Army became an increasingly effective fighting organization.

"Would you say, then, that the Nazi Army has struck its maximum blow, and that Hitler will never again be as strong as he was this winter?" I asked.

The General paused and then slowly he said: "The enemy is still very strong. On certain sectors he will be able to attack with great vigor. But from now on his strategic objectives must be of limited aim. The German Army will not launch another offensive on such a vast scale as the one we are now defeating."

That gave a solid impression of the importance the cautious Russian generals attached to the current operation. Later I tried to cable his statement from Moscow, but the censors struck it out, as they did from all other dispatches. I never could get them to explain why.

We came then to the serious part of the day, filing out behind the General to another room where there was a long table spread with a generous feast. Large tumblers stood before each plate, but they were not filled with the water of the Don. Vodka rose to the brim of each glass. Malinovsky lifted his promptly and toasted: "My aim is to go on with this offensive till we reach Paris. To the author of this offensive, Comrade Stalin, and to our common victory!"

Whereupon Malinovsky drank—and drank. Out of the corner

of an eye one saw that he was emptying his glass, and, as an appreciative guest, one could hardly do less. There was a strong aroma of kerosene on the drink; it must have been carried to the front in fuel-oil containers; but if Malinovsky could take it, so could a visiting fireman.

"Will it be your first trip to Paris, General?"

"No, my second. You see I fought on the French front in the last war."

"So you were in the French Army?"

"No, the Russian forces. In 1916 the Tsar formed two infantry brigades for the purpose of 'reinforcing' the French. His idea was probably to demonstrate the limitless reserves of Russian manpower and hearten the French." He chuckled at the reminiscence and went on: "We sailed by way of Vladivostok and via Hong Kong and Suez and finally arrived at Marseille. At that time the French girls were quite surprised by us; they had imagined that all Russians had long beards." A mischievous twinkle came into his eye. "But they discovered we were quite young—and capable of hard labor."

"So it was then you first met your present allies?"

"Yes, I suppose I am the only Russian general who has already had the pleasure of fighting side by side with Americans. In July, 1916, we found ourselves fighting next to an American division. In spirit we got along with them better than with the others. When it came to having a drink, or breaking glasses, it was always the Americans and the Russians!"

He had even picked up some English, the General said, but he regretted to state that the only words he could recall were "kiss me!"

After the October Revolution Malinovsky's detachment was surrounded by the French and disarmed. Some stayed on in France, some escaped to Africa, and Malinovsky himself eventually found his way back to Siberia, again around Singapore. There he joined the bolsheviks and fought against Admiral Kolchak. Ever since then he had been in the Red Army.

Such pertinent information emerged between numerous toasts, all of which the General accepted with a graceful little response of his own, and all of which, without exception, ended up, we never knew quite how, in eulogy of Comrade Stalin. But just before he left us (rather the worse for wear) to go off somewhere and win another battle, he touched what was then the theme song of every gathering of Russians with foreigners. I had never heard it done more diplomatically.

"We Russians have fought successfully without a second front," he said, "and we shall go on and on till the enemy is finally crushed. But our faith is constant in our Allies, and in their determination to come to our aid. It is inevitable because our warm triumph is inevitable, the triumph of all those who want to organize life on a basis of liberty. Beside the grandeur of our common cause the various shades of opinion and difference of ideas behind our striving are without significance, simply without significance!"

And another tumbler of vodka bit the dust.

A month later, after he had taken Rostov, Malinovsky was promoted to the rank of full Army General. And a little more than a year after that his Ukrainian Army down-swept the Dniester to enter Rumania, and mangle almost to utter ruin twenty German divisions, in one of the most notable battles of the war. As if that were not enough, Malinovsky then turned southward to capture Odessa. When I read about it the scent of cologne suddenly seemed to fill the room again. These Ukrainians were indeed capable of hard labor.

IV

Interview with Fritz

IN STALINGRAD nearly 200,000 trapped Germans were slowly starving to death. They lived on the horses of the Rumanian cavalry, and such bread as the Nazis could fly in by air, and they were losing hundreds of transport planes in the effort. When one of these was shot down outside Kotelnikovo the Russians brought in some survivors for us to question. In these and other interviews Robert Magidoff and Alec Werth, who both speak flawless Russian, usually interpreted for us. Nearly every foreign correspondent was indebted to them not only for that, but for endless acts of generosity in helping him to get oriented to life in wartime Russia.

Gerhardt Schewei was a shifty-eyed, sickly and mean-looking officer of twenty-nine. The Russians said his comrades had declared he belonged to an S.S. detachment. Schewei himself said he was a non-party man; but all captives said that. He had been radio operator on the plane shot down and it was his first mission in Russia, "a kind of holiday, a change from my teaching work in Germany." But German captives also usually stated that they had just arrived in Russia.

Schewei declared that few Germans doubted the war would be won. "It may go on for five or ten years but we will win in the end." He admitted current defeats also in Africa, but believed that Rommel would stage a comeback. He ridiculed the idea that America could send any troops to Europe in time to affect the outcome and said flatly that it was impossible for us to ferry bombers to Britain and Africa. A shrewd gleam crept into his eye as he noticed we were divided into British and American correspondents. Piously, he said:

"My own hope is for a compromise peace. The voice of reason will be awakened in America and the European people too will realize the futility of war and make a demand to end it. The voice of reason should tell America that Europe does not want her to interfere but wants to live in peace. Americans will realize this is not their war and they will try to get out of it through a compromise arranged by Europeans among themselves."

We had had enough of Schewei. In this vein he smelled too much like Goebbels. Siegfried Beck, a flight corporal, aged twenty-one, came up next. Beck had wavy golden hair and handsome "Aryan" features. His cheeks were red with frost and he kept rubbing his numb hands as he talked.

"I say," remarked Matthews, "what a pity he wasn't born in England. He would have made a first-rate scrum half."

Beck said he was from Thüring and had been in the war since April, 1942. He had been machine-gunner on the wrecked Junkers. Someone asked him why he had tried to escape after the crash, rather than surrender.

"We have been told," he said, "that the Russians do not take any prisoners but shoot all Germans." He looked around nervously. "And it may come yet." He added: "Nobody likes to come to Russia; either you are killed in your plane or shot on the ground. We Germans prefer to fly over England."

100

He denied that prisoners were maltreated in Germany and said the Russians taken there lived better than they had at home. He thought they were happy and contented. Some of them were even allowed to sit at the table with their masters. The inference was that no greater honor could be conferred on a mere Russian.

"Anyway, there are no Russian women in my home. My father is a poor bookbinder. We cannot afford any slaves."

"Then what are you fighting for? If not for slaves, for what?" demanded one of the Russians, flushing angrily.

"That's for the statesmen to say. I am a simple youth. I don't have an insight into the mind of the Fuehrer. But the war would soon be over if the Americans hadn't come into it. Now it will be dragged out."

"But still, Germany will win?"

"I don't know. But we won't surrender. More likely we'll all die." He gulped at the thought; tears filled the wells of his clear blue eyes.

When Beck had gone the pilot was brought in, but he had little to say, except that Germany would win. After him we interviewed a ground soldier, an anti-aircraft gunner of twenty-six, named Reindhardt, of Dresden. He, too, had wandered the countryside several days after his unit had been cut off, afraid to surrender.

"All soldiers believe it is better to commit suicide than to fall into Russian hands," he said. But he made no complaint now. "I have been much surprised," he emphasized.

Reindhardt was more candid than the fliers, and struck me as the most honest of the lot. He said he had joined the Hitler Youth in 1933, at the insistence of his boss, a butcher; and in 1938 he had been mobilized for the army. We asked whether the Germans still thought they could win the war.

"At home everybody believed we would destroy Russia in 1942. Now they think we will do it in 1943."

"What do the soldiers think?"

"In my regiment 80% of the men are sick and tired of the war. They think it can't go on much longer like this."

"Are they worried about the opening of a second front?"

"I don't know what others think, but I myself am convinced that sooner or later the Americans and British are going to break into Europe somehow."

"So you think Hitler will finally collapse?"

"I am convinced of it."

"And what will take his place?"

"That I can't say. The people may decide—unless we are all wiped out. That's possible, too. We are now hated by every people in Europe. I wouldn't be surprised if the conquered peoples desire to destroy Germany altogether."

Reindhardt left and we talked next to a sly Rumanian muzhik, one Alexander Nicolai, who had been taken prisoner when his whole division surrendered near Kotelnikovo. He was eager to talk and eager to curse the Germans.

"We never wanted to fight the Russians," he said. "It was our officers and corrupt government who led us into it. Now even the officers are disgusted. At home the Germans are running our country. At the front they run our army."

Nicolai had memorized down to a gram the difference between the food allowances given German and Rumanian troops. "The Germans get 800 grams of bread a day, we get 500. They get six cigarettes, we get three. They have brandy and vodka to drink. If Rumanians ask for a drink they get a kick or a blow on the head."

"Then why do you fight, Nicolai?"

"Why? I'll tell you why. If you don't obey an order you are flogged twenty-five lashes with your pants down. I got my twenty-five lashes, oh, yes! I was glad to be captured."

The Russians laughed and shrugged their shoulders as Nicolai warmed to his subject. They seemed to say, "Just so, but the poor devil is only a Rumanian. If only the Fritzies would talk this way, the war would soon be over."

The long-haired, black-eyed Nicolai was pleased that he had made a good impression on us and he bowed low, cap in hand, as he left. It was too much for the public-school training of the redoubtable Matthews. He selected a chocolate from a plate on the table and "Here you are, my good man," he said, handing it to the wretched Rumanian. Turning to us, Ronnie remarked brightly, "After all, we are gentlemen, you know."

The Russian officers stared at him, dumfounded.

I

Concerning Collectives

BACK in Moscow, while waiting for another trip to the front, I visited several collective farms, to find out how they were managing under war conditions and without much help from the male of the species. I first asked to see a farm close to a combat area and I was sent off to a place called the *Plamya*, or the Flame. It lay on the Moscow River, above Tula and not far from the enemy lines.

Flying up from Baku to Kuibyshev and Moscow I had seen hundreds of collectives spread out around their toy-town villages. Each had its main street joining little peak-roofed log-cabin huts and its solid-looking silos and great barns, the whole usually converging on a green where often a white church raised its blue or gold domes—sometimes surmounted by a red flag instead of the orthodox cross. Before coming to Russia I had heard reports that the labor shortage was so acute that the harvests would rot in the fields. But flying over in mid-October I had not seen a farm that was not swept clean, with its grain already stacked in long golden loaves that from the air looked highly edible.

To meet the emergency the government had passed laws which made women as well as men (between sixteen and sixty-four) subject to labor conscription, and made all women between fourteen and fifty, not employed in war industry or transport, available for farm labor during the planting and harvesting seasons. Even before the war there were more women on farms than men; by 1942 they outnumbered males nine to one in many collectives. Over 70% of the skilled agricultural workers in the whole country were now women. In the agricultural schools over half a million women were learning to handle tractors and harvester combines which were in the past almost exclusively man's domain.

103

Millions of urban people had been mobilized to bring in the harvests, including 110,000 school children from the Moscow oblast alone. Everywhere efforts were made to increase crop acreage; virtually nowhere outside the occupied areas was there a decline. Siberian farmers had opened 3,750,000 acres of virgin soil in 1942, and Central Asian states had moved toward self-sufficiency by greatly increasing the cultivation of basic crops. In 1943, Victory gardens covering 2,500,000 acres were cultivated by ten million city folk, and, in addition, twenty-eight different industrial associations operated factory auxiliary farms of about the same acreage. Beyond that, twenty million acres of new soil were brought into production by the collectives and state farms.

During the war Russia had temporarily lost nearly half her normal sown acreage, however, and while the new efforts could alleviate, they could in no adequate sense compensate for so gigantic a blow. It was only the high level of efficiency achieved by Soviet agriculture that had made possible the feeding of the Red Army and the population, and without which the nation would have faced total disaster. With only half the cultivated acreage at its disposal, the Soviet Union in 1942 produced a greater crop than Russia of 1914. And the surface reason for this was, of course, collectivization and the use of modern machines.

In the First World War Russia had practically no tractors and only 4.2 million steel and iron plows. The soil was turned mainly by 17.7 million wooden harrows and ten million wooden plows. By 1940 Russia claimed to have the greatest mechanized farm system in the world, with 523,000 tractors in use and 182,000 harvester combines. More than eighteen million peasant families lived on collective farms and 99% of all products of the land came from collectives or state farms. In 1938 only 2,250,000 acres, or less than 1% of the total crop area, was still cultivated by uncollectivized peasants. Russia had under cultivation the world's largest acreage and ranked first in seven basic crops. The production of grain had doubled, and cotton was up four times since Tsarist days.

At what cost in human anguish all the advances had been achieved this writer cannot begin to compute here. The levy of life and liberty on the ruined classes was certainly extremely heavy in the years when the bolsheviks broke the spirit of the individualistic peasant and bent him into the collectivist pattern. But it was an upheaval on so elemental a scale that judgment could be passed on its technique, its aims, and its results, only in terms of contrast with the whole history of Russia that had led up to it, as well as with social progress elsewhere in the world, past and contemporary. Few observers on the scene managed to preserve enough objectivity to see what was happening or were competent to present it, in that perspective. And still fewer critics abroad were able to do so.

Such is the perversity of human nature, however, that even if the whole world tells man he is sinning, worshipping false prophets, and certain to perish, he will not give over and repent as long as he is succeeding with his enterprise. And Soviet socialism was succeeding, though that was not to be generally conceded as a fact until it was demonstrated.

Such reflections passed through my head as I gazed at the neck of our driver, an obstinate old fellow of sixty-three, who was taking me out to the Flame—where I knew in advance I would hear a success story. For the Goon, that amazing gentleman who headed the Russian press department, was obviously not going to waste precious petrol and rubber to send me out to talk to any kulaks.

II

Comrade Kashchiv

EARTHWORKS and tank barriers were in evidence on the road and occasionally we passed bombed buildings and shell holes. We were stopped at several points and we presented our papers. The last and most impressive sentry of the lot, bundled to the ears in khaki, saluted me smartly, and I did not notice till we passed on that she was a girl. Russian women are the only females in the world who manage to look so natural in uniforms that very often you can't tell them from men. But this ceases to apply at all once they peel off their winter clothing, let down their hair under the summer caps, and reveal other unmistakable anatomical distinctions.

At last we came to a dirt road leading off to the Flame. The driver looked at it long and gloomily; he was an old Muscovite and at ease only with the solid pavements under his wheels. He hated all this indecently exposed earth and kept complaining that he would get stuck somewhere, but he finally decided to slither in toward the farm. Getting out at the bottom of an alligator-backed road we struggled up between two rows of the usual unpainted wooden cottages. Firewood was cut and piled in neat stacks and the wooden walls were reinforced with abutments of earth a foot thick, such as you may sometimes still see in New England in the winter. These windbreaks become solid as bricks and keep out the worst of the frost.

In his office at the head of the village, which picturesquely faced the Moscow River, we located the chairman of the kolkhoz, Sergei Vassilyevich Kashchiv. He was tall and strongly built, about forty years old, and had big hands hardened by toil and an honest intelligent face, burned and lined by wind and sun. Encased in black-leather boots he had a pair of long legs which had a stride exactly like Evans Carlson's, I soon discovered, the stride that imperceptibly eats up miles. He was a native of the village and the peasants had voted him into office five years straight.

Sergei was a dirt farmer. Though there was an agronomist and cattle breeder working with him, who was a college graduate from Moscow, and was doubtless party representative on the farm, he himself had never been to an agricultural school. But he knew the Flame as a man knows the body of a woman he loves. He could see every corner of it right there in his office and he answered my questions without any reference books or notes and without any hesitation.

It seems that before the Flame there was one farm called *Iskra*, which means spark. When it merged with an adjoining farm in 1930 to become one of the first collectives, the peasants voted to adopt the new name. "Lenin," explained Sergei, not at all displeased at the opportunity to edify, "said that in political struggle two sparks made a flame."

You may remember that Lenin's old bolshevik paper was called *Iskra*. But here there was a third spark, I discovered later in the day, which Sergei had neglected to mention. She was Anastasia, the red-cheeked cowgirl, who could drink her vodka like a man. But I shall be coming back to that.

In contrast with the average American farm of about fifty

106

acres, the average collective is 1,228 acres, and before the war there were 243,000 of them in Russia. The Flame was larger than most. It was 1,339 hectares,* or nearly 3,200 acres, and it was interesting because of its diversified economy. The larger part of the land was in pasture for cows and horses, including some specially bred animals. But 950 acres grew wheat, barley and potatoes, which was becoming the big war crop in Russia, incidentally, and there were nearly 200 acres laid out in orchards.

"We have our own nurseries," Sergei inventoried. "We have eighty hectares in vegetables of all kinds. We have hothouses, 1,200 frames of them, and we keep chickens and geese and have a fine pig barn, besides the cow barns and horse barns. We have an apiary, too. Here at the Flame we are not dependent on rain, either, *tovarishch*. We make our own rain. We have 8,000 meters of pipes and our own spraying system."

"How many people do the work?"

"We were 285 families before the war, but most of the men are gone now."

"That's quite a town. Do you have your own school here?"

"Our school goes up to the seventh grade. We've also got a nursery, a village library and a cinema house which shows sound pictures."

"I suppose you have the best farm around here?"

"No, not the best. It's just average. But come and look. Talking is not so good as seeing." He strode ahead, climbing a little knoll to a white church which stood at the crest.

"Do you go to church, Sergei Vassilyevich?"

"No, we are not religious here. The church has not been used for a long time. Our comrades have voted to remodel it for use as a recreational hall."

We halted before a new building with a floor raised well above the ground and inside I felt warm for the first time since leaving Persia. A big-breasted peasant woman in a white robe and with a kindly face greeted us cheerfully. When I expressed my admiration for the great Russian stove, she smiled and patted its smooth white tiling. "This," she said affectionately, making a pun in Russian, "is where our Flame begins!"

In the nursery playroom were half a dozen inmates ranging from a few months to a year or more. Two babies with hair the color of honey and texture of silk were absorbed in erecting mys-

* 1 hectare=2.48 acres.

terious edifices with wood blocks. "Do they play according to plan?" I asked, trying to be facetious.

"Yes," the nurse came back quite seriously, "everything you see here is part of socialist planning to make good citizens of tomorrow."

Across the hall was a classroom for older children and decorating its walls were colored posters which denounced the Nazis and praised the works of Stalin. There was a large sleeping porch filled with small spring beds and enclosed by sunlit windows. Here a dozen children wrapped in hooded arctic bags peeped from their cocoons or contentedly slept off the effects of that last drink. We tiptoed out, fearful of waking the little emperors and interrupting socialist planning.

"If they weren't asleep, you could ask one question they all like to answer: 'Where is your daddy?'" said the nurse.

"And what would they say?"

"My daddy is fighting *Nemtsev!*"*

So the earliest memories of many of these children would be this fixation of hatred against the Germans. All over Russia children were going through the same conditioning. And millions of them would never see their daddies again.

We went on to the movie, a simple one-room building with a cheap screen and hard wooden chairs for seats. It was like the old nickel shows where I used to see Westerns, except that its walls were festooned with red banners, slogans and posters.

"Of course it isn't the Bolshoi Theater," apologized the chairman, "but it is ours and we like it. We have a movie every night and we see the face of the whole world here. In the old days a peasant knew nothing outside his own village."

"Do you ever see American pictures?" I asked the theater manager, who hovered near the projection booth.

"Oh, yes! Last week we showed *Melody of the Waltz* and this week we had *The Great Waltz*. Everybody thought *The Great Waltz* one of the best pictures we ever had here."

The leather boots strode on to another modest wooden building, where we stopped to see the library. Inside, I noticed some translations of European classics, Shakespeare and some French and German novelists; and the cards showed they had seen plenty of use.

"How many here can read?" I asked.

* Germans

108

"All of us. Several years ago we had an illiteracy-liquidation drive and now even the old people read."

We went down the bank of the Moscow River until we came upon a pile of great bronze bells taken from the village church. The Germans had at one time been only a few miles away and all day long the kolkhoz had resounded with the noise of cannon.

"It was our idea, moving the bells," Sergei remarked. We didn't want the Nazis melting them to use against our boys. We were ready to burn everything we couldn't move or bury."

Cabbages lay in neat piles beside one of the barns and I commented on their enormous size as we passed them. I assumed this farm's output must have fallen off since the war and I said so. "It must have brought you down a peg or two on the honor roll, hasn't it?"

Sergei denied it. "Production hasn't declined at all and that's a curious thing. Take those cabbages, for example. We produced a third more this year than ever before. We also got a record yield of apples, an average of fifty tons to the hectare, which is pretty good for hereabouts. So it was with berries and vegetables. At picking time, an army of school children came out from the city and in no time the crop was taken in. They'll be out again to help us in the spring." Actually over 100,000 school children were mobilized from Moscow to help sow the crops and harvest.

We went past bare black trees of the orchards, and at the chicken-and-goose farm stopped to watch an old woman who gabbled interminably at her charges. They seemed to understand every word she said. The black boots led on through the apiary and through the greenhouses, where winter vegetables were beginning to sprout.

"How much land does one farmer get for his own use?" I asked.

"He has his house and lot. Besides that, he gets a third of a hectare to farm as he pleases. He can plant fruit trees, or a vegetable garden, or he can keep bees. On our farm every family owns a cow."

"How much does the farmer get for the labor he contributes to the collectives?" I kept saying "he" all the time, out of habit, but it was "she" who was doing nearly everything.

"That depends on the crop, naturally, and it depends on how much the farmer overfulfills the norm."

The *norm*, Sergei explained, was determined annually by the

109

Gosplan, or State Planning Commission. It was the minimum number of work-days required from each member in a collective, which might be described as a kind of state-supervised producers' co-operative. Formerly the law fixed the norm between 100 and 150 work-days a year, but now the demand had greatly increased. A woman farmer now did far more work than a man had before the war. For a norm of labor a kolkhoz member received an equal share of the profits, in terms of produce and cash. He could dispose of the rest of his time as he wished, either on his own plot of land, or as overtime on the main farm, for which there was overtime pay.

At the end of a business year a certain percentage of all farm products was sold to the state, in amounts and at prices fixed by decree. Normally this was less than half the crop, but during the war the margin was sharper. Payments in kind were also made to the motor and tractor stations (M.T.S.) and reserves were set aside for hired labor, seed grain, insurance, and for care of the old and the invalid.

After collective members had received their payment in kind for their norm of labor, plus overtime, the balance of the crop was sold in the open market or to various state trading organizations. Theoretically the "free" market price was supposed to influence state grain prices and bring about adjustments, but in practice the state disposed of such tremendous reserves of commodities that the open market price could readily be controlled by the monopoly. During the war, as we shall see, it was another matter. Even though there was practically no non-government market except that created by the individual peasants selling their own surplus, the unsatisfied public demand sent black market prices ballooning.

Proceeds from the sale of the collective's products were allocated as reserves to cover depreciation and for various communal needs: education, public health, entertainment and recreation, village improvements such as housing, light, water, and so on.

At the Flame the work-day pay norm was, according to Sergei, three kilos of grain, three kilos of vegetables, cattle fodder and three rubles in cash. It will be seen that this was considerably better than the daily rations allowed workers in the city. Three kilos of vegetables, for example, were worth about 300 rubles on the urban market and three kilos of grain were worth another 200 to 300 rubles. In addition, the peasant family had its own garden plot and cow, which as a rule more than supplied personal needs, and left a good surplus for private sale.

110

It was evident at the Flame, and at other farms I visited later, that a thrifty and hard-working peasant family with access to city markets, might make as much as 5,000 or even 10,000 rubles a month. Or, at official exchange rates, U.S. $1,000 to $2,000 a month! But money meant little where few consumers' goods existed. It just accumulated. It was small wonder that a state loan of twelve billion rubles, issued in 1943, was oversubscribed at twenty billions, in one day, despite billions previously contributed by peasants for the purchase of tanks and airplanes.

And all this made it perfectly clear why Anastasia, to whose domain Sergei was taking me, was only one of millions of Russian women who much preferred living and working on a collective to any job the cities had to offer during the war.

III

Anastasia

AT THE cattle barn, on our way to the dairy, a girl wrapped in a padded coat and with yellow hair hanging down from her fur hat waved a bucket and determinedly motioned us to turn back as she ran toward the gate we had just entered.

"You don't come in here till you disinfect your shoes, comrades," cried Anastasia, shooing us toward the fence. "It's the rule," she said to the sheepish-looking chairman. "You made it yourself, now let's see you obey it."

We trooped back, while the mistress of the dairy poured her carbolic solution on a straw matting under the gate and we doused the soles of our shoes. When we had performed the rites, her personality transformed; the keys to the cow barn were ours. She led us into the clubroom where the milk girls could rest, smoke, gossip and, for all I knew, read detective stories.*

Anastasia pointed proudly to a chart showing the rising curve of production. "In 1937 our cows gave only 2,000 liters

* They don't, I found out later. In Russia the "thriller" type of literature is virtually unknown.

a year. Now they are nearly up to 5,000 liters! You see how they love me?"

In her laboratory she demonstrated how milk is tested for purity and fat content. "I learned this only a few years ago myself, and now I am teaching it to others. Isn't it miraculous?"

Anastasia, now twenty-one, was not a mere phenomenon of the war. She had been manager of the cow barns since she was seventeen. Her cows had taken prizes and she had been decorated. She had been offered scholarships to study in Moscow but she wasn't interested.

"Who would look after my cows and pigs if I went to the capital? They depend on me, I could never leave them behind, I am not so cruel! Get up, Masha!" she shouted, striking her prize milker on the rump. "Get up and show yourself off. Believe me, comrades, she gives forty-seven liters of milk every day without fail. Can you imagine such generosity?"

Proudly she exhibited her magnificent bull.

"He weighs a ton, and he loves me," sighed Anastasia, tweeking his nose. "But don't you try that," she warned as I approached. "He only likes women."

At the door she paused to demonstrate the electric milking machines, and how they fitted over the teats. "It's a grand life for a milk girl nowadays, compared with when I was young. Once the machine begins to work, my milkmaids have nothing to do but sing songs and dance." Whereupon this surprising girl burst forth herself:

"Every night at sunset, there's a fellow round my house,
He blinks his eyes and doesn't say a word.
Who knows why? Who knows why?"

We couldn't get away without seeing Vanya, Anastasia's personal triumph. She introduced us to a young, white pig, with a room all his own. "Isn't he lovely?" demanded Anastasia. "When he grows up he'll be as strong as I am." Oh, terrifying thought!

It was already dusk when we started back to the village. At a cottage like all the rest we turned in to warm up before starting for Moscow. Inside, I noticed a bright icon in the corner. Evidently religion still had its followers at the Flame despite Sergei's atheism. I looked around with amazement at the table groaning with river fish, meat, eggs, vegetables and mounds of bread, butter, cheese and milk.

112

Sergei poured me a tumblerful of vodka and an equal amount for the others, including Anastasia. The collective was run by an elected committee of a dozen members, most of whom were there to greet us. One professorial-looking old man, full of dignity and wearing a peg-leg, proposed the first toast, and to my astonishment it was not to comrade you-know-who. Unexpectedly he struck a grave note.

"To the triumph," he declared, "of all that is good in humanity."

I noticed that Anastasia tossed down her drink like milk from her prize cow. I followed her example and my glass was refilled at once. We might as well dispose of Topic No. 1, I thought, and so in offering the expected response I proposed:

"To our common victory, and the speedy opening of a second front in Europe."

Everybody reached for his glass, led by the professor with the peg-leg.

"I never drink," he said, "except with old friends. But in honor of that toast I am going to drink!"

"Now, that's a fact, I'll confirm it," echoed the lady of the house and the icon, from her end of the crowded little table. "He hardly ever touches a drop, but we all pray God for the second front."

"America is going to fight the Nazis, all right," said the professor. "We have every confidence she'll make a good job of it. But when? At what time will the invasion commence? That's what we want to know."

"So would Hitler like to know, I imagine. But don't expect it soon. I ask you to be patient and remember all the places we have to be at once and how unprepared we were when we got into the war. Do you know that when France collapsed America had produced up to that time less than 400 tanks since the First World War? We did not have even one armored brigade! But don't ever doubt that Americans are as anxious as you are to get the war over with. When they begin a job, they like to get it done quickly."

The old professor looked somewhat dejected. He had expected more from me and now he seemed to think if he could convince me of the urgent need then I could advance the date of the invasion. "My friend," he went on, "all I have to say is this: Time is of the utmost importance, and what used to happen in

113

ten years now happens in ten days. I have one thing to demand of you. Just write a letter to your President and inform him that we of the Flame give it as our judgment that the front on the Continent must be opened this year—or it will be too late."

I am glad to say he was wrong about that and I frankly told him there was no such early possibility. I told him also that the President had better advisors than myself; but I mollified him by promising to cable the Flame's opinion to the *Post*—which I did. And having taken care of that as gracefully as I could I asked the professor what change the Revolution had made in the village. He was old enough to remember more than the rest.

"I am only a self-educated man myself," he replied, "yet I know this place must not seem very grand to you, coming from America. But compared to old Russia it is heaven above hell. The greatest difference is simply that we tillers of the soil no longer starve in the winter. In the old days we never had bread for more than three months after harvest. We had no seed grain for spring planting and had to borrow from the landlord and were always head over heels in debt. Six out of ten of us had no horses and had to pull our plows and harrows by hand. Now, it's a fact, we were beginning to enjoy a rich life when the Nazis spoiled it all. Just imagine, according to plan, this little village would have had running water in every house this year . . ."

Anastasia suddenly leaned over and handed me a vast pitcher of sour milk.

"I never drink sour milk," I said, "except with old friends. I loathe it as much as the professor loathes vodka. But in honor of the cow barn and its mistress I am going to drink this and like it." Whereupon I did, and all at once I understood why vodka made no impression on Anastasia. She took it on a solid foundation of butterfat.

IV

The Rich Life

AN HOUR later we walked up to the broken bridge where we had left our car. We told everyone goodbye but it turned out to be a false getaway. Sergei had warned us that we had taken the wrong road coming in. We had not gone a mile when the driver managed to get himself hung up on a ridge, with the back wheels in a hole, where they froze fast as a clam to its shell. For three hours Lydia and I made futile efforts to extricate ourselves. At last a wagon rolled up, driven by a couple of half-grown lads bound for the Flame. We climbed onto the straw and went back to get a tractor to give us a tow.

Perhaps it was a good break, I thought; now I could see the village when it was not on its company behavior. All along I had been a little skeptical about that display of good food, somehow; and it was not till after my second visit that I decided to write about the Flame at all.

Music and voices and laughter drifted toward the road from the black silhouettes of cottages, flattered under a full moon. Each house had its own radio amplifier and most of them were turned on. But there were still no sidewalks; the street was a frozen river of muck. One of the boys seemed to sense my thought and, turning back from the horses, he shouted, "It's a mess now, but it's a pretty little street in summertime. You ought to come out here when the berries are ripe. That's the time to be at the Flame. We were having a rich life when the fascists spoiled it all."

We found Sergei at the clubhouse and the whole village was with him. He sent somebody off for a tractor and invited us to join him at a big table shaped like an L. It was spread with the same dishes I had eaten earlier that day and with the same great pitchers of thick milk. Judging by the heaps of untouched food on the table there was no want around here.

On one side a knot of girls crowded in shyly from another room and began singing to the accompaniment of an accordion. In the center of the floor a good-looking young army officer, whose left arm hung useless, was doing a fast folk dance with a shapely girl in a tight-fitting skirt and a pale blue sweater. She was a Russian version of pin-up girl. It was nobody other than Anastasia.

"What is it, Lenin's birthday?" I asked.

"No, it's a welcome-home for one of our boys who has come back injured. We want him to feel nothing has changed. At the same time, it's a farewell party for Sergei Vassilyevich."

"Where is Sergei going?"

"He's been called up. He's leaving for the front tomorrow."

"So Sergei's going to war, too? He never mentioned it to us."

"That's Sergei Vassilyevich."

I noticed now that there were more than a hundred females in the place and only a dozen men, nearly all white-haired. Women and children were doing the work on this farm, and now it was already getting back invalids.

Later the armless lieutenant came over and we shook hands and when I asked about it he told me how he had won his decoration. At the Bryansk front he had commanded an anti-tank battery and during a German offensive he was ordered to withdraw. It happened to be the anniversary of the founding of the Red Army; the lieutenant felt ashamed to retire. He went on holding the position and kept the battery's fire on the Germans at point-blank range. This tenacity so disconcerted the enemy tanks that it disorganized a considerable sector of the attack. And so he had got the Red Star for changing the course of a battle.

We had a drink or two and he became talkative. I asked him what Russia wanted to do with Germany after the war.

"This is what I think," he said. "We had no quarrel with the Germans, did we? They saw us leading a good life, they envied us, and wanted to steal our land and factories. For those who tried to take what belongs to us we have an answer." He held up his good arm and doubled his good fist. "We will crush them and utterly destroy them. That's what every Russian wants to do with Germany!"

"That's right," chipped in a white-haired woman across the table, who had been throwing words at me ever since I had sat down. "Nobody can take our Russian soil away from us."

116

Lydia asked her if she had been evacuated when the Germans were near.

"Evacuate? Never. I would have gone to the forest with the young ones and fought. What could I lose at my age? These German pigs, ruining our country just when we were beginning to enjoy life. Think of it, electric lights and radios, mind you, and that isn't half . . ."

A messenger arrived to say the tractor was on the way to our car, and it would soon be ready to drive. Sergei Vassilyevich begged us to spend the night, but the old driver was itching for the security of his city pavements. As it was, we would not get back till after dawn.

"We had plans, too, beautiful plans," the old lady droned on, not to be put off. "We could have built many things this year. For example, we would by now have running water in every house . . ."

Anastasia walked up the moonlit street with us, humming *Every night at sunset* until we reached her cottage, where she broke off and ran inside, asking us to wait. When she came out in a minute she had three of the handsomest cabbages I have ever seen, and she pressed them on us. "They're from my own garden. Think of me when you eat them."

She did not have to press very hard. Sergei had boasted of their bumper cabbage crop and I knew people in Moscow who had not got around any fresh cabbage for months. I made three Russians very happy with those cabbages. And often now when I see a fine head of cabbage anywhere I do think of the sparkling Anastasia and of her prize pig, Vanya, who already had running water in his quarters before any cottage on the Flame.

I

The Germans Give Up

EARLY in the battle for Stalingrad a Young Communist, consumed with patriotic zeal, wrote a letter to Stalin in which he swore never to cross the east bank of the Volga till Stalingrad was liberated. "For me," he declared simply, "there is no land beyond the Volga."

Everyone knew that Stalingrad meant much to Josef Stalin. It was a quarter of a century since he and Voroshilov had organized the defense of what was then called Tsaritsyn, and had successfully repulsed the White Russian forces. Now the Communist Party seized on the Komsomol's phrase and made it a slogan in the defense of which tens of thousands gave up their lives. The whole army took it up; it swept across the nation; every schoolboy repeated it. And in the end the Russians turned it into a wry jest to fling into the face of Adolf Hitler, who had promised the world Stalingrad would be his—and the land beyond the Volga, too.

On February 4, 1943, I was with the Red Army near the Don front, and on my way to Stalingrad at last. Two days earlier the German forces in the city had capitulated and the rout and extermination of twenty-two trapped divisions was completed. During the battle I had several times asked permission to visit the city, but the Russians continued to refuse to accredit foreign observers to accompany troops in active combat, a policy to which they made no exceptions whatever, as far as I know. I considered myself lucky to be getting into Stalingrad at all. American military attachés had been unable to visit it, and up till this time no member of the large British Military Mission had been allowed near any part of the front since the beginning of the war.

The Russians took 91,000 prisoners at Stalingrad, including

250 officers, twenty-four German and two Rumanian generals, and one German Field Marshal, Frederick von Paulus. We were promised an interview with them. As no single person from the outside world had yet seen the Stalingrad battlefield, we figured the Russians had decided some verification of their claims was in order. "Barkis was willin'." but in my case also from Missouri.

We got into an old ambulance and rattled across the snow-covered steppe toward the City of Stalin, alleged to be only thirty-eight miles from Proleskaya Selo, which we had left a day before, but the journey was to take still another day and a night, through the creeping cold. Our conveyance had broken sides through which blew an icy wind, and had broken seats and rear doors that would not stay closed. On the climb out of every ravine we crossed the engine coughed and died and had to be slowly coaxed back to life. We thought it a little strange that at least one of the hundred thousand American trucks arriving here could not be loaned to transport a few of us to the front; but "everything for the fighters," said the Russians, "all for the front." We were super-cargo.

A vast ocean of oncoming white surrounded us and seemed ever about to engulf us. There were not even trees except before the rare dark nondescript villages which rose up like derelict ships. We marveled again at the big gap between the machines and efficiency of the Red Army and this primitive countryside. A casual traveler would never believe a modern army could emerge from such a background and perhaps it was such little things that misled the Nazis. The deadly monotony, the bleakness, and the melancholy stillness now that the guns were quiet, all added to the oppressive bitterness of the intense cold.

"Did you ever see anything like it?" demanded Dave Nichol, of the *Chicago Daily News* from the back of the ambulance. He gazed out incredulously. "No trees, just nothingness! It's like going through an endless cloud. Imagine living here! Imagine wanting to conquer this place! Imagine *trying* to conquer this place!"

At the village of Zovarikino we found we had lost thirteen miles somewhere; we were now fifty miles from Stalingrad. In a small overheated room there we met Lieutenant-General Michael Sergeivich Malinin, Chief of Operations under Colonel-General K. K. Rokossovsky, Commander of the Don forces which had closed the northern pincer in the encirclement of Stalingrad. Malinin, who joined the Red Army as a private, and finished military academy only in 1931, had been at Smolensk and was again at

119

Moscow with Rokossovsky, who played a major role in halting the blitz of 1941. He was a big bull of a man, Malinin, and, as he gave a résumé of the battle just concluded, he threw his sentences at us pugnaciously.

"The Sixth Army," he opined, "was the most experienced army Hitler possessed, and he sent with it, against Stalingrad, his best armored divisions. Their aim was to break through to the Volga as part of a grand encirclement movement. Our resistance on the Germans' left flank along the Don compelled them to throw in greater and greater reinforcements, however, and they exhausted the reserves they needed for the break-through.

"By mid-November we had attained an equilibrium of forces and the Soviet High Command ordered a counter-offensive. The aim was to encircle the enemy at Stalingrad and to destroy his forces along the Don. We of the northern group covered fifty-six miles in four days and the southern group did the same. On November 24th we met on the Don. The Germans were at first not alarmed by their predicament; they expected to break our encirclement with their counter-attack through Kotelnikovo. But our Stalin plan had foreseen that attempt and, when it failed,[*] the doom of the Sixth Army was sealed."

Malinin claimed that their victory more closely resembled the pattern of Hannibal's perfect encirclement of the Romans at Cannae than any other example afforded by history, not excepting the celebrated battles of Sedan and Metz.

"The battle of Sedan, fought in 1870, resulted in the complete encirclement of 80,000 Frenchmen. But Schlieffen, the German military historian and teacher, did not consider Sedan an ideal Cannae. Two ways of escape had been open to the French, though they failed to make use of them. Compared to Sedan, we encircled 330,000 Germans. We encircled 6,700 guns at Stalingrad, as compared to the capture of 400 at Sedan. We took 1,482 trench mortars and 750 tanks, and 1,550 planes—and of course those weapons were unknown at Sedan.

"Another thing. In the case of Stalingrad millions of troops were involved, spread along a continuous front over 2,000 kilometers long, and all necessary to our break-through across the Don and the Volga. How does that compare with Metz? The victory at Metz was considered a classic by some German authorities, but it was a simple fortress battle. Metz was not an area in a continuous

* Thanks to our friend Malinovsky. See p. 94

120

front and the forces involved were small. At Stalingrad we had to mass for a double break-through and at the same time maintain our vast front intact. Bear in mind, too, that the Stalingrad victory came at the end of a Red Army retreat, and that it was achieved by switching directly from large-scale defensive operations to large-scale counter-offensive."

Back in our ambulance it struck me that if the German generals, whom we now drove off to see, could speak frankly and truthfully to us, it would be the first time a group of observers had ever been privileged to interview the principals on both sides right after a battle of historic and decisive proportions. Had there been a military historian on the scene, granted the right to do exhaustive questioning, what an authentic symposium of how to win a modern war, and how to lose, might have emerged from it! But we were to be given no such opportunity.

II

Twenty-Four Generals and a Marshal

WE STOPPED before a group of low-roofed buildings where the two dozen generals were ensconced, about seven or eight of them to a hut, in which they hardly had room to stretch. Among the occupants of the first hut were Major-General Moritz von Drebber, Lieutenant-General Adler von Daniels, Lieutenant-General Helmoth Schlemmer (who commanded the Nazis' crack 14th tank corps), Major-General Wolf (artillery chief), and Brigadier-General Homilu Dimitriu, about whom Lieutenant-General Chuikov, commander of the Russian 62nd Army, later on told me this story.

"After the surrender, the generals were fed and given some vodka," Chuikov said. "Dimitriu got to his feet and asked if he could propose a toast, to which we agreed. Looking right at his German allies he held up his glass and declared, 'To the victory of the Red Army and the defeat of Hitler!'"

In the little hut I noticed that Dimitriu hovered in the background and looked thoroughly miserable and spoke to no one. All these men used to aides and valets and command and dignity now looked helpless and forlorn, like bewildered small boys whose toys had been snatched from them for the first time, and when they had been doing everything according to the rules. One or two still kept their arrogant manners. Schlemmer, for example, who wore the Iron Cross at his throat, and the Knights Cross, the swastika bordered in gold, and the German Helmet, on his chest. He had fought through the Lowlands and France and had driven the British across the Channel at Dunkirk. Now a lesser Napoleon come to his St. Helena on the lonely steppe, he did not want to discuss the battle that had brought about the disaster. He quite humanly complained of the food.

"Look at it!" he growled, reaching over for a plate filled with bread crusts, "this is what we are getting to eat." He shrugged his well-tailored shoulders. "It's worse than they feed to our common soldiers!"

Schlemmer's preoccupation was understandable; food is a trivial subject only to a man with a full belly. But for one in his predicament, I thought, there was the consolation of an old Chinese proverb: "It's better to go hungry with a pure mind than to eat well with an evil one." No longer in a position to do any more harm to his fellow man, Schlemmer could enjoy sound sleep. Or could he?

The captured generals were permitted to retain their marks of rank and their decorations, but some of them apparently expected to retain their privileges as well. A Russian staff officer told me that one old roué had winked at the Soviet girl barber who was giving him a shave. Emboldened by her expression of astonishment, and in his enthusiasm forgetting for the moment where he was, the old general followed up his advantage by pinching her on the buttocks. She brought him back sharply with a resounding blow on his ears. "He is now growing a beard," ended the Russian.

General Moritz von Drebber, who was the first German commander to surrender, struck me as the most human of the lot. He stood out sharply as a Potsdam man, the professional German officer-type in contrast with some of the others who had won promotion through adoration of the Fuehrer and Nazism. He was about six feet two, erect and soldierly, with snow-white hair, blue eyes, and a sensitive, not unkindly face. Rosenberg, correspondent of a Red Army front paper, interpreted for us. The poor fellow had a wretched cold and his nose was running all the time; and that, I suppose, together with the fact that he was a Jew, seemed to infuriate some of the Nazi generals, who glared maliciously through their monocles and answered him with sullen insolence. But Drebber spoke evenly and courteously and favored Rosenberg with a polite bow when we departed.

"Why did you continue to fight after you were encircled, General?"

"We were ordered to do so," he replied, "by our highest command."

"Then when you surrendered were you not disobeying orders?"

Drebber winced and seemed somewhat vexed. "We were ordered to defend a certain line, you know." He threw up his hands. "When that was lost it was senseless to continue fighting."

"If you had tried a large-scale flanking movement and a retreat toward Rostov, you might have broken through in the early days of the encirclement," I suggested. "Why did the Sixth Army never attempt it?"

The General hesitated a moment. Then: "I cannot say. Only the highest command was responsible for that decision."

It was the nearest any of them came to a direct attack on the Fuehrer, but it was enough to confirm what the Russians were then suggesting, that Hitler alone had insisted on holding Stalingrad, at the cost of 240,000 Germans. In this little remark we saw the wide crack in the German wall, the fissure that would spread and spread from this time on until confidence of the army in Hitler's leadership, and then the confidence of the entire nation, would be broken, and with it all hope of victory abandoned.

Some of the Stalingrad generals, who had fought so doggedly and fanatically, would, before the year was out, be leading the organization of German soldiers captured in Russia in a movement to overthrow Hitler. One of them, General von Seidlitz, would become vice-president of the "Free Germany" national committee, and tell his fellow officers that "Hitler's fateful interference has led our armies from defeat to defeat," and call upon them to negotiate a peace while there was still time to "preserve German life for a German future."

That day we drove on to the edge of the village where Marshal Paulus, with two aides, was guarded by Russian tommy-gunners. Before surrendering, Paulus had asked (I learned later

123

from the young lieutenant who captured him) that he "not be killed by the soldiers, exhibited any more than necessary, or treated like a tramp." Respecting his wishes, the Russians did not permit us to interview him; and I believe they exhibited him publicly only this once.

He came out on the little porch now, his six feet or more emphasized by a long leather army coat, and he stood looking over our heads so that our eyes never met. "I am Freiderich von Paulus," he said, in answer to the only questions our Russian liaison officer put to him, "fifty-three years old."

Paulus had a handsome face, but with hard brutal lines around the mouth, though at the moment there was plenty of reason for an expression of bitterness. Perhaps he was thinking that the Russians were already breaking their promise not to show him off. It may have occurred to him that never in German history had a captured field marshal been displayed before the press of the entire world. Or was he merely wondering whether these Russians really meant to try him as a criminal who had (it was said by Red Army commanders) ordered Russian prisoners of war, and even women and children, herded as a screen before his advancing troops? Most likely his mind was occupied with none of those thoughts, but merely with the wish that these sons-of-bitches would quit gaping, crawl on, and leave him to his bruised, dazed peace.

One thought kept coming back to me through all this. I wondered what the Japanese would think of it. The surrender of one general, not to mention twenty-four generals and a marshal, would be incomprehensible to them. Only suicide could wipe out such a disgrace to one's Emperor. Adolf had encouraged the idea, but without getting any takers.

As we left, the thermometer stood at thirty-seven below zero and the wind was a sharp lash in the face. Hours passed and after dark the wind increased. It came at us through the broken panels, through the floor, through the battered doors; it penetrated blankets, several layers of wool, and sheepskin-lined leather coats. It crawled along your spine like a live thing. We drank the little vodka we had and tried to sleep. We gave up and pounded each other with both fists to relieve the ache and stiffness. We sang to drown out the howling wind. And at one o'clock in the morning, when it must have been well under forty below, the car slowed to a walk, and we heard voices outside, and the creak of wagon

124

wheels. Thinking we had reached the city we untied the doors and looked out.

The wind was blowing the floury snow across a column of hooded, sheepskin-robed figures, and over horses obscured in their own frosty steam. Several light field pieces rolled by, followed by motor-driven supply wagons, field kitchens and ambulances. Some of the figures unhooded and, holding their rifles ready, came over to us.

"Who are you?" they demanded.

"Nemtsev!" said the playful Dave Nichol, to our horror. We quickly contradicted him, the Russians lowered their guns, and we produced cigarettes. They were on their way to the front, they said, and had already marched eight hours.

"Aren't you freezing?" we yelled.

"Nichevo! It's fine weather for war, but if you ask Fritz he won't agree!"

They all laughed and marched on and disappeared like ghosts in the oblivion around us. The encounter left a vivid impression of the way in which, under cover of night and a witches' brew of weather, the Russian offensive gathered the momentum that was carrying it to successes from which the Nazi Army would never recover.

At four o'clock, in the light of pre-dawn, we crept slowly into dim, smoking and still-mined shades of Stalingrad, into a death's head that had once been a city of 600,000 men. In the warmth of a dugout built into a railway embankment surmounting a bluff high above the frozen Volga, we fell into an exhausted sleep.

III

Blood in the Volga

I DID not wake up till around noon, when the smiling face of a black-haired, black-eyed girl in a soldier's uniform appeared in the doorway, to announce that dinner was ready. Her name, we learned on prompt inquiry, was Clara Yeramachenko. She was twenty-three, a Ukrainian, and before the war was a schoolteacher. She had been in Stalingrad with the service corps from the beginning of the battle. Now she inquired if we had slept well and upon being answered affirmatively seemed relieved.

"During the battle the dugouts were regularly inspected for bugs," she said, "and when a bug was found everybody in the dugout had to be deloused. We could not risk getting typhus, we had to keep our strength for the Germans." She paused and smiled wanly. "Of course death was commonplace enough. We were like animals, everyone able to think only from one action to the next. Comrades died all around us and we paid little attention. We never had time. Now I can neither believe it ever happened nor that it's all over."

Clara ran off down the hill and we did not see her again till that night, when she made a remark I would never forget.

The wind had died now and the only sound came from mines being detonated by the sappers, who all seemed to be Asiatics. Under the clear sky we saw the flattened remains of the great industrial heart of Southwest Russia, spreading along forty-one miles of waterfront. Quite near our dugout, just on the brow of the bluff, and in a very exposed position, stood a little house with whitewashed mud-brick walls. It was pockmarked with shrapnel holes, but by some humor of fate remained literally the only structure still intact for miles around. Going up to it I found some Red Army shoemakers inside, fixing the soles of their shoes with wooden nails. To my surprise I found a middle-aged mother and her small child were living there and on inquiry I learned they had stayed throughout the battle. She told me she had waited too long to cross the Volga, until it was actually safer inside the battle lines.

"The Germans never stopped shelling and firing at the river," she said. "The steel fell over it just like rain all day and night." And yet that river was the Russians' only supply line for five months, and during the worst weeks they never had more than two days' supplies in reserve. The story of how those supplies got across under constant fire is an epic in itself.

At the bottom of the cliff we entered the blindage which, throughout much of the battle, had served as headquarters of the 62nd Russian Army. It was an apartment cut deep into the frozen earth with a number of warm, dry rooms, much like the loess caves people build in China's Northwest. And here I saw our host, Lieutenant-General Vassili Ivanovich Chuikov. He was a big man, not tall, but with a big body, big hands, big face, and a big heart, I came to know. He had a wide mouth and when he grinned he exposed two rows of all-gold teeth which made me remember Mme. Pushnestikov.

Chuikov had an interesting background. He was a Russian, born in Tula, the son of illiterate peasants, and he became a worker at the age of twelve. He joined the Red Army six years later, in 1918, and fought through the revolutionary war and later attended military academy, graduating in 1925. He specialized in artillery and became a recognized expert in this branch. In 1940 Stalin sent him to China, as chief of the Russian Military Mission at Chungking. I never met him there but I knew he was credited with having organized the Chinese campaign at Changsha, in 1941. At that time the Japanese went into a trap, taking their tanks and guns across a long stretch of devastated country. The Chinese counterattacked, completed a minor encirclement, and drove the remnant Japs fleeing in rout back to Hankow. The Generalissimo thus won his only important victory since the battle of Taierchuang, in 1938.

But not long afterward the Russians withdrew their Mission, reportedly on the advice of Chuikov himself. It was said he had become convinced that measures he advocated for the reorganization and retraining of the Chinese forces would not be carried out. It was also stated that the Russians had become dissatisfied with the Generalissimo's practice of using their supplies to equip his First Army, which was engaged not in fighting the Japs but in blockading the Chinese Communist forces. At any rate, Chuikov returned to Russia in time to be given command of the 62nd Army, which Stalin ordered to fight a delaying action against the German advance toward the Volga.

"We first met the enemy on July 22nd, west of the Don," Chuikov told us, "so that we actually engaged the Sixth Army for half a year. In August they broke through to the Volga, but we checked them in the middle of the city till September 10th, when they began their heavy attacks to drive us into the river. It was just fifty days since we had first made contact. On September 14th, after they had broken through on each side of the city—they held a total of about five miles of the Volga shore—they began raining blows with all their force against the center, defended by the 62nd Army.

"That day we received a message from Comrade Stalin, saying

127

that the city must be held. He ordered us to stand fast and save Stalingrad. So we knew then that it was 'do or die.' We could not retreat."

Chuikov said that the Germans threw in men recklessly at first, hoping to break Russian morale; and in four days they lost over 50,000 dead. They seized historic Mamayev Kurgan—the height which dominated the city—but failed to break the main Russian lines. By the beginning of October some buildings had changed hands more than twenty times. On October 12th Paulus shifted his attacks and concentrated five divisions of infantry and two tank divisions in the factory district, along a front of two to three miles. The heaviest weight was grouped within a mile, where an attempt was made on the Red October Factory, the largest metal works in the world, which covered a path to the river. Here stood the Siberians, of whom more later.

"It was the worst day of the war," Chuikov went on. "We could not hear a single bomb or shell burst. It was just a deep unbroken thunder. The enemy made 2,500 plane flights and launched twenty-three separate attacks. We could not see more than five yards ahead because of the pall of smoke and dust. Glasses standing on a table in my blindage disintegrated into a thousand pieces, just from the concussion."

On that day Chuikov's own headquarters was only 200 yards from the front. One of his officers was killed as he stood talking to him. Altogether sixty-one of his staff were killed that day. Another time, when Chuikov was flying in a slow plane over the German lines, personally to observe their artillery position, he was shot down, but he escaped unhurt.

"At the end of that attack," he continued, "the Germans had advanced only a mile. They made their gains not because we retreated, but because our men were killed faster than they could be replaced. The enemy advanced only over our dead. But we prevented him from breaking through to the river. The Germans lost tens of thousands of dead in a half mile of soil and they couldn't keep it up. Before they could renew their ranks with fresh reserves the Red Army launched its general offensive and Stalingrad was encircled."

I asked Chuikov what important tactical errors the Germans had made, but he said he had observed none. "The only great error they made was strategic."

"What was that?"

"They gave Hitler supreme command."

But it was more than that which decided the outcome, he said. "On any battlefield the contending forces are never absolutely equal. If there is numerical equality there is variation in countless other factors. But once you are given approximate equilibrium, the side with better training, better equipment and greater stability will win. We had greater *stability* and we won."

At one time the Germans possessed immense tank superiority. On October 9th, when the Germans attacked with two tank divisions, the whole 62nd Army had only nine heavy tanks and thirty-one light tanks. But the Russians had superior artillery and made good use of it. Everywhere it was the might of Russian guns that stopped, wore out, and finally pushed back the enemy, and this was particularly true in the winter, of course, when the Germans' mechanized equipment lost much of its greater mobility.

"The Germans underestimated our artillery," Chuikov said, "and they underestimated the effectiveness of our infantry against their tanks. This battle showed that tanks forced to operate in narrow quarters are of limited value; they're just guns without mobility. In such conditions nothing can take the place of small groups of infantry, properly armed, and fighting with utmost determination. I don't mean barricade street fighting—there was little of that—but groups converting every building into a fortress and fighting for it floor by floor and even room by room. Such defenders cannot be driven out either by tanks or planes. The Germans dropped over a million bombs on us but they did not dislodge our infantry from its decisive positions. On the other hand, tanks can be destroyed from buildings used as fortresses."

The Germans learned that costly lesson at Stalingrad and later they were to apply it most effectively against the Allied troops in Italy. The tactics Chuikov used were employed a year later, with little variation, by the Germans who held up our advance for weeks at Cassino despite our complete mastery of the air. There is an answer to this kind of ground-hog defense, but our generals had not learned it, and Chuikov told us that, too.

"Our counter-attacks," he said, "were not led by tanks but by small storm groups of 'armor-piercers' who knocked out enemy firepoints, assisted by tanks. These small groups, of from five to eight men, were equipped with tommyguns, rifles, anti-tank rifles, hand-grenades, knives, flame-throwers and shovels. They usually attacked at night and they recovered each house as a fortress."

Here the Guardist troops of young Major-General Rodimstev proved to be most expert. Rodimstev himself had fought at Saragossa and University City during the civil war in Spain and he told us of his experiences there which had been useful in this battle. There was a Spanish detachment in Rodimstev's division, incidentally, and among others killed at Stalingrad was the youthful son of Dolores Ibarruri, the *La Passionaria* of the Republicans.

We sat down with Chuikov to a dinner of beef stew, potatoes, salt pork, butter, fish, herring, and the inevitable vodka. Chuikov knew quite a lot of English and he understood the toasts that were offered. I said that millions of people would perhaps like to be where we were, dining with the General who had won the battle of Stalingrad, and in the name of those millions proposed a toast to Chuikov. He quickly amended it.

"The Soviet Union and the Red Army are the heroes and not any individual commander," he said. All the same, he was deeply aware of the significance of his victory. "This is Hitler's black day. He will never again be able to take the offensive on such a scale. For Germany this is the beginning of the end."

After dinner I wandered into the kitchen with Henry Shapiro, looking for some drinking water, a rare commodity at the front. There we ran into Clara Yeramachenko, the Ukrainian with the schoolgirl complexion. She told us to wait and disappeared in the darkness. After some minutes she returned, lugging a bucket of water. She handed us a glassful. It was icy cold and tasted like nectar.

Looking at us quizzically, she said, "It's better than wine, isn't it?" and I nodded agreement.

"Of course it is," she exclaimed with sudden pride, "it's holy water—the Volga River mixed with our Russian blood!"

At that moment I felt ashamed to have her serving me; the roles should have been reversed. Clara was just as much a hero as Chuikov or anyone there. All through the battle she had helped cook for other heroes now dead. She and hundreds of girls like her had carried hot food to the trenches, so that a man could die with a warm stomach, and in his mind the image of her fresh youth and fine dark eyes, the personification of his beloved Russia. Hundreds like Clara had perished in this war, carrying wounded back through the squalls of lead and steel and tending them in dressing stations where you could not hear your own shouts and doing the menial tasks of the sanitation corps.

It was not an easy thing to offer up soft young flesh that way, to which everything cried out "Live!" How much Clara had left behind—love, perhaps, or a career and anyway the sweet spring of the Ukraine—to come to this river where blood mingled freely with water, and to do the little-sung, seldom-decorated work of a servant! How far away our American women seemed right then, with their inane talk of meatless days and "sacrifices" of gas and butter! How could they know what war meant to Clara?

IV

End of the Line

NEXT day we went through the half-buried corpse of the city. Streets and roads had been erased and we stepped carefully over footpaths broken through the mine-strewn debris. At the railway crossings the tracks themselves were gone and only the rusty signs still warned, "Beware!" and "Danger—Train."

Everything I had seen of war's destruction elsewhere fell into a common background of picayune damage and I realized that here Stalingrad was the pattern that would be laid across the face of all Europe before the catastrophe had spent itself. It was demolished Chapei, in Shanghai, magnified twenty times and the bombed districts of London could have been lost in a corner of it. Ronnie Matthews said he had seen Ypres after the last war, when it was shelled steadily for three years; but beside this it was a bagatelle.

Along one of the paths behind a pile of scrap iron, we saw a woman and several children peeking out of a hole in the ground, and we stopped to talk to them. They had been here throughout the fighting. Caught between fires, they had lived on dead horses. At night the mother and her children dragged in the frozen meat and cooked it underground. A near-by rubble was the scene of their former home. She said they would stay in their hole in the ground till the house was rebuilt. Why move now? And where to?

"They were not the only ones who ate horses," one of the Russians with us remarked. "When the Rumanian cavalry general, Bratescu, surrendered, we asked him where his horses were. 'Sir,' he replied indignantly, 'I regret to state that they have all been eaten by our allies!'"

We walked from the factory district up the famous Mamayev Kurgan, or Hill 102, which changed hands so many times. "The enemy," said young Captain Piotr Kostean, who was conducting, "considered the capture of Mamayev the key to Stalingrad. It commanded a view of all troop movements along the river and it enabled the Germans to hold our river-crossings under fire. To take it, the Germans threw in three divisions."

Mamayev Kurgan was named after Mamay, one of the last chiefs of the Volga Mongols, whom the Russians drove from the region in a decisive battle fought in 1380 at Kulikovo, not far from here. Kurgan simply means "burial ground," and the legend is that the chief was entombed here when the Mongols withdrew. It surmounts the long bluff on which the whole city is built. Just below, and separated from it by a ravine, is a strategic ridge which General Rodimstev's Guardists wrested from the Germans. But the latter had clung on to the highest point till the end, fighting back with hundreds of machine-guns.

From the eminence you could see for miles on all sides and in this world's-end scene only two things were recognizable works of creative man. Riddled with holes like long-running syphilitic sores some chimneys still stood; and the other things were the bedsteads. They seem as indestructible as the earth itself. It is always the same in every ruin. Churches collapse, idols and images fall apart, beauty and ugliness alike are obliterated, but no general has yet been able to wipe out all the chimneys and bedsteads, these pathetic affirmations of the eternal verities of work and rest and of fire and procreation.

From Mamayev we drove through more wreckage, to Revolutionary Heroes Square in the center of the city. Large buildings near by were burned or half-demolished; one had been filled with German corpses and burned as a huge crematorium. In the basement of a big department store, Universal No. 2, Marshal Paulus surrendered with his staff. Some of the top stories were shot off. The courtyard was littered with piles of personal letters, broken

132

guns, ammunition, and German corpses. Inside the building freckle-faced twenty-one-year-old Lieutenant Yelichenko, from Kiev in the Ukraine, showed us the tiny room where he had found Paulus, stretched out on a cot, and taken him prisoner.

Across the Square was a former Red Army Club which the Germans had used for a hospital. Only the walls and the foundation still stood. In a back corner we came upon a stack of half-naked Germans, the corpses of wounded men evidently thrown here by other inmates too weak to bury or burn them. Many of the dead had rags wrapped round their feet and hands; thousands of Germans froze to death. All of them looked half-starved. In the last weeks of the battle the German soldiers lived on two ounces of bread a day and an ounce or two of horse meat and then even that failed.

Scattered round the corpses were photographs of pretty girls, gay frauleins in canoes or sports scenes. A Russian who read German translated one of them for me. "Love, from Gretchen," was written on it. "Remember this, Hans?" and "Kill me a Russian, Siegfried!" on another. Tied with a piece of string around the neck of an Aryan youth, who lay so that you saw the rolls of frozen flesh on his withered belly, was a snapshot of a voluptuous blonde in a Varga-girl bathing costume. On it was written, "To my only one, come back to Bertha."

While we stared at this gruesome scene a figure seemed to detach itself from the corpses and stagger toward the open lot behind, which was filled with excrement and filth. We pulled back in amazement. Looking at the spot whence he had risen, as from the dead, we saw a small opening leading to the basement. As we leaned over it a nauseating stench rose up; evidently others were still alive below. The Russians were so busy burying their own dead that they had not yet brought in all the living Germans.

But it was at the Red October Factory that you best saw how this soil had been fought over, inch by inch, where one contestant understood that the limit of trading space for time had been reached, and the other knew that if the conquered space were lost now then nothing could restore the precious time consumed in winning it and all past victories would be rendered pyrrhic. Of the once great metal works, its acres of buildings, sidings, warehouses and docks, its thousands of homes and schools, parks and gardens, its fine machines, nothing remained but scrap and rubbish. It was a total loss.

Here and there pieces of buildings still stood, but you could not tell what they had been—an arm of steel jutting pointlessly into the sky, a half-gone wall; nothing else. In between these torn bones of industry, the lost labor of billions of hours of honest toil, were snow-covered foxholes, irregular trenches, and huge craters, where half-exposed corpses showed bits of saffron-colored waxy flesh and dull red patches frozen on their green rags. Guns and ammunition and sidearms lay about attached to booby traps. Sappers had not yet cleared the area.

At last we came to the end of the factory grounds and stood upon a knoll that rose fifteen feet above the remains of a modern building which marked the limit of the Germans' advance. Hardly more than a hundred yards beyond, the bluff fell away sharply to the river's edge. Hundreds of miles, all the way from Berlin, Fritz had come to this point—Hitler's "utmost sailmark"—thus far and no farther. Why? Was it possible that you could actually see, as clearly as the line of a receding tide upon a shelf of rock, the place where man would in after years say, "Here the evil spent itself?"

All the insides of the big building were missing, but the walls and the columns and the pillars stood. You could see how the defenders had found cover and how anyone trying to take the place must have been caught in a murderous crossfire. In front of it the terrain was cut up with deep bombholes which ruled out the use of tanks. The Russians' left flank was protected by a deep ravine running to the water's edge. On their right flank the little hill had guarded the building.

The Siberians who defended the Red October Factory area were the honored Eighth Guardist "division" under General Guriev, rushed here just before the Nazi onslaught of October 14th. Against it the enemy had thrown giant tanks, armadas of dive-bombers, and artillery ranging from long-range heavy guns and howitzers to six-barreled mortars firing thermite shells. At night the Germans turned the place into day with flares and fires; and burning buildings and smokescreens camouflaged the day. On an average 6,000 tons of metal was dropped on every half mile of the Stalingrad front. Preceding that day of the twenty-three attacks led by tanks and automatic-riflemen, they had saturated these two miles for eighty hours with shells and bombs. At the height of the battle 13,000 machine-guns were firing. Somehow the Siberians held against it all and did not go mad.

Even after seeing the positions I could not understand how a huge crushing machine could have been stopped a few tens of yards short of its goal. I asked some of the soldiers still on the river front, assorting booty, how it was that the Germans, having come that far, could not take the land which might have given them strategic victory. "They couldn't get it," they said, "because we could not retreat." Perhaps in final analysis it was that simple. Chuikov had said the Germans could advance only over the Russian dead. In the end there were more Russians in that small space than the Germans, with all their means, could kill.

But of course it was men who stood there, with frail destructible life at stake. So individual valor in men properly trained and equipped, confident in an intelligent leadership, determined to die rather than yield; belief in a sacred cause, or perhaps in the case of these Siberians the rugged plainsman's regional pride, or *esprit de corps*, what our Marines had later at Makin and Tarawa; or you might say simply discipline, the incalculable group will which, attaching to a tradition, subordinates the normal instinct to survive: all those intangibles that go to make up what is called "morale"—whatever it is, those Siberians had it. Once again they proved that it is still that strange human quality, high above self— it is that, and not machines—which turns the fate of men in battle.

Near by, under the bluff, we met Major-General Guriev, a man of medium height, with a strong face and taciturn manner of speech characteristic of Siberians. "Our whole front," he said, "was at no point more than half a mile deep. In places it was much shallower, and it was shallowest of all at the building you saw. We could not maneuver tanks in such terrain and, besides, we had very few. But we managed to destroy all the enemy sent against us."

Guriev told us that one of the reasons the Germans could not make full use of their tanks here was because their own bombing had so pitted the terrain with deep holes that they could not use their armored equipment effectively. Stalingrad proved that the dive-bomber has but a limited value in close fighting of this kind and, in fact, if used too extensively becomes an asset to the defending side, for it simply throws up new barriers which can be easily utilized by a close system of subterranean defense. We were to learn that lesson also—at Cassino.

It was not anything he said—he added little to what we already knew—but the feeling of strength behind this man, perhaps what Chuikov meant by "stability," that impressed us. He showed no sign of strain and smiled faintly when he denied suffering from shell-shock. A curious thing about the whole battle was that practically no "war neuroses" appeared. In Moscow, later, I met a woman psychiatrist who had worked in a base hospital behind Stalingrad. She told me that a number of cases had been referred to her, but that only two were genuine victims of shell-shock. She had finally been transferred to the rear, because there was too little for her to do at the front. This phenomenon has since been explained scientifically by Dr. Walter B. Cannon of Harvard, who states that when the combative spirit rises to a high pitch the "self-saving, self-protective instincts become secondary"—and it is the normal reaction of these instincts, not the shellburst itself, which causes so-called "shell-shock."

General Guriev was killed leading his troops in an attack not long after I saw him. But he and his Siberians live in the memory of Stalingrad, where young people, walking along the right bank of the Volga, pause to salute the monument which here marked the end of the line for Hitler.

It seemed to me that what I had seen and heard in and around Stalingrad was so important, in contrast to every other battle or battlefield I had seen, that I wrote out my notes in full and they alone made over 20,000 words. When I got back to Moscow I turned the whole thing over to our Military Attaché. I hoped there might be something helpful in it, since none of the foreign military observers had been to the front. Later I asked him whether he thought there was anything about this battle or the strategy and and tactics of the Red Army generally which we Americans could learn and usefully incorporate in our battle practice. "No," he replied, "their generals are not as well educated as ours." Then he corrected himself. "There is just one thing we could learn from them—something about cold-weather flying. But they won't give us the information we want."

PART - V - BEHIND   THE   ARMY

I

Travels of Industry

·····❦⟦❧·····

IT WAS the Russian workers whom the enemy perhaps under-estimated more than Russian soldiers. In other words, he under-estimated the whole Russian people: men under arms at the front, and women, children and old people at the rear.

Russian officials claimed that they completed, in the six months after the war began, a task of converting and reorganizing industry for war purposes to which Hitler had devoted six years. The statement astounded me. For one thing, I had assumed Russia was already pretty fully mobilized for war before the invasion began. Evidently not. Total mobilization, meaning elimination of virtually all non-military industry, came only after June, 1941. In 1943 the head of the Labor Power and Employment Division of the State Planning Commission, A. Karmalov, said that there were actually more skilled workers in the Soviet Union than ever before. And he claimed that they were producing more planes, tanks and other munitions than before the war, notwithstanding all the losses suffered in Western Russia.

How was it done? Nobody gave me a better answer than Anna Mikhailovna, a woman of fifty-two, whom I met as I was leaving a munitions plant and feeling a little dizzy from watching a furious pace of production. She was crating weapons near the door. As I started past her it seemed that she wanted to speak.

"It looks like heavy work for a woman your age," I ventured. "Don't you get tired? How is your health?" I knew she had already stood on her feet eight hours that day and that another three hours of labor lay ahead of her, in the draughty unheated room.

"Heavy work? Yes, of course," she hurried through her answer, anxious to ask a question of her own. "Of course we get tired;

137

everybody in Russia is tired these days. But we aren't often ill; we can't afford to be ill if we want to win the war. Right here in this factory we're killing plenty of Fritzes, and that's what matters now."

Anna's own husband was in the army and she had a grown daughter there too. A woman beside her had two sons and a husband at the front. Another was over sixty. After working all day in the factory she went home to look after her grandchildren, she said, whose parents were both in the forces.

"Well, but what are you Americans doing to beat Hitler, tell me that?" Anna interrupted my questioning in a challenging tone. I told her the usual thing: production, mobilization, training an army, fighting the Japs in the Pacific, getting ready to invade Europe. I reminded her too that some of the machines in this very shop had come from America. She listened; but she was not visibly impressed. Picking up her hammer she replied:

"Your help is good and we thank you for it. But fighting for yourself is better than letting other people fight for you. That's what we think here in the Soviet Union. The only kind of help we depend upon is the help we give ourselves." Anna spoke with feeling and confidence and behind her words I could easily see the factory leader, some Komsomol or the commissariat, telling her that each nail she drove was a blow at Hitler. I sensed from her how proudly conscious of winning the war even the humblest Russian was, as a result of this daily indoctrination. Other nations might expect America to fight their battles; Russia, never. Fundamentally it was just this profound conviction of their own strength, this unfaltering faith in themselves, that enabled the Russians to do the impossible.

Russia devoted to the cause of production for war nearly every minute and every bit of manpower and horsepower that could safely be taken from rest, play and the enjoyment of life. She won on the industrial front because her workers understood their peril, because the government realized what was needed for her salvation, and because about 99% of the energies of the United Republics seemed to have been mobilized to realize a single plan embracing more people and more territory than ever before was used to battle an invader.

There were practically no jobs in which women did not substitute for men. Women built the new subway in Moscow, women engineers constructed the defense works, women were the police

138

and the locomotive drivers and the miners and steel workers. It was the same way with youth, who by the age of sixteen could undertake almost any man's job. Even boys between the ages of twelve and sixteen probably averaged a third of a manpower day of production each. Little ones under twelve, organized as Pioneers and Timors, went about collecting scrap of various kinds or hauling wood or doing odd jobs after school. Except among the definitely disabled and aged and very young, non-producers were almost unknown.

Despite German seizure of areas which less than a decade ago held some 2,000 units of basic industry, the Russians managed in a little more than a year to better their pre-war output of weapons in many lines. Here is an example I happened to know about personally. Between my arrival in Russia and my departure six months later the government planned, built and put into operation, in a region once partly evacuated as a war zone, an entirely new aircraft plant, which by the end of 1943 was turning out about 300 fighter-bombers every month. An American expert called them "the finest in the world."

Leningrad was partly blockaded for two years and under German artillery fire, but we learned that production continued in many factories. Refugees coming out told me that the Kirov plant was still making munitions. Most of its workers were evacuated to the Urals, but a skeleton staff remained, and it was 70% women. They bricked up the factory windows and mounted machine-guns behind narrow slits in them. Shells dropped on them from German artillery positions only two or three miles away, and many buildings were wrecked. Over a thousand workers were killed or wounded, but the rest went on living in the factory and kept up some kind of production. For over a year they ate only black bread and thin cabbage soup.

The way this country solved its complicated problem of production was illustrated by the remarkable history of a garment factory I visited near the recovered town of Mozhaisk, then about twenty miles behind the central front. The factory had been organized fourteen years earlier as an industrial co-operative. By 1941, when it was purchased by the government, it had 600 workers. On October 14th, a few days before the Nazis marched in, the factory with its machines and many of its workers was started off to Kuibyshev, about a thousand miles to the southeast where some units resumed operations.

139

When Mozhaisk was retaken by the Red Army on January 20, 1942, the thirty-year-old factory director, Georgi Lismikov, at once reported again for industrial duty. He was still in the neighborhood because after safely evacuating the factory he had returned to organize and command a guerrilla detachment. On January 24th he received an order to restore the factory on its original site. Most of the former workers meanwhile had been scattered, many to be absorbed in new industries farther east. But seven skilled men from the factory had stayed with Lismikov in the guerrilla outfit. With their help he located machinery, raw materials, workers and transportation.

The Red Army had advance field headquarters near by and the neighborhood was still being bombed. Transport priorities were all held for the military. Most of the surviving population was living in holes dug in the frozen earth near the ruins of their former homes. But Lismikov and his mates worked fifteen hours a day and brought together enough skilled workers to clean and repair the wrecked building. The Red Army understood the importance of his work and fully co-operated; so did the quickly re-established Soviet government. On February 18th the factory was again producing.

The recuperative powers of local labor fully matched the physical restoration of the factory. All the women and girls I met here making goods for the front within a few minutes' flight from the German lines, were well, optimistic and not in the least worried about security, although only a short time earlier many had been near death from starvation and exposure. They toiled ten hours daily and after work many attended night classes or study groups. The Russian physique is one absolute among factors favoring a speedy post-war recovery.

It was the sequence of dates about this story that struck me as amazing, as Georgi told it to me when he took me through his plant. Here skilled labor and labor authority had shifted as a team from civilian life to military activity, then again just as quickly commenced reconstruction. Obviously that could not occur without extraordinary co-operation on the production line among military, party and government power. A demarcation clearly existed among the three, but it was not so much a line as a hyphen.

Now, a thing like that could happen elsewhere. In case of an invasion of the United States we could perhaps get that much co-operation between workers and managers; anyway, I hope so. I know personally of a similar happening in China, where a whole printing plant of 600 workers moved from a battle area behind the Japanese lines, to a guerrilla base—and got out a daily paper a few hours later. But except in the guerrilla areas run by the Chinese Communists such a thing would be inconceivable in China. The factory manager would run off to the nearest place of safety and he would never dream of debasing himself to fight guerrilla war. In Burma and Java the factory manager was everywhere a foreigner and he cleared out, often leaving his plant for the Japs and abandoning the workers to shift for themselves. In the case of Burma the workers took pot-shots at him as he departed.

Sophia Andreyovna Tolstoy, the granddaughter of Leo and now director of all the Tolstoy museums in Russia, told me how the Communists had evacuated her and her entourage from Yasnaya Polyana, the ancestral home, along with the most precious of the Tolstoy treasures, on a few hours' notice. When the Germans neared Orel in 1941 she appealed to the local Communist Party branch for help. All available transport was mobilized for military purposes and the evacuation of industry, and it was only a matter of hours before the Germans would arrive. Nevertheless the Party the army, the Soviet authorities and the public organizations all contributed personnel and transport sufficient to meet this emergency.

"We reached Moscow in a couple of days," Sophia told me, "and managed to bring with us nearly all the really important books, papers and furnishings, which never would have been possible without the co-ordinated help given to us."

II

Making Haste Swiftly

COMPETITION is the life of business and since there isn't any "business" in Russia, in our sense, some people think there can be no competition. But when you break it down to its Latin origin that excellent word really means "to strive after *together*." The Soviets did everything to promote competition in that literal sense. They realized it is a good old human instinct to want to excel, whether one lives in a capitalist or a socialist world.

And in this period the incentive was nothing less than the life of a nation. To secure the banners, awards and decorations offered by the government during the war, individual Russians began to work as nobody had ever seen them work before. Sergei Lukin, the People's Commissar for Light Industry, said that the launching of all-union competitions for higher output was one of the most fruitful ideas ever tried in Russia. He gave it as a main reason for the remarkable speed of Soviet industrial recovery. Very few factories, once the "game" began, failed to exceed the "norms" set for them by the defense council; and individual workers doubled, trebled and even quadrupled the minimum output demanded of them.

I found factories competing for honors with as much enthusiasm as Americans vie for sports titles. Top workers kept training as carefully as football stars and they had about the same following. Their pictures appeared in the papers, they were photographed with Kalinin and Stalin, they were decorated with many of the medals a general could get. Children sought their autographs. Their prestige was underlined by an interesting fact: the only medal Stalin ever wore was his decoration as a Hero of Socialist Labor.

"Coaching" factory teams was not so much the job of factory managers as of the most highly politicalized element of workers consisting of a few hundred thousand Communist Party members and millions of Komsomols. The Young Communists themselves were roughly a quarter of all the workers in the armament industry. Once I was walking through the busy aisles with a factory director when he suddenly stopped to read a big placard.

"Good, that's all right too," he commented as we moved on. "I see they've pledged to produce an extra 500 parts this month."

"Who has pledged it?"

"The workers."

"You mean you knew nothing about it till now?"

"That's not my affair. The Komsomols have done this. They probably called a meeting of the workers early this morning and got their promise. The Komsomols all have to do the same work themselves, so it's hard for others to refuse."

In the press one read at the end of every month stories of how

142

factories had won their banners. In a Novosibirsk factory some Komsomols made an extra squadron of planes by working faster and longer; in Azerbaijan a group of workers produced a couple of extra trainloads of oil; in a Urals factory some student-workers turned out enough field guns above their norm to equip three extra batteries of artillerymen.

Side by side with the names of war heroes appeared names of workers decorated for service on the labor front. Thus a woman garment maker of far-off Alma-Ata became nationally known because she noticed one day that a centimeter of cloth was wasted in a factory operation and she suggested a change which saved thousands of meters of material. In Moscow, a young steel smelter in the Hammer and Sickle Works, Nikolai Yanin, acquired the halo of a hero because he discovered a way to charge his furnaces in twenty minutes instead of the normal fifty minutes. Nikolai was a glorious fellow; he added about three hours to his labor productivity and that many more shells for the Red Army.

Another interesting thing the Russians discovered was that they could train women and 'teen-age youths into skilled workers in about a third of the time required in the past. One famous factory manager told me he could make a good worker out of the average housewife in two weeks and in a month she would more than fulfill her norm. Many youths who began part-time work at sixteen exceeded their quotas in a fortnight.

Before the war the Soviet Government anticipated that thousands of trained people might be killed off or maimed in battle and the Gosplan laid down a quota for each field of enterprise. It set up a system of developing "labor reserves" in every part of the country. Compulsory education had earlier gone only as far as the fourth grade; then it was extended to the seventh grade. In 1940 all youth was more or less conscripted under what amounted to a commissariat of labor reserves, headed by M. Maskatov, and a new educational plan went into operation in full force in 1941. Not much is yet known about this system abroad, which provides the human basis of Soviet reconstruction.

At the end of the seventh grade in city schools a selection takes place in which about half, and sometimes more than half, the students are earmarked as "labor reserve trainees," to be assigned to technical schools of various levels. Poorer students may drop out and go directly to the factories. Top students compete for scholarships which carry them through *tekhnikums,* colleges or universities, where they can branch out into the professions and sciences.

Selection is conducted somewhat as in our army we choose men for candidates to officers' schools. Past scholarship and personal history, physical and mental aptitude, personal preferences and the needs of the State plan, all enter into the Russian decision. Graduates of the workers' schools may later on apply for professional training also, and get it, if the record justifies it.

I visited several labor-training institutes in Moscow and found them a kind of cross between our polytechnic and vocational training institutes, but with important differences. Students were between fourteen and seventeen years old and courses which normally would take three years were being covered in two. There was an eight-hour day of class and field work. Half the time was devoted to general education and half to technical, including military training. Some students spent a month in the classroom and alternated with a month in the field.

The State furnished clothing, lodging, and part of their food, for which students paid 500 rubles, or half of the monthly 1,000 rubles allowed each person by the government. On graduation they were guaranteed jobs at a minimum wage of 1,000 rubles a month. About 30% of those I talked to were Komsomols and the goal was to raise this to 90% during the war. Most of the students said they hoped to become engineers.

By the spring of 1943 the new plan had provided the Soviet Union with over a million trained technicians for the iron and steel, metal, electrical, mining, railway, building, and other industries. The system was still being expanded and could theoretically draw upon a mass of forty million grade-school students for future trainees, so its possibilities were enormous. Soviet technicians were also trained in schools operated along similar lines by factories, mines and railways, for older workers as well as youths.

In Moscow I visited the famous Vladimir Ilyitch Factory, where Lenin was shot by Dora Kaplan while he was making a speech. As if to make up for its notoriety, this factory had during the war repeatedly won first place in the munitions industry, in competition with all contenders in the Soviet Union. Yet in 1941 its operators had been almost utter strangers to the machines and 70% of them were girls and women freshly recruited from households, offices, schools and farms.

In ten months the productivity of labor at the Ilyitch factory increased over 500%. The women defended their national record by working at almost superhuman tempo. Virtually, they dedicated themselves body and soul to the factory and what little leisure they had was devoted to needed rest. Their working day was twelve hours, with an hour for meals; sixty-six working hours a week. Machines moved at such break-neck speed that it seemed to me an hour here must equal the wear and tear on the human constitution of two hours of normal work. I don't know how they stood it. The mere sound of the place was a dentist's drill in your head.

But the extraordinary stamina of Russian women is no myth. Here they thought of themselves as troops and manipulated their lathes like machine-guns aimed at Nazis. It sounds terribly in earnest and, believe me, it was. I hesitated to break in on them, they seemed so utterly absorbed. When I ventured to speak to several I found they were positive zealots about their work.

I remember Zina Ivanovna, a big blonde of twenty-one, with a wide grin and arms like pistons. She had been in the factory a year and ranked as a Stakhanovite: she had just been decorated, together with thirty-five others in that plant. I hardly needed to ask her about her health; she looked good for another 100 years.

"I can go on making shells at this rate as long as Hitler can take them," she laughed. "My husband is at the front. Every time I finish a shell it brings him that much nearer home!"

Zina was producing three times the required norm. In terms of the fifteen-pound shells she tossed around like baseballs that meant handling 165 to 170 a day. She was paid on a piecework basis and earned about 750 rubles a month, she told me. That was quite enough for ordinary purposes and normally it would have bought luxuries too. As a super-worker she could now buy at the factory canteen extra rations of things like butter, milk, sugar and eggs—no small additional incentive. The Vladimir Ilyitch Factory also had a farm of its own and its director, Georgi Alexandrovich Pregnesky, told me it was a grand thing for morale.

Pregnesky himself was thirty-five, and had a handsome, radiant face. He was walking on air when I visited him because he had just got news that he had been awarded the Order of Lenin. "It's the greatest day of my life," he exulted. Probing for his secret of success, I asked him whether he had a workers' council to help him run the plant.

"We don't have such a system any more. We find it neither necessary nor desirable. The workers do their jobs and I do mine."

"Don't the labor unions have a voice in the direction of your plant?"

No again. "They have other work to do, they don't interfere with management in any way. But they have an indirect voice in all industry, of course, through representation in the Supreme Soviet."

"But who are your directors? Who fires you if you fail to make good?"

"The commissariat that hired me is my board, but it doesn't tell me how to manage the plant, either. Does a good board in America interfere with the manager? Certainly not! That's why you have efficient factory operation there. Of course there is this difference. In this country labor runs everything, there are no bosses and no dividend collectors. In this job I am just a delegate, you might say, of the whole working class of the Soviet Union."

Nevertheless, Sergei was tremendously enthusiastic about American industry. It turned out he had spent a whole year visiting American factories. He seemed to know as much about what we make between New York and San Francisco as his friend Don Nelson himself. But he had one regret. He had been so busy crawling in and out of machines that he had never got around to a thing the comrades had been asking about ever since his return.

"You won't believe me," he said, "but I never did know an American girl. Not even *once!*"

III

Spine of Russia

LENIN always preached the industrialization of the East and flayed the Tsarist government for not developing the Urals, except as a source of pretty colored stones. Long before this war Lenin's disciples had already turned the region into what Russians now call "the iron spine of the Soviet Union." Without the Soviet industrial bases there the Red Army might well have been driven out of Europe and come to disaster in the deep hinterland of Asia.

The U.S.S.R. is all one color in our textbooks, but when you begin to move around here you soon see it is more polyglot than Europe. With its 175 different nations and tribes, it has more peoples than India and is scattered over four times more territory. There are eleven independent republics in the Union, with many autonomous republics to accommodate all the economic and cultural differences of some forty-nine officially recognized nationalities.

Largest of the "Union Republics," and largest republic in the world, is the Russian Soviet Federated Socialist Republic, which is twice the size of the United States. By far the greater part of it lies in Asia. From the Urals it stretches eastward for more than 3,000 miles to the Pacific Ocean. Included are all the Soviet North, all Western and Eastern Siberia, the Buryat-Mongolian and Yakut autonomous republics and a number of other autonomous areas. Its Far Eastern territory, reaching from Vladivostok to the Bering Strait, is only six minutes by fast plane from Alaska, and hence the Asiatic part of the Soviet Union is America's nearest neighbor and closest concern.

Russia is over 6,000 miles wide, and the Urals lie a good 1,000 miles east of Moscow. Geologically much of this huge continent is unexplored, and complete data are lacking even on the Urals. During the war extensive surveys were completed which revealed even greater resources than had been estimated, with especially amazing wealth in iron, coal, oil, aluminum and manganese. A. P. Fersman, of the Soviet Academy, has declared that this mountain range contains all but four of the known chemical elements, "a concentration of reserves found nowhere else on such a grand scale." Radium, he asserted, is extant here not in ounces but by the pound.

In 1939 the Urals already accounted for a third of the nation's total productive capacity; since then the percentage has probably doubled. Added to this pre-war construction, much of the armament industry evacuated from the West was brought to the Urals and put to work again. Among others, the great Kharkov tank factory moved some 1,500 miles. By the middle of 1943 it was making more tanks than it ever produced in its old home. A cable company brought the same distance made more cable and a Ukrainian metal works, one of the largest in Russia, was in 1943 almost back to normal production. Workers of the great Mariu pol Metal Tubing Works, evacuated from the Ukraine, installed a similar mill in the Urals in one-seventh the time taken to erect the original. The general rate of growth of Urals industry was indicated on a Soviet graph published in 1943. This showed that, taking January, 1942, as 100, the September construction figure for the same year was 215.

Few people realize that most of the Urals' mineral wealth lies on their Asiatic slope. For example, the Kuzbas (Kusnetsk Coal Basin) holds six times more coal than the Donbas itself. It became the greatest coal producer in Russia in 1942. In Kuznetsk the Russians claimed to have built a larger metal works than the one destroyed at Stalingrad, which was the biggest on earth, they said. Siberia boasts the largest iron and steel works in Russia and the largest blast furnace in Asia or Europe. One Kuzbas furnace alone makes more than a million tons of steel a year.

The foresight embodied in the Third Five-Year Plan simplified the transplanting of key industries to Asia. It prohibited the building of more new enterprises in Moscow and Leningrad, as well as in Kiev, Kharkov, Gorki and even Sverdlovsk, so that before 1941 maximum allotments of building materials were already being diverted to the East. After 1938 a third of all new iron and steel factories were erected there and three-quarters of all new Soviet blast furnaces.

Double-tracking of the Trans-Siberian railway was followed by other construction, including further work on the Turksib railroad, which connects Central Asia with the Urals and the Far East. The 1,000 kilometers of single- and double-track originally scheduled in the Third Plan came into use in 1943, and improvements on the northern sea route gave better communications with the Orient. Power plants, cement factories and truck plants were operating as planned, along with many new light industries.

Machine-tool plants worked in Irkutsk, Vladivostok and even in Ulan Ude, capital of Buryat Mongolia. Aircraft flew out of Tomsk and Irkutsk. The fine steel of the East became fine tanks, and not only for shipment westward. Hundreds of millions of tons of tinned fish and mountains of fur hats and coats poured to the Red Army from the Far Eastern territory, which is farther from Moscow than America is from England. The Far East had everything needed for an industrial state and the Soviets decided to make it self-sustaining.

Down in Central Asia, too, industry was developed. Open-hearth furnaces began to blaze, and blast furnaces were prepared for modern industrial centers technologically autonomous from Western Russia for the first time. Stretching from the Caspian to the Altai Mountains, and beginning in the North at the Urals to end on the high frontiers of Iran and Afghanistan in the South, Soviet Central Asia includes a half dozen republics which are together bigger than British India. Tashkent, Samarkand, Tajikistan, Turkmenistan and Bashkiria were a generation ago romantic-sounding places but actually little but camel towns and wild steppe, mountain fastnesses and lonely deserts. The old Tsarist colony of Turkestan was still largely the domain of the nomad. Today they are already sufficiently changed to offer highly effective contributions of men and materials to the cause of Soviet arms.

Bashkiria, with its "second Baku," and its new oil wells sunk at Fergana, Bokhara and in the Kirgi and Turkmen Republics, gave promise of a Soviet oil production which might eventually equal our own. The Karaganda coal fields in eastern Kazakhstan became the second largest in Russian hands. Central Asia's cotton clothed the whole Union, and now its own mills could produce all the textiles needed. Formerly the cotton had to be hauled 2,000 miles to the mills of Moscow and Leningrad. Kazakhstan's huge new meat industry accounted in part for the high morale of the Red soldier, for it changed his diet from dried herring to tasty tinned meat.

Here in the Soviet East there had been a decade of migration as dramatic as the settlement of the American West. There was gold in these hills, too; but other inducements were offered to lure the adventurous of all ages. Collective farms were exempted from forced grain sales for ten years. "Private enterprise" was encouraged. Individuals were permitted to work their own farms and to sell produce in the open market. Teachers, doctors and technicians were given good bonuses and even Red Army pay was higher than elsewhere. Propaganda campaigns among youth represented going East as a crusade. One of Siberia's greatest industrial cities, Komsomolsk, was built almost entirely by Young Communists.

Great cities and new nations grew out of the wilderness. It is said that more than 100 towns of over 100,000 each have arisen here since the Revolution. That would mean about 10,000,000 people uprooted and resettled in a couple of decades, most of them shifted by decree. Karaganda is one example. A few years ago it did not even exist and now it has a population of 200,000. Stalinsk, as recently as 1936, had only 3,800 "souls," as the Russians still say; now it is an important Siberian steel center as big as Karaganda. Novosibirsk quadrupled in size in three years. After centuries of slow growth Tashkent suddenly quintupled its population in a little more than a decade; today it is a metropolis of nearly 2,000,000 people.

In strange ways the war helped to people all these frontiers, as refugees from European Russia, together with factory workers, poured in from the West. How many people were involved in this resettlement is not yet known. *Pravda* once laconically described the evacuees as "numbering tens of millions." More recently it was officially stated that fifteen million people live in the Urals area and that is about three times the "pre-Plan" population. What is certain is that this war migration exceeded anything seen in the past. One result has been the opening up of millions of hectares of new land in Siberia, the Soviet North and Central Asia.

In Uzbekistan more than a million acres were stolen back from the desert, to be transformed into enough new fertile soil to make the Republic self-sufficient in grain. A remarkable thing about war-time construction in Siberia and Central Asia was that it was mostly done by people who never before were builders. Uzbekistan's irrigation projects were the work of old men and women and children, led by young graduates from local trade and engineering schools. Formerly a backward pastoral country, this state now has a production 75% industrial.

Industrialization also spilled into the neighboring agrarian Republics of Tajikistan and Turkmenistan and even little Kirghistan. The Tajik Republic, bordering on Chinese Sinkiang and Afghanistan, was formerly only an isolated frontier, landlocking Russia behind the high barrier of the Pamirs. Now railways and roads reach into it and bring its cotton to the white buildings of Samarkand, where modern mills hum across the street from the blue-domed Gur-Emir mausoleum of Tamerlane.

I remember going to see Olga Mishakova, the good-looking blonde secretary of the national Komsomol organization. It was the day after she returned from an airplane trip to Tashkent and she was ecstatic about her experiences. She told me stories of Uzbek and Tajik women running collective farms and factories, operating tractors, trucks, locomotives and anything on wheels. "The last of the veils have disappeared during the war," she said. "Every woman is now out working either in a factory or the field, and you can't work with a curtain over your face."

She was genuinely excited by the way Soviet Asia's youth was responding to appeals for help. In Uzbekistan, she said, 400,000 children were working in the fields, sowing and reaping grain and cotton, before and after school hours. Here the Pioneers and Komsomols had themselves made and shipped off more than 80,000 sets of winter clothes. They had raised or bought more than 3,000 crates of oranges, for the cold and hungry children of blockaded Leningrad. Here youth and women were caring for homeless people from the devastated regions.

From far Lithuania and from the valleys of the Don and the Dnieper, from White Russia and from the Caucasus, thousands of little refugees were coming to live under the warm southern sun, and in the rich fields of Tashkent and Fergana, of Bokhara and Samarkand. Many of them were orphans, sons and daughters of soldiers and civilians killed in the war. Hundreds of State homes were opened to care for them, but thousands of the fair-haired children of the North were being adopted by Asiatic families, sometimes three or four to a single family. Russian and Ukrainian boys and girls would grow up to speak Uzbek or Kazakh or Kirghiz as well as their native tongues. Many would spend their lives here and help build up this land.

It was all very interesting, this enthusiastic support of the war by Asiatics whose own lands were still very far from any menace. In Burma the British had found themselves attacked by the natives; in India they had been obliged to put Nehru and Gandhi in jail. Even in China the army still brought in conscripts with ropes around their necks. What made the difference? Not just the law and not just politics. A lot of it was explained by the Soviet Union's policy of social and racial equality, in spirit as well as law, which made it acceptable to everybody, apparently, for brown men to foster white orphans.

There was another side to this picture, of course. I was reminded of it when I talked in Moscow to a member of the British Military Mission. I remarked upon the success of the Soviets in socializing Asia and bringing them into the war. "We could do that in our colonies, too," he replied, "if we wanted to interfere with their freedom and their personal rights. But we would never do it. That is against English principles of fair play."

It was not as paradoxical as it sounded. It never occurred to the bolsheviks that in imposing their way of life on Asiatics they were doing anything but liberating them, and just as secure in that

151

knowledge as the British in their own, they had intervened to a maximum degree against the old society and its privileges. In Soviet Asia Gandhi would probably have been shot or put to work spinning in a concentration camp, as an enemy of the people and wrecker of socialist property, instead of being immured in a palace. So also with other "civilly disobedient." But it wouldn't have been done to preserve the capitalist system or to protect the rights of minorities to be princes or Untouchables, as the case might be. It would have been avowedly for the opposite purpose of doing away with that particular kind of minority rights.

IV

Asia Versus Hitler

Do you realize," a Russian professor remarked to me one day, "that this is probably the first time in history that Asia has saved so-called Western civilization? Could the United States win its war against Japan without China as an ally? Could Britain recover her colonies at all, without the help of India, or could she even defend herself in Europe? As for Russia, where would we be today without the Asiatic territories?"

Not long afterward I saw, standing in a resplendent yellow silk robe on which hung a couple of Red Army decorations, and gazing meditatively at the sparkling towers of the Kremlin, the Commander-in-Chief of the armed forces of the Mongolian People's Republic, Marshal Choy Bolsan. He had just returned from the front, with a large delegation that had traveled over 3,000 miles to bring gifts contributed by the nomads of this ancient nation of warriors. I could not know what thoughts lay behind the old Mongol's wind-burned face as he looked at those crenellated walls, built when Genghis Khan still dominated this part of the world; but he was a richly symbolic picture. After seven centuries of incessant warring, the gap between Mongol and Russian seemed to be closing forever, as they stood together now as allies.

152

In reality there was no line drawn between European and Asiatic in the planning and organization of Soviet war. Military detachments were made up of people from all parts of the country, without special concern for racial backgrounds. There were some all-Asiatic regiments and there were also mixed regiments. There were Asiatics commanding Russian troops and vice-versa. Kurban Durdi, an Uzbek, was an outstanding general. Uzbeks were among the Siberians who defended Stalingrad, Mongols were mixed with the tankists outside Kotelnikovo, and Tajiks among troops in Mozhaisk. In a military hospital I met a Kazakh who had been fighting the Nazis in American tanks, and I became so interested in him that I decided to call on Tovarishch Sharibov, chief delegate of the Kazakh Republic, to learn more about this distant colorful people.

Sharibov's own story partly answered the question of Soviet success in Asia. He was born on the Caspian, where his father was a poor fisherman, and until he was fourteen he was a fisherman too. Then he went to work in a factory, where he heard about the Revolution and the opening of free schools. At the age of sixteen he learned to read; soon he knew both his own written language and Russian well enough to become a teacher. He was elected chairman of a local executive committee; eventually he became a government minister in Alma Ata. And now in Moscow I found him very much the efficient executive behind his battery of telephones. At the age of thirty-seven he was chief delegate to the all-union Council of Commissars, representing a republic over half the size of India.

Sharibov looked much like any Mongol, though he might have passed for a Northern Chinese, too. He was in appearance youthful for his age and had the smooth pale-brown skin of his race. But he was Russian in his thinking and knew little about Asia beyond the Union's own frontiers. He got down to serious talk at once, without the Oriental preliminaries, when I asked why Kazakhs felt that a fellow as far away as Hitler was a threat to them.

"Distances separating friends and enemies are unimportant in this war," he told me. "The Soviet Union is a big family and the important thing to us is the Kazakhs are equal partners in it. When one house is on fire all the neighbors have to help put it out. The Soviet Union is our motherland too. We could not stand idle in this war and have a right to survive."

153

Sharibov asked me something about India. Did the people support the war? I told him a little about the divisions between castes and religions; of contrasts between the enormously rich and the majority living in beggary; of the fear and suspicion dividing Hindus and Moslems; and of a general indifference to the war and antagonism toward the Allies. He seemed genuinely perplexed to hear all this.

"Well, do you have such differences in Kazakhstan?" I asked.

"Before the Revolution we had some wealthy princes, and the Tsarist regime promoted fights between the Moslems and the Orthodox Church," he said. "Maybe it was somewhat similar to India in those days. But the princes were wiped out. As for the Church—for a while we opposed all religion—the old Churches were pretty corrupt, you know. Now Churches are tolerated, but young Kazakhs are not very religious. But such a policy as playing off Moslems against Catholics could not exist nowadays."

"Do you feel satisfied with the Soviet policy for the nationalities?"

"In general it is satisfactory and I will tell you why. Our nation isn't discriminated against and we've made great progress; nobody can deny that. Kazakhstan was only a poor colony under the Tsars, but now it is an independent republic with its own elected local and national governments. In the beginning it was the Russians who led us, but now we have trained and educated Kazakhs in charge of affairs. The majority of both the government and Communist Party are Kazakhs. But we don't think about these things; we aren't afraid of Russian help, we welcome it. Russians have equal status in our state, as we have in theirs; they vote in the same electorates with us."

Warming up to his subject he went on: "Before the Revolution our national culture was suppressed and the Russian language was forced on us. Today we have our own opera, we have our own music and literature. Some Kazakh opera stars, ballet dancers and cinema actors are leading artists of the whole Union. Our artists are in great demand at the front; Kazakh writers and poets are nationally known. Take, for example, the poet Gumbil. You may never have heard of Gumbil in America (he was right about that!) but he is a People's Poet of the Soviet Union. The whole country reads him, in all our languages. Before the Revolution his works couldn't be published even in Kazakhstan."

This fellow Gumbil was a picturesque patriarch, ninety-seven

154

years old, who wandered the steppe composing epics which he sang to his own musical accompaniment. In Tsarist times he used to recite revolutionary poems recalling the vanished glory of his people and more than once he was thrown in jail. He became an ardent follower of the bolsheviks and sang the praises of the reforms. Now he composed ballads of hate against Hitler.

"In Tsarist times," Sharibov continued, "we did not have a single university. We had very few schools and 93% of the people were illiterate. Today even most old people can read and write and literacy is well above 90%. We have twenty colleges and universities and 130 technical training institutes."

He told me how Kazakhstan had benefited economically, changing in only one generation from a semi-nomadic colony to an agrarian-industrial republic. Railway mileage had more than trebled and industrial workers had increased six times, until industry now accounted for more than 50% of the total production.

"These gains are understood by Kazakhs; they are the concrete reasons why we fight. We know what we have won and we know what the Nazis would take away from us, and the test is that today we have conscription but most Kazakhs volunteer for service long before they are called up. Many of our soldiers have returned and told us what the Nazis are like and how cruel and bestial they are and we have seen movies of their crimes and heard our men describe them. We know also that Hitler especially hates all Asiatics. Have you not read *Mein Kampf*?"

Sharibov referred to the remarkable letter written by the Uzbeks, which was published all over the Soviet Union. Signed by two million Uzbeks, it declared that if Hitler conquered Russia all Asiatics would either be killed or made slaves of the "Aryans." It quoted Hitler's description of Asiatics as "ape-men," one rung on the ladder below the Russians who were "sub-men." With *Mein Kampf* the letter contrasted Soviet teachings of racial equality and harmony. Here was an ideal already realized, said the Uzbeks, for which they were prepared freely to mingle their blood with Russian blood on the field of battle.

"That's how it is with all of us," said Sharibov. "Caste, religious difference, racial hatred? We don't acknowledge them and such things don't worry us, we've left them far behind! We still have plenty of problems to solve in the future, but our changes will be made to strengthen racial solidarity and co-operation—that is fundamental."

155

This interview with Sharibov would come back to me very forcefully some months later, when the Supreme Soviet adopted laws granting national armies and much increased powers of autonomy to the member republics of the U.S.S.R. But that belongs in a later chapter.

PART - VI - WINTER IN MOSCOW

I

Around the Kremlin

THE winter of 1942-3 was grim and tough, the worst months of the war. It was better in Moscow than in some other Russian cities and towns, but cheerless enough to make foreigners who had never seen real famine say to each other darkly, "Things can't go on like this, next winter there'll be riots and revolt." But Moscow was never at any time in danger of social disintegration. It was the most thoroughly organized war capital I have ever seen.

Nevertheless, that winter made a melancholy impression on the new arrival and on the foreign residents, who of necessity lived pretty much to themselves, in their embassy buildings and other relatively cozy quarters where they ate far better than 98% of the Muscovites. On November 7th there was no parade or celebration of any kind, for the first time in many years; and even after the offensive began there was little rejoicing over the daily communiqués of victory. Russians knew what those successes were costing them and they mourned their dead. They guessed how far away the final triumph still lay and they suspected their Allies were waiting for more of them to be killed before making a landing in Hitler's Europe.

Moscow must have always had a rather dreary look, though the Russians apparently used to find something endearing even in its winters, if you can believe Tolstoy; but this year at the mere approach of zero weather people's faces shut in hard unsmiling lines, as if setting out on a perilous sea journey. Buildings were insufficiently heated and coal was unobtainable; most people managed to keep warm only in bed. Every family had to haul its own wood in from the forests miles outside the city and anyone not otherwise usefully employed was obliged to collect timber for the State. It was said that 80,000 people were busy all the time chopping wood.

"Economize" was the watchword not only for fuel but for everything else. There was never sufficient light anywhere and ditto for hot water. Many Russians never had a bath all winter, though you didn't notice it, olfactorily, perhaps because of the cold. Taxis were unobtainable; the Metro, the busses and the street cars were so crowded that "by comparison a sardine tin could be considered a vacuum," as Philip Jordan remarked. At night the blackout was complete, and innumerable accidents occurred on the pavements and sidewalks thickly coated with ice. You were lucky to get home from the theater without at least one fall; you walked braced for a collision with an immovable obstacle or a fellow pedestrian.

I never ran into such an exasperating blackout; the hazards of Chungking or Cairo or London were nothing to compare with it. In daytime the city was in a dim-out; for months dusk came between two and three in the afternoon. Even when you could see, the ice-covered façades of the buildings seemed to warn you to keep your distance. How a Moscow winter made you wonder what you ever found to complain about in the tropics!

Most of the shop-windows were boarded up, which added to the austerity. It was like putting dark glasses on a woman, or putting her into purdah. A few *gastronomes* still kept up a bright display of huge hams, sausages, cheeses, bread and cake of all varieties, and chocolate, wines and vodka. But these heavens from afar on closer examination proved to be clever imitations in cardboard, while the bottles were totally empty.

Just before the war the Russians had been enjoying a life of plenty for the first time since the Revolution, as my friends on the Flame had made clear. Rationing had been abolished and there were foodstuffs of various kinds in abundance, and luxuries, too: wine and fruit from the Caucasus and Central Asia, over a hundred varieties of sausage and even "Birdseye" type and other processed foods, and hundreds of kinds of confectionery and pastry. Now the cardboard window displays seemed to me an obscene offense to an ever-hungry people; but the Russians didn't react that way, apparently. They considered them legitimate reminders of the good life that was and a promise of what would be again, after victory.

But cardboard clothes wouldn't keep people warm and here the emphasis was decidedly on the practical. When I first came into Kuibyshev I thought I had never seen anywhere a population so uniformly drab in appearance, so down-at-the-heels. Everyone seemed to be wearing somebody else's handed-down clothes. Then I realized that though they were wretchedly dressed, no one was in real rags or without shoes, as were thousands in Peking, Shanghai, Delhi, Calcutta or some cities in Europe and South America, where you could also see the most expensively gowned women in the world. Here they were just shabby, no one very richly dressed but nobody in obvious beggary either.

Moscow streets showed more variety in dress than Kuibyshev's, but still everything was somber and black. If you wore a bit of color you stood out like a red apple in the snow, and people looked at you and muttered "foreigner" or "second front." Yet Maurice Hindus was right when he wrote in *Mother Russia,* "a visit to the theater in any city quickly dispels the impression of shabbiness in dress, and evokes a Russia bright with color." It turned out that most Russians did own one party suit or dress, but were saving it for the theater, New Year, their wedding, or the end of the war.

For all that, when I saw the Kremlin towers beyond the magnificently broad but otherwise undistinguished Gorki Street, and the domes of St. Basil's rising beside the red marble of Lenin's tomb, with the silver-white of the river below, I decided I liked Moscow.

The day after I arrived Lee Stowe and I went for a walk around the Kremlin. After that I never let a week pass without going to the top of Moskvoretskaya Bridge, where you could see the walled citadel in full panorama, with its many-spired cathedrals and once-imperial chambers. A vast camouflage had been painted over the red walls, more than a mile around, and the same pointless landscaping effect was carried out on the buildings inside. It made the place seem even more chaotic than it is. There is no pattern or symmetry about the Kremlin; it just grew.

People call it "Oriental," as they call Moscow itself, chiefly because of the bulbous domes on the cathedrals, I suppose. But compared to the splendor and dignity of the Forbidden City of Peking, with its spaciousness and balanced conceptions, or to the perfection of line and detail of the Taj Mahal, it seems crude and even barbaric; there is little Oriental about it. All the same the total effect is uniquely Russian, and somehow a striving to blend Europe and Asia. St. Basil's concentrates the effect in smaller space, with its nine chapels unified as one, yet each retaining its wholly independent architectural mood, and with domes of all shapes and colors. It's a fantasia in stone, wood and tin, a gorgeous gingerbread house of Hansel and Gretel, which belongs exactly where it is, at the head of Red Square; and when in the pale moonlight of a Moscow winter night its roofs are frosted with snow it seems the very incarnation of historic Russia.

No city holds quite so much of the heart of a people as Moscow. In other lands nations arose, formed, and found their natural boundaries, more or less, before they found a capital; but here it was Muscovy first and then Russia grew up around it. Moscow's chronicles begin only after the Norman Conquest of England. If you omit the early Slav communes and the city-states of Kiev and Novgorod, Russian civilization is hardly much older than English. In fact it wasn't till the fifteenth century that Ivan III finally threw off the Mongol yoke, and Russia emerged as a true independent state. Thus virtually all we know of Russia happened within the Ming and Ch'ing dynasties, which the Chinese consider their recent history.

But it was no winter for archeological study in Russia. Nearly all the museums were closed and the best art had been removed; even the Lenin Library had been stripped of its best books. Lenin's Tomb was not open to the public and St. Basil's was also locked up. Black-coated members of the N.K.V.D. (*Narkomindel*), successor to the Cheka and Gaypayoo, known among foreigners as "the Y.M.C.A."—to the lasting mystification of the Russians—were everywhere on guard. They readily discouraged any tendency to stand about gawking at the scenery. Even on a walk around the Kremlin we usually had the company of the Y.M.C.A. boys, who were never objectionable, however, in any way. The gates of the citadel themselves were always closely guarded.

Not long after I arrived I did the usual thing; I wrote a letter to Mr. Stalin and took it over myself to his letter box in one of the Kremlin gates. I gave him a number of reasons why he should break his established practice and see me. He was, of course, the least accessible leader in the world; no newspaperman had inter-

159

viewed him for publication since he had received Roy Howard, a decade ago. He never holds off-the-record conferences or even mass interviews, as most other leaders do. It is extremely hard even to get a look at him from a distance. Usually the press has that opportunity on November 7th, when it is seated near him in the Red Square, or at annual sessions of the Supreme Soviet, of which he is an elected member for Moscow.

Admittedly Stalin was a busy man; as Secretary-General of the Communist Party, chairman of the Council of People's Commissars, and Supreme Commander-in-Chief of the general headquarters, he was understandably shy of press parleys. Our standing argument with the Foreign Office was that if we had a few contacts with Stalin and other commissars—who were almost as hard to see—we could "humanize" them in America and Britain, and correct the impression there of a sinister, aloof and scheming group of Orientals.

One of the great illusions among our people is that Moscow is always looking for ways in which to "propagandize" the world and sell its system to us. The Russians save their indoctrination efforts for their own people. The complaint of the foreign correspondents is just the opposite: that they seldom get the co-operation needed in order to dramatize the Russian story in the epic terms which they themselves feel it. No government is so economical with explanations of its motives or methods, and none makes such a poor effort to give the press access to its official personalities. At the same time it carefully scrutinizes every word written about it overseas, and has its own system of weighing the importance of all foreign comment.

"I've been here over a year now," Walter Kerr once remarked rather plaintively, "and nobody has yet tried to convert me or propagandize me. I wish to God somebody would. I'd like to know the Russian answers to a lot of things here, but I can't find anybody even interested in telling me what they are, and least of all in selling me Communist ideology."

Even when the big brass flew in, always on "imperative" secret missions and unwilling to settle for less than an audience with Stalin himself, the Russians kept them cooling their heels for weeks. It did not matter that they carried letters from the President or the Prime Minister, as most of them did. They stood in the queue just the same. General Patrick Hurley waited for a fortnight before seeing the Marshal and Lieutenant General Folet

160

Bradley fretted about two months before he got his chance. Others of more or less note stood around even longer, fuming and raging sometimes, but (to the malicious delight of humbler onlookers) they went on waiting.

I thought nothing more of my letter; it was just a card dropped onto the lap of chance. One day one of the Kremlin interpreters drew me aside at an official dinner and asked me just what questions I proposed to put to Stalin if I saw him. My hopes rose slightly. But I heard nothing more from him; mine must have been the wrong questions. By the time I left, Marshal Djugashvili owed me replies to four other letters. He is a notoriously bad correspondent. One newspaperman in Moscow had been writing to him for eight years and had yet to receive a single acknowledgement.

II

Business of Living

EVERYONE on the streets of Moscow seemed inevitably to be clutching a briefcase under his arm. It was always a black case and when occasionally I appeared carrying a brown one it seemed to arouse intense interest, just as my brown-leather coat, instead of the customary black, also made me a curiosity. At first I assumed that all the briefcases were filled with state documents and they invested their owners with an air of importance and mystery. Then one day I was with a young Russian writer when she opened her briefcase for some purpose and inside I saw that all it contained were slices of black bread and some old copies of *Pravda*. I felt embarrassed and quickly turned my head.

Later I noticed that emaciated old people in the Metro, unable to wait till they reached home, would occasionally open such cases and tear off a piece of bread, chewing it surreptitiously. Presently the sight of those little black cases everywhere was a reminder that (unlike myself) most Muscovites were hungry nearly all the time. And even more depressing were the little black-net bags with which housewives went to market. When they were carrying anything it was usually of such an unsubstantial nature as to arouse pathos; and when they were empty, which was generally the case, you saw why the Russians bitter-humorously called them "perhaps bags."

Russia had lost her best wheatlands, millions of farmers were in the army, and most of the means of distribution of food were mobilized for the primary task of hauling military supplies to the front. Moscow, like many other cities, had to exist largely on products grown in the immediate environs, after it quickly exhausted its reserve stocks of food. Only the most rigorous enforcement of food rationing saved some two million people from actual starvation.

In war as in peace the rationing system was based on the principle "from each according to his ability, to each *according to the work performed*," and its relative importance in the eyes of the ruling party authorities. The army and navy, the N.K.V.D., certain party people, high officials, privileged foreigners, and very essential technicians and professional people got special allowances and could buy at stores not accessible to the general public. The mass of the population fell into four categories. The first group included workers in war industries, who received a slightly higher bread ration, and workers in essential services and utilities, and in general those engaged in manual toil. The second group consisted of professional people, office workers, bureaucrats, white-collar employees, secondary brain-workers in general, and people like watchmen, waiters and clerks. Third came the housewives, people partly or wholly unemployed, usually the aged, dependents and school children. Category four was for children under the age of six, who received a milk ration not available to others and a mid-day hot meal served at the neighborhood school, when their parents were working. Monthly allowances of basic foods were as follows:

Group No.	Bread	Sugar or Candy	Meat	Butter, Oil, or Fat	Cereals	Salt	Fish
I	40 to 53 lbs.	1.10 lbs.	5 lbs.	2 lbs.	4 lbs.	1 lb.	2 lbs.
II	33 "	.66 "	3 "	1 "	3 "	1 "	3 "
III	26 "	.44 "	1 "	$\frac{1}{2}$ "	2 "	1 "	1 "
IV	26 "	.66 "	1 "	1 "	3 "	1 "	1 "

It can be seen that even Group I wasn't getting fat. Probably in no other country were the working man and woman doing their eleven-hour shifts on so little. The allowance of fat, so essential in a Moscow winter, was especially severe. Furthermore, some things like sugar, butter and meat often weren't obtainable at all, even for Groups I and IV, which otherwise usually got full rations. Housewives and dependents came off worst. Until the victory gardens began producing, many of the old and sick died of diseases aggravated by undernourishment or slow starvation. On the whole, however, the system worked without noticeable corruption or favor and if India, China, Persia, or Egypt had enforced rationing half as well, tens of thousands need not have died of starvation.

I found a sample cross-section of Moscow's households in the apartment building where some friends of mine lived. They were a couple who had good jobs and were in Group II. They had fourteen square meters* of space and considered themselves fortunate; the standard allowance was eight meters. Though half the population had left the city, the housing shortage was as acute as ever. Heating and lights were furnished in only a minimum number of dwellings and transportation difficulties ruled out whole sections of the suburbs.

Under the Moscow Soviet there was a Housing Group which assigned dwellings to citizens, according to their work. In every block were housing committees headed by a "Komindant." The Komindant who lived in my friends' apartment was a girl of nineteen and worked full time at the job. She was responsible for the upkeep and repair of several buildings and the conduct of the residents. A woman bookkeeper collected the rents and paid the Moscow Soviets. A third girl was a kind of registrar who had a little biography of each tenant, took custody over their passports, handed out food cards, and kept a record of overnight guests. Thus the police usually knew where every Muscovite was and if anyone didn't have a passport entitling him to live in the city he was quickly found out.

One of the residents was the wife of a naval officer on duty in the Far East. She had two children, a boy of nine and a girl of eleven. She herself worked all day at home, knitting on a piecework basis, and thus got an "essential worker" card. Her little girl, Lucia, knitted after school hours, too, and if she fulfilled her

* 1 meter = 39.37 inches.

norm she also got a worker's card. She did so for several months in a row. The little boy preferred to play and read my friends' books. He said he got enough to eat at school.

Another apartment was occupied by primary school teachers, an elderly couple who had two grown children. They ate relatively well because the girl, eighteen, was a blood donor and the boy, seventeen, a student-worker in an aviation institute. There was a special store for blood donors, where Leila got extra rations of canned milk, butter, sugar, meat and even eggs. She actually gained weight instead of losing it, in spite of her regular contributions of blood. The boy, with his worker's card, also got a free uniform and the State paid him 500 rubles a month. These four people shared thirty meters of space.

There was another resident in this apartment house, which was really a converted private residence, dating back to Tsarist days. She was an old maid named Tanya, who worked in an armament factory eleven hours a day. Tanya got an allowance of half a pound of bread a day and made 600 rubles a month. She spent most of her money on clothes and dressed in what passed for style in Moscow.

All these people used a common kitchen and common bathroom. My friends told me they had lived in a number of other houses in Moscow and that this apartment was no worse, though not much better, than the rest. I did see quarters which were in more advanced disrepair (all houses were deteriorating rapidly) and I also visited friends in three apartment houses which were much better. The latter were about the equivalent of flats occupied by lower middle-class American families; they had "modern" kitchens and private bathrooms. But only people with upper-bracket incomes, usually intellectuals or professional workers, could rate such comparative luxury. Housing in Russia was very backward compared to America, and Russians never denied that. But industrialization had priority over housing until the Third Five-Year Plan, which had provided for an impressive program. Had the war not interfered there would doubtless have been an immense improvement in Soviet dwellings.

My two friends together made about 2,500 rubles a month, the equivalent of U.S. $500 at official exchange rates. But the husband was of draft age, deferred as a special worker, and furthermore they were a childless couple. His income tax, deferment tax and childless-parent tax relieved him of roughly one-third of

Literacy Campaign in a Gujrath Village   Pandit Jawarhalal Nehru

Congress Procession at Ramgarh

Gandhi's Hut at Sevagram

Women Workers at a Factory Meeting

P. C. Joshi, Communist Leader

Abdul Ghaffar Khan,
the "Frontier Gandhi"

A Street Meeting
under the Hammer and Sickle

Hooded Indian Woman at Work

M. A. Jinnah,
President of the Moslem League

Major Fred Eldridge Consults with Negro Soldiers on the China-Burma-India Road

Ruins of Red October Factory Stalingrad

Ambassador Standley and a Group of Russian School Teachers

Field Marshal Frederick von Paulus, Captured at Stalingrad

The Frozen Volga River at Stalingrad

Partisan Leader Litvak

Budanova, Ace Russian Woman Pilot

The Author and Delegates from Outer Mongolia

Mao Tse-tung

Armed Local Defense Unit
in North China

North China Partisan
Tries Captured
Japanese Machine Gun

The Author Interviews Partisan Leaders in a Cave in Yenan

A Gathering of Partisans in North China Addressed by G. Martel Hall

Traveling Propaganda Unit Entertains Chinese Soldiers and Peasants

Women Students
at Yenan

Eddie Rickenbacker, Quentin Reynolds and Edgar Snow at Kuaming

his earnings. Yet these friends as well as most Russians I knew always had more than enough money to pay for everything they could buy on their food and clothing cards. Rent was a negligible item. With the balance of their earnings, several hundred rubles a month, they tried to pick up odds and ends in the market to fill out their diet. Money was useful for little else and most Russians attached no other importance to it. The manufacture of civilian clothing had virtually ceased for the duration, but there were State-owned "commission stores" where second-hand stuff was sold. There was a thriving black market in clothing too. Operations on all black markets were fascinating to watch. The government complacently tolerated the operators, apparently because it knew it could relieve them of their profiteering gains, when the time was ripe for it.

III

Black Markets

I GOT an education in petty trade and barter when I was minor host at a Chinese dinner for some Americans and Russians. It was arranged by Commander Kemp Tolley, assistant American Naval Attaché, and Miss Hu Tsi-pang, the attractive Press Attaché of the Chinese Embassy, and the only Chinese diplomat who lived in Moscow that winter. Until late in 1943 she was the only Chinese the Russians permitted to visit the front. Up to Stalingrad, the Chinese military attachés were, like some Anglo-American observers, convinced that the Red Army was destined to defeat. Little Hu Tsi-pang made a reputation for herself in China by predicting the contrary.

I was assigned to locate some vodka and three pounds of fresh beef. The vodka was easy enough, and I had expected to get the beef from the chef of the Metropole Hotel, where I was staying. At the last minute the usually accommodating Jack, Cockney-born manager and now a naturalized Soviet citizen, told me he was fresh out of beef; it was really impossible to obtain. I could not lose face; beef was the principal ingredient of the *pièce de résistance*, so I appealed to one of the guests, Colonel ("Pop") Hill, of the British Military Mission. "Pop" Hill was a noble character who always came through in an emergency and he magically filled my request from his own larder. Blithely I promised to repay the debt next day.

Most correspondents in Moscow lived at the Metropole and were relatively well fed there. We were allowed small additional rations of luxuries at a local store: chocolate or sugar, eggs, cigarettes and matches, caviar, tinned milk and a few oddments, and a generous ration of four quarts of vodka a month. Naturally we could not buy meat, butter, bread and such items supplied in our daily meals at the hotel.

So I first referred my problem to the director of the Metropole, whom I arranged to see by appointment. He received me in his spacious carpeted office and indicated a heavily upholstered leather chair. He was a busy man and I hesitated to bother him about three pounds of meat, but I explained it was a point of honor to return the same to Pop Hill, whose mess would otherwise lose its ration.

"Impossible!" he exclaimed. "Our kitchen feeds over 2,000 people a day—guests who live here and other comrades who are entitled to use our dining room. If I sold you meat I would be depriving some of them. What's worse, I would be breaking the law."

"Then why not give me my own meat ration in advance, and let me go on a vegetarian diet for as many days as the three pounds cover?"

He wouldn't hear of that. Meat could not be issued in advance.

"I can see that," I said, and with the deep interest of my colleagues at heart I went on, "but why not give the correspondents a meatless day? They all eat too much meat anyway; it's not good for them."

The director conceded that; Russians were generally ready to agree that foreigners ate more than their labor justified. But he said that this suggestion could also end in his being liquidated. He said he could not fall in with any other proposal I made unless it was specifically authorized by his boss, the head of the Intourist Bureau, which operates hotels of the Soviet Union. As I could not see any alternative at the time, I had my secretary write a formal letter and take it to Intourist.

Now, praise God for Intourist! The girls who ran it were the most helpful people we found in Russia and you only had to ask them and they went to work for you. If we had had our way we would have converted Intourist into the Press Department overnight. In our dealings with Intourist, at least, we got the impression that efficiency in a Soviet bureau is perfectly possible. Wherever they had the power they came through with banners flying. Unfortunately they had no influence with the meat department. Within twenty-four hours I got a polite reply from the chief stating my "demand" for beef could not be fulfilled.

It was then that I began to take a really thin view of my future. I went with a certain Natasha to visit the Arbat Market, over near the Metro station. It was a bitter day, but the narrow lanes between the open stalls were filled with a grim crowd. In the stalls were kolkhozniki in from the farms, with the precious products of their little pieces of "personal" land. There were vegetables of all kinds, and eggs, milk and bread. And here are the prices they quoted for them, compared to the controlled market:

Product	Open Market Price	State Store Price
Bread (per lb.)	60 rubles	½ to 1½ rubles
Milk "	40 "	1 "
Carrots "	35 "	1½ "
Onions "	400 "	1½ "
Butter "	400 "	1½ "
Sugar "	500 "	3 "
Flour "	50 "	2 "
Cabbage "	40 "	1½ "
Eggs (each)	20 "	65 kopeks

By diplomatic agreement, Americans got twelve rubles to the dollar instead of five, but even so such prices were prohibitive. For a Russian worker, buying outside his own store, it would take nearly a month's wages to buy a pound of butter.

A standing joke in the Moscow Circus was of a gag man who, meeting a farmer carrying one huge basket and one very small basket, asked what each one was for. "The little one," said the farmer, "is for my vegetables. The large basket is for my money." Toward the end of 1943 urban resentment against exploitation by the kolkhozniki mounted rapidly and the big drift of money

167

toward the collectives also aggravated the inflation problem. The Party decided the time had come to "de-capitalize" these newly rich farmers. Instead of expropriation or taxation it put the whole thing on a patriotic basis, appealing for contributions to buy airplanes and tanks. Fortunes in the tens of thousands and even hundreds of thousands of rubles were thus revealed. Rich collectives and even individual peasants either voluntarily, or under "social pressure" too strong to be safely ignored, came forth to buy one or two airplanes or tanks for the State. Even the priests and mullahs bought thousands of rubles worth of bonds or tanks. In reward the weapons were named after them. So much for the results of hoarding and profiteering under this system!

But kolkhozniki who came into the Moscow markets were already shrewdly preferring goods to money. Most customers brought with them pieces of wearing apparel, clocks, watches, rings, leather goods and articles of personal use. The peasants had become very choosey and could only be interested in something good. In the lanes stood people who had articles no farmers wanted, which they offered for cash or trade to other Muscovites. Few young or able-bodied people were among the customers. Some of them were unashamed in their urgent hunger and when they managed to buy bread or milk they consumed it standing on the spot.

The whole market was carefully patrolled by policemen. They never interfered, except to disperse the crowds when the lanes grew too congested.

But the expedition brought no solution to my problem. There was no meat on this market though it was rumored a little had been sold earlier in the day for 400 rubles a pound. At that rate it would have cost me $100 to pay off my debt.

The memory of the suffering in some of the faces I had seen around the stalls stayed with me for a long time. We could not invite guests to the Metropole dining room, but after that I ate in my own room as often as possible, with a Russian—any Russian I could lure into the hotel.

Across the street we entered a little park and sat down for a few moments to watch some children playing in the snow. They were robust, healthy and happy-looking, as all Russian children were; here, at least, the bony fingers of war were not allowed to reach. A charming red-headed boy, about five years old, supervised the making of pies and pastry out of the wet snow. He had

168

"mobilized" three little girls, who were busy bringing him "materials" for his "ovens." Turning to us he asked for our order, recommending the sweet buns as the *pièce du jour*. But Natasha told him we wanted a *parouzhni* with cream stuffing and chocolate icing.

"How much are they?" she asked.

"Fifty rubles each," responded the little baker, not batting an eye.

"It's an outrage," declared Natasha, "you are a bandit!"

"It's the regular market price, lady," he came back. "Everything has gone up since the war."

We decided to be extravagant and ordered a dozen. They were the best imaginary cakes I ever ate.

After a fruitless visit to two other markets that week I finally thought of confiding my problem to a Chinese boy I knew, who had been in Moscow some years. It was a way out which should have occurred to me at once. "Get me a liter of vodka," he said, "and I think I can solve your problem." I asked no questions but got the last of my month's allowance from our store and turned it over to him. In a couple of days he returned with the goods.

I had learned the key to the black markets. Vodka would buy virtually anything. But I took care not to borrow any more meat.

IV

Marriage in Moscow

IT HAS become a fashion in the West to say the Russians are 100% realists, with absolutely no sentiment in them. "Nothing moves them but the facts." Of course it is nonsense, the Russians are almost as sentimental as the British—about themselves and their own institutions. Even in war they found time to expend a little sentiment on marriage. Take the case of Ronald Matthews.

Ronnie and his excited bride, Tanya, who came from Grozny, invited me to witness their ceremony, along with Alec Werth and

Marjorie Shaw, the *Daily Mirror* (London) correspondent; and with us also went a Russian lady whom I shall call Anna. She had spent her childhood in Moscow and loved every tower of the Kremlin, but Anna had a sense of humor about it, too; and a subtle ironic laughter of her own.

Marriage in the Soviet Union has gone through almost a complete cycle and now it is nearly restored as the sacred ceremony on which the once more glorified family is founded. As everyone knows by now, the Soviet fathers, having discovered that many old Russian traditions could be adapted to socialist aims, with beneficial effects in stabilizing the regime and invoking social and patriotic fervor, began to refurbish many accepted symbols and institutions of the past, which were formerly considered "bourgeois" or "counter-revolutionary."

For a time divorce in the U.S.S.R. was obtainable merely by mailing a postcard to notify the spouse that the match was at an end, and by "writing out" the contract at a marriage bureau. Abortion was legalized and free; birth control was encouraged. Women were to be as independent as men and not mere childbearing machines. For complex reasons—and the fear of war was not least among them—all this began to change. By 1936 the State had adopted new laws making abortion illegal, except for reasons of health, and rendering divorce a more elusive matter. In the old days, Maurice Hindus said, "it was easier to obtain a divorce than to buy a new pair of shoes." As a matter of fact that was at the moment probably still true; it was an extremely difficult matter to buy any shoes during the war.

Nowadays the Russian theoretically can still get a divorce by mailing a card; but the spouse has to be heard from first, and if he or she raises objections more than likely the action won't be admitted. Communists used to be foremost among the wifechangers and husband-changers; in some cases it was seasonal. Today it practically ruins a Party member's career to seek a divorce. If children are involved, the party makes it virtually impossible for a Communist to secure a divorce except on grounds of flagrant infidelity.

"So you see you are now about to be chained for life," remarked Anna, as we discussed the prospects for the not-so-young Matthews. But he was too far gone; nothing could now save him from throwing freedom to the winds.

We squeezed into a street car and gradually were processed

170

toward the front. I fancied our fellow passengers resented our exhilaration. It was a biting day and people wore looks which seemed to say, "Don't aggravate us with anything pleasant before next spring." They glanced at the good stuff of our clothes and sniffed suspiciously. Even Tanya was impressive in a borrowed fur coat; clearly we were foreigners. In his British correspondent's uniform Matthews was a dead giveaway.

"Second front, second front," came from the corners of several closed mouths. "Is it cultured, *Gospadin* Englishman, to knock a lady's hat off her head? Why not attack Fritz instead?" This when the huge Matthews unavoidably dislodged an old lady's bonnet.

But the bride and groom were oblivious. Innuendoes rolled from them like marbles off Mussolini's bald head. In the marriage bureau itself we found a bespectacled woman in a heavy overcoat under a sign, "Births, marriages and deaths registered." She scowled at us but brightened when she heard it was a marriage.

"That's good, comrades, we get too few nowadays; there are no men left it seems. A birth would be better, of course." Examining Matthews' passport she pronounced his name as it had been transliterated by some hasty Soviet inspector.

"Matzoos Ronnal," she said aloud, as she wrote in her book.

"But that's a mistake, Matthews is the last name," exclaimed Tanya.

Looking over her glasses the old lady shook her head decisively. "I'm sorry, comrade, we can register here your birth, marriage or death, but we cannot change your husband's name. Matzoos Ronnal it is in the passport and it's only as Mrs. Ronnal that you can be married here."

Poor Tanya! Argument availed nothing. What's in a name? Mrs. Ronnal she became. As we left, the old woman gave us a sweet smile in compensation and declared:

"Marrying an Englishman! We approve; it's a good thing, too. Maybe your son will grow up in time to open the second front!"

And so we left for Moscow's only cocktail bar to drink the health of the newlyweds. I felt awkward on such an errand on this gloomy day, but it was different when outside the bar itself we found a long queue of thirsty Russians. Inside there was a crowd of men and women in uniform and some Russian intellectuals

171

dressed in dark unpressed clothes. They looked at us as only a Russian crowd could look, half curiosity and half hostility.

We ordered Tailrammers—named for the Russian daredevils who specialize in cutting the tails off Nazi planes, when they are out of ammunition, by diving straight at them. And the drink, made of camouflaged vodka, does hit you right about there.

Suddenly Anna cried out above the subdued voices, "*Gorko! Gorko!*" and raised her Tailrammer in a toast. Near us the shut Slavic faces opened like winter flowers. A buzz went round and the room filled with grins.

"Anna, what magic is that?"

"*Gorko, gorko*—it just means 'bitter, bitter,' and we Russians always say it to a new bride and groom. But don't ask me why."

I found out later; it isn't what a cynic might think, a word of commiseration to the poor soul about to acquire a ball and chain. When Russians complain at a wedding that it is "bitter, bitter," the bridegroom is expected to kiss the bride and sweeten the atmosphere. Everybody is content for a while, until the bitterness again becomes unbearable and the bridegroom has to repeat the same business.

Anyway the word proved an open sesame at the cocktail bar. Our neighbors leaned over to shower good wishes and invited us to drink.

Anna and I left the place before the Matzoos Ronnals. The manageress bowed us out with a smile as wide as Red Square. "Congratulations, comrades, you make a lovely couple. All happiness to you!" *Gorko! Gorko!* trailed after us as we faced the angry wind.

We did not trouble to contradict the manageress and explain her mistake. After all, in this hour when every Russian believed that by Russian blood alone the world was being saved, a bolshevik was actually feeling sentimental about a pair of foreigners. The picture was too good to spoil. But I wish I had known then what a bridegroom was expected to do about *gorko*. Anna was a very attractive female.

I

Three Girls from Smolensk

I TALKED to a lot of partisans in Moscow and to some at the front, and they all had absorbing tales to tell, such as you may have already read in books by Maurice Hindus and Walter Graebner and Quentin Reynolds. But the case of the three girls from Smolensk had a special meaning for me. I met them after they had made their way back through the forests and swamps, and across the swollen rivers of the raw early spring, from far behind the German lines to the Red Army and Free Russia again. They were Panya, aged twenty-one, Liza, twenty-five, and Kenya, twenty-three.

Panya was a robust Russian country girl with wide, frank, greenish eyes, very red cheeks, a ready grin and a head of taffy-colored hair. She was wearing a black cotton coat and skirt—her uniform, she said. She had been in high school when the Germans had taken Smolensk; and like thousands of others she had fled to the forests. There she had met Liza, a weaver from a Smolensk factory, and Kenya, another school girl. Liza seemed rather shy at first; but she had unusually fine blue eyes, and when she turned them on you you felt instinctively that here was an absolutely straight and fearless personality, passionate in her faith. She was obviously the leader of the trio and I was not surprised to learn she was a Komsomol.

"How did you get started?" I asked.

"We met others in the forest," Liza explained, "and we held a meeting and decided to fight. There were about fifty of us at first, thirty girls and the rest young boys and old men. We raided a village where there were 170 Germans and we took them by surprise. It was a big success. We got lots of tommyguns and rifles

173

and we got a field kitchen on wheels which we later used to mount a gun! It worked, too."

"But who taught you how to fight? Were there military men with you?"

"Only a few old men. They taught us something. We also learned a lot from a book called *Red Star Over China* that we brought from Smolensk. We got many ideas from it. Nearly every Komsomol in our group has read it by now."

If Liza had not just come in out of the forests and if I had not met these three by chance, I would have thought the thing had been rehearsed. If so, it was the only time I was flattered by that much attention in Russia.

"It's a good book," I said. "I wrote it myself."

From that point on it turned into a counter-interview on China and they wanted to know all about the "Komsomols" whom they supposed existed there. I had to bring them up to date before we could get back onto the guerrillas of the Ukraine.

I can mention this because the chapters in that book on guerrilla warfare were none of my doing, but the statements of Peng Teh-huai, Mao Tse-tung and other Chinese leaders. I merely printed verbatim what they said and the credit was entirely theirs. Still, it gave me a good feeling to know the written word could travel that far and still have meaning and find people ready to act upon it.

"More and more peasants came to join us," Liza continued, "until the forests soon became full of them, especially young girls. They found out it's impossible to live under the Germans. Sooner or later a woman is bound to be carried off to a brothel in Smolensk, or be sent back to Germany to be sold into slavery." This was no exaggeration: German papers seized by the Russians carried reports of Russian women and children sold as chattel. "Women keep coming to join us every day now; everyone believes Smolensk will be liberated soon and they know the Germans will drive the rest of our women to the West with them."

The villages themselves were disappearing one by one, and old people were left freezing on the streets, with a, "Go where you like; it's no business of ours to find a roof for your head," from the Germans. For thirty miles all around Smolensk four-fifths of the settlements were already in ashes.

"The people live in dugouts," said Panya. "They are starving by hundreds and it's a terrible thing to see the children. People

174

make their bread out of sawdust. When the Germans come to the villages and see this bread they pick it up and hold their sides with laughter. 'Look what the Russians call bread,' they shout to each other. They have eaten up everything in the country—chickens, pigs, cattle and grain. Last year little of the land around Smolensk was sown and this year it will be fallow again. There's only one way to live now, the hunter's life in the forest."

"Is there enough game, then?"

They all grinned. "Fritz is the game, comrade, and there's plenty of him!"

"You sound pretty dangerous, Panya. Have you ever actually killed a man?"

"Not a man, exactly. I've killed some Nazis."

"How do you know you killed them?"

"I shot them and saw them fall. Later I saw their dead bodies."

"And how did you feel afterward?"

"I felt good because I am a girl. I knew that they had ruined our towns and beautiful buildings where our youth was enjoying a happy life. I was proud that I, a mere girl, could bring vengeance on them."

Suddenly I saw behind Panya the long shadow of a whole generation of Russian youth, say sixty to eighty million boys and girls, going through experiences the traces of which will not entirely disappear as long as any of us still live. It is an experience that people lucky enough not to be invaded will never quite understand or fully share. No one getting his impressions of this war from photographs, newsreels or words like mine can believe the filth and savagery of it.

Literally tens of millions of young Russians, from infants upward, have seen their parents or brothers and sisters or relatives or neighbors lynched or murdered or mutilated, or have seen them starve or freeze to death, or nearly to death, or have seen their homes go up in smoke while they were carrying off all the little possessions of intimate significance, or they have themselves gone through such experiences. It is never quite credible until it happens to you. The death of your beloved on some distant battlefield or sea is a cruel thing, but it is far from the same thing as watching it happen in your own back yard.

Panya, Liza and Kenya told me, in a matter-of-fact way, of crimes committed by the Nazis in their neighborhood, of murders and hangings, rape as a daily occurrence, torture and all the rest of it. Many of the victims were their own friends. How could they tolerate the sight of a German again? Yet, when I was about to leave, Liza said something about the Germans and Czechs fighting in their detachment.

"I shouldn't think their lives would be worth a kopek with you," I said frankly.

"Why not?" asked Liza. "We are fighting only Hitlerites, and we don't want to exterminate the good Germans. Our best machine gunner is a German and we like and trust him. He is a fine man."

It was good to have allies like Panya and Liza and Kenya, people who could still talk about "good Germans," after what had happened around them. These Russian youths are worth our knowing far better, they are worth going the whole way to understand.

II

Rzhev

TWO or three days after its recapture by the Red Army I went to Rzhev and from a distance it appeared to be still largely intact. But as I drew into the city I saw that it was a stage-set thing, all façade and no insides to it. The walls stood in many places but everything else was burned out or wrecked by shells or dynamite. It was a ruin, except for a few small houses and in one of those freshly fumigated and deloused I spent the night. Coming out onto the street after dinner I heard a concertina spiritedly playing *Moskva*.

It was such lively music to be heard in these somber streets of the dead that I turned and felt my way into the house next door, where it was coming from. Inside, I found that the artist was a freckle-faced, tow-headed boy of thirteen, named Victor Volaskov, whom I keep thinking of as an American lad, I suppose because he reminded me so much of my nephew, Johnny Snow. His mother was there, and his grandfather, Alexander Volaskov, who was a veteran of the Russo-Japanese War. There was also a little orphan girl named Ilena Markova. These four were among the 200 people left in Rzhev, out of an original population of 65,000.

It is of Ilena I want to tell you, because she seemed to me the personification of all the pointless misery and tragedy that the war was inflicting on millions of bystanders. Caught behind the German lines, and unlike Panya and Liza, not able to get into the war, they were also quite unable to get out of it either.

Ilena wore a soiled gingham dress and a faded red sweater above much-mended black stockings and broken shoes. They were her only clothes. She had a well-made head, but it was too large now for her half-starved little body. She had fine black eyes, underlined with deep half-moons; her whole face, drawn by sharp lines of grief and suffering, might have belonged to a woman of forty who has learned everything sorrow can teach. At the age of thirteen Ilena had lost everything she had treasured and nearly everyone she had cherished.

The Germans occupied Rzhev in October, 1941, and were there until March, 1943. Before they came, Ilena said, she was in the fourth grade of a school that was now destroyed. She had been an enthusiastic Pioneer in a unit of which she and Victor were the sole survivors. It was Victor who, seeing her wandering on the streets after the Germans left, had brought her to the Volaskovs' shell-shaken house.

Smoothing out her little soiled gingham dress, smoothing it out again and again, she looked at me with those great solemn eyes and talked in long breathless sentences, with long pauses in between. Her father and mother had had good jobs and had made good money, quite enough to pay for their comfortable little house and look after Ilena's grandmother, who had lived with them. "Then a bomb fell on our house," she said. "It was badly smashed, but I wasn't hurt because I was in the basement with Mama. Then the Germans came to Rzhev and they took our house and they could live in one part of it after they fixed it up and they put us in one room and then we had to work for them and we cleaned the house and washed clothes and shined their boots."

"I suppose they fed you?"

"No, they didn't give us anything, but we made soup from potato peelings and things they left in their dishes."

"How did they treat you?"

177

"Treat us? They couldn't speak Russian so they only shouted at us and we had to guess what they wanted."

"But wasn't even one German ever kind to you? Think, didn't they give you some candy or something good to eat at least once?"

Ilena deliberated for a long moment and then she looked back at me and slowly shook her head. "The big officer who lived with us ate bonbons out of a foreign box every day and once I asked him for a sweet when I brought him his boots and he pushed me out the door. The next time I asked him he hit me on the head."

Ilena's grandmother became ill with typhus. There were no hospitals open in town. She died in a few days and the Germans ordered her father and mother to bury her at once. Although they both were already ill, they were obliged to carry the body to the graveyard in the middle of a winter night. Ilena went along. When they returned her father went to bed with a high fever. In the morning he was dead. Again that dreadful trip with her mother and this time her aunt helped carry the body to the cold, frightening cemetery.

The Germans drove them from the house now, and they set off for a near-by village to live with her mother's sister. Soon afterward both mother and child were struck with typhus and went to a little village clinic which had not yet been closed.

"I was in the clinic eight days," Ilena said, in her sad sweet voice. "We had nothing to eat but a hundred grams* of bread daily, bread and water were all I had. As soon as I was well enough to stand Mama told me to leave but when I got out I found my aunt's family had been sent to Germany. And there was no place for me so I went back to town to stay with mother's brother. He had seven children and they were all sleeping in one room because their house was full of Germans, but they took me in and made a place for me."

"And your mother?"

"About a week later I was walking on the street when I met a woman from the village and asked her about Mama and she said, 'Your mama is dead.'" For the first time in the recital of her tragedy, Ilena's eyes filled with tears.

I put my arm around her tiny waist and felt choked myself and we both looked across the dark little room in which we sat. All the windows had been broken and the frames boarded over,

* About ¼ lb.

with the exception of a single pane of glass. Through it filtered a feeble gray light, the pale sun of Russian spring. On the window ledge was an open book of Gogol, in an old edition bound in faded tan leather. I thought the old man must have been reading, but I learned it was Victor; grandfather said he didn't know the letters. In a corner hung a large icon of the Virgin and Child, brightly polished. The mother and the old man were religious persons, although both children professed atheism. A few rickety chairs stood about the rough board tables. Otherwise the room was bare. The rest of the house was occupied by Red soldiers. They drifted in now and then, but quickly drifted out again when they heard the conversation. It was an old story to them, heard from many Ilenas and in many places.

"How did you live at your uncle's place then, Ilena? Did the Germans feed you?"

"I worked on the road after I came back to the city. I carried stones and bricks."

"Did the Germans pay you?"

"They gave us half a tin of flour and water once a week, about a pound."

"Was it enough?"

"I also ate scraps from the table and I always had a stomach-ache."

After the Russian offensive began and the Red Army neared Rzhev, the Germans drove away nearly all the civilians who had survived the winter. Ilena's uncle was taken west with the rest, but she hid and somehow managed to live on until the city was retaken. Two days before they left the Germans rounded up the remaining Russians and herded them into the only church still intact in Rzhev. This time Ilena obeyed. Those who argued or tried to escape were killed.

So Ilena said, and I believed her because of what I had seen that morning. Down one muddy street stood a few houses relatively undamaged, and with a Russian officer I went to have a look at them. In one we came upon a grisly tableau where a whole family had been wiped out. The house itself was untouched by bombs or shells, but chests and cabinets had been torn open and their contents strewn upon the floor, pictures slashed and furniture broken and overturned.

First there was the mother, a frozen corpse which blocked the narrow hallway. Her head was flattened on the side, probably by

179

a rifle butt. Farther on, lying half-naked on a wicker couch in the living room, lay the body of a fine-featured boy with very fair hair and wide blue eyes. He was emaciated from illness, and his arm, bent as if warding off a blow, was hardly thicker than its bone. In his chest and head you could count seven neat bullet holes drilled in at close range. Behind him in a little alcove were the bodies of two younger children almost embracing each other. They, too, had been murdered in the same way, while in another room lay the body of a second woman, also shot by the supermen.

Right across the street was another scene quite like it, where an old woman had been killed in her bedroom and the house looted. In another street, the Russians told me, were the corpses of a family named Sadov; the father and mother had been shot, the daughter stabbed, the son shot through the right eye. Another daughter of eighteen was violated and then strangled. Near by a baby girl, five months old, had been shot in the head.

Ilena told of seeing an old woman near her house shot down by a Nazi because she was ill and begged not to be forced to go to the church—possibly the reason the Nazis had wiped out other families too. It was testified in many other cases that the Germans had locked up civilians in towns about to be abandoned, mined the houses with delayed-action explosives and thus sent them to death. Red Army men told me that they had removed mines from under the church in which Ilena was put by the Nazis, with 150 others. She said she was there two days and three nights, while bombs and shells burst all around. There was a sudden hush one morning and at dawn she looked into the street and there was the first Russian soldier she had seen for more than a year. She rushed out, embraced him, and then ran as fast as her legs could go to her own house. While it had been occupied by the Germans it had miraculously escaped harm when everything around was destroyed.

"And how was it, Ilena?"

"Nothing was there," she said with her queer little smile and her eyes wide with surprise. "Nothing at all, not even the samovar; the Germans set fire to it all before they went home." Such was the tale of Ilena, or a pale reflection of it.

As for Victor and his family, they would still be prisoners of the Germans but for the wit of his mother. She had stood leaning on a chair, her face heavy and impassive, listening to Ilena's story. Now she began to speak herself. She was, at thirty-six, prematurely an old woman. Like Ilena, she had lived a couple of decades in a year. She herself wore a cheap red-cotton print dress and a tattered green sweater, but I noticed that she had somehow kept Victor warmly clad in a fur-collared mackinaw and a pair of felt *valenki*.

Her husband was in the Red Army and her brother also, she said. A second brother of seventeen had been carried off to Germany. She had not heard anything from either one for more than a year. She had been working in the post office when the Germans came and did not leave soon enough and, like most of the population, was caught in the city. The Germans put her family into one room and made her clean and sweep for them. They gave her no food, but she ate potato peelings and sometimes made trips to the village where she bartered belongings for food. Each time she came back to Rzhev, the Germans took most of the produce for themselves before letting her into the city.

"What about people with nothing to trade?"

"They starved or went to Germany to work."

She continued: "A few weeks before the Red Army came back, the Germans began driving everybody in Rzhev along the road to Smolensk. There was wet snow and our *valenki* got soaked through. Most of the people were sick or half-starved and there were thousands of women and old men and children among them. Many dropped dead along the road. My boy and my father were both very ill and Papa had a high fever. We begged the Germans to let us stay behind but they kept driving us ahead. At last we managed to fall out of the column and hid in some shrubbery not far from the village of Korobeynich. Every time Germans came near us we cried at them 'typhus' and they turned and ran. For about ten days we hid that way and then the Red Army came to Korobeynich. When we saw the first Russian soldier we wept and got down on our knees and hugged him."

III

Murder, Inc.

W HILE Admiral Standley and I were visiting some orphans, we asked a few of the children what had happened to their parents. In several cases they had seen them shot or hung or bayoneted before their eyes. One of them broke into tears when she started speaking of it, and, realizing this was a form of torture, I dropped the subject. One day I mentioned this to Olga Mishakova, saying that there must be hundreds of thousands of Russian children who would carry such memories to their graves and that it was bound to influence Russian thinking about Europe for years to come.

Mishakova agreed and she told me that she herself had adopted three orphans whose parents were killed in the war. She told me how the eldest, a lad of six, had seen the Germans slowly beat them to death, as a man might leisurely beat out the life of a helpless rat with a stick.

She paused and looked at me sardonically and said: "But you won't write about such things; your editor wouldn't print them, I know! Americans don't want to face such facts about the enemy. Why is it? Yet you have a big appetite for stories and movies glorifying fictitious gangsters and murderers, isn't it so?"

Mishakova had not been to the United States, so I suppose she must have heard this from Russian monitors of our press and cinema, or perhaps from Ludmilla Pavlichenko, the girl sniper who toured this country. Her mother told me she had remarked on the squeamishness of Americans. Anyway, Mishakova was partly right. Few of us sent home news of that kind, even after hearing accounts directly from eyewitnesses. I have seen some shut their notebooks when interviews turned in that direction. My own experience in the Far East taught me how hard it was to get such facts generally accepted. In a book of mine I reported some atrocities, when I had either seen the evidence myself or got the story from eyewitnesses in whose integrity I had confidence, but these items (concerning the Japanese) were often questioned by fastidious reviewers. They considered them "not in good taste," or exaggerated anyway. Later I met people who asked me incredulously, "Now tell me, did that incident really happen?"

I remember lying in bed one night in a billet in Scotland, in the same room with an R.A.F. flyer and a young American bomber pilot who had just come in from Sicily. "We had some captured German pilots near us," the American was saying from his bed in the dark room, "and we went over to talk to them through an interpreter. What surprised us was what nice fellows they were. I think we've been fed an awful lot of bunk about the crimes of the Germans in Russia. Why, they're just like us; they believe in this Nazi ideal of theirs and they have to fight for it, but they are just as civilized as we are."

I felt like yelling at him about some of the places I had seen in China and Russia. But what was the use, I thought; he would think I was a liar. At the same time I marveled again at the professional *esprit de corps* of our Air Force, which made it a fighting organization of splendid morale despite the political vacuum in which a lot of its heroes apparently lived.

Was it just a reluctance, as in the case of this boy, to believe ill of other human beings like ourselves, or a national hangover from the debunking of Allied propaganda in the last war, or because such things hadn't happened on American soil, that made it so hard for us to accept the facts about Hitlerism? Probably it was the last, because belatedly we seem ready enough to believe in the sadistic nature of Japanese fascism, now that it is Americans being tortured or beheaded. I have known Germans who were fine human beings and I have known Japanese who were ditto; I don't believe either race is physiologically or congenitally any more paranoiac than I am. But that is no reason for not studying their behavior under the leadership which launched this war. Not to do it is to shirk our duty to analyze and correct the causes of it. And between the Nazis and Japs, in their worst moments, there was not much to choose, as far as I could see.

Personally, I was born in Missouri and a native skepticism was further trained by years of running down reports in the Orient, where rumors often drive out facts. But in Russia I heard of so many crimes from the lips of survivors, coming all the way from Leningrad to the Caucasus, and myself saw so much evidence of terror, that it ceased to occur to me to doubt the main charges pub-

183

lished by the so-called Soviet "Atrocities Committee" for "investigating and recording" enemy acts violating human decency. It was enough simply to remember some of the things I had seen, without trying to compete with that busy committee, which kept an account book of human depravity with a thoroughness never before attempted in history.

I thought of the kindly peasant woman, for example, who told me how the Germans came to live in her house, and first took her cow, then her poultry and pigs, and then the boots from her feet. After five months the Red Army returned and her guests prepared to leave. As a parting gesture they threw some hand grenades into the house and set it afire, because they said it was the home of a Red soldier, her husband. When her sister ran out of the burning house with the children, her baby was tommy-gunned in her arms.

There was Vera Galkinova, a young schoolteacher who worked in a village near Mozhaisk. She told me how the Germans, suspecting her of sheltering guerrillas, had tortured her to extract a confession from her. Among other things they applied a hot iron to her cheek, where there was an ugly scar. They locked her in a barn without light or air, packed tight with other wretched souls.

"One day they threw us some rotten horse meat," she said. "That was all we had to eat for many days. There wasn't enough room to sit down in the barn and we even slept standing up. One man died near me, but there was nothing we could do about it. He just kept standing there, held up by others around him."

Vera was repeatedly beaten to unconsciousness. At last her sister was permitted to take her home. When she woke up six days later her sister told her that as she had undressed her most of her skin had peeled off with her garments. "When the Red Army came I was still sick," she ended. "I hadn't eaten anything but rotten potatoes for weeks, but still I got down on hands and knees and crawled to the street to hug our men."

There in a few words is a story it took many painful minutes to extract. Questioning like this is an ordeal for the interrogator as well as the victim. Yet I suppose it doesn't mean much to anybody sitting in a comfortable office or home under free, sunny skies. All I know is that I won't forget Vera's face and the look of terror which came into her eyes when weeks afterward she had to think about it again. But cases like Vera's had happened to people known to nearly everybody you passed in a Russian street.

Even when you speak only of what you have seen yourself you

know how little of it you convey. Who could write more than a fragment of the catastrophe of just the ruined cities, not to mention the countless obliterated villages? Each was in itself a cataclysm too large for any one mind to encompass. In beautiful Kiev, for example, the Nazis carried out horrible massacres and pogroms. Premier Molotov backed up with formidable documentation his awful charge that they had "murdered 52,000 men, women, old people and children."

No one can study Nazism in action, from the organized looting and pillage to the enslavement of millions of abducted civilians, and the destruction of museums, hospitals, schools and churches, without concluding that it was the fulfillment of a deliberate policy Hitler was determined to realize even if all else failed. "If our hearts are set on establishing our great German Reich, we must above all things force out and exterminate the Slavonic nations," said the Fuehrer in one of his rare bursts of candor after invading Russia. "Twenty million people must be wiped out. From now on, this will be one of the principal aims of German policy."

But if twenty million corpses was the price this madman expected Russia to pay for his own victory, what would he exact as the hour of Germany's defeat and his personal catastrophe drew near? He could not kill that many Red Army men, but it was within his power to kill or starve to death millions of civilians. As the Red Army drove them back to face disgrace in Europe the Nazis would make of every city and village they left behind a desert as bleak as man ever created over so large a section of this earth. People spoke of bacterial warfare or gas as if, as long as they were not used, the war was being conducted with relative humaneness. But this campaign of annihilation already constituted an ultimate terror.

It is a difficult thing for one people to understand the sufferings which explain the moods of another. It is impossible for us to understand Russia unless we force ourselves to think what all this would mean in terms of our own daily lives. We ought to think about war not as just a map crossed by long battle lines made up of rows of colored pins but as an apocalypse tearing asunder the fabric of life for millions of little people, and leaving them still with fear of death and always with the memory of death around them.

This requires a positive act of imagination on the part of Americans in particular. You hear our men returned from abroad criticizing the home folks for "not taking the war seriously," and

185

what they mean is that Americans do not act as if they were aware of the catastrophe that has struck Europe and Asia, in which they are involved. This criticism is probably unfair, in a sense. We cannot expect people to act something they don't feel, and no one can feel war except by being in it. It is natural that for home-staying Americans the war should seem faraway and unreal and impersonal. It is also "natural" that our own troops should continue to be the least educated, politically, of all the forces in the war. Our own soil has not been devastated, our people have not seen war as a neighbor for two generations as the Russians have, nor have we had to defend our political system in our own gardens against a horde of homicidal fanatics. Such experiences are the conditioning which creates a high degree of "political conscious-ness" in an army and a people. But we are not exempt from the effort to put ourselves in other people's shoes; to remember their experiences and make allowances; to remember especially that for nearly every Russian the word "atrocity" now connotes one or more personal tragedies which have directly altered his life.

Wars between the Slavs and the Germans, and wars in the past between the Russians and Poles and Finns, have often been, it is true, wars of no quarter between troops. I have no doubt that there was good reason for the Germans' fear of capture in the early months and I imagine few of them met mercy at the hands of Russians at the front. But ruthlessness as between armies is one thing and the wholesale destruction of civilian life is quite another. There is no evidence in recent wars of a high command adopting extermination of the civilian population as a general policy, until Hitler.

"We must resort to all means," said Hitler in *Mein Kampf*, "to bring about the conquest of the world by the Germans. If our hearts are set upon establishing our Great German Reich we must above all things force out and exterminate the Slavonic nations—the Russians, Poles, Czechs, Slovaks, Bulgarians, Ukrainians, Byelo-russians. There is no reason why this should not be done." And elsewhere Hitler gives this blessing to mass murder: "Man is a born sinner; he can be ruled only by force. In dealing with him all means are permissible. When policy requires it we should lie, be-tray and even kill." By all means kill, echoes the monstrous Goer-ing. "Kill everyone opposed to us. Kill, kill! Not you will answer for this, but I! Hence, kill!"

On the body of a German soldier, Lt. Gustav Ziegel, a native of Frankfort-on-Main, was found a copy of a speech delivered by Ziegel's Nazi commander. "You have no heart or nerves," it declared. "They are not needed in war. Eradicate every trace of pity and sympathy from your heart—kill every Russian, every Soviet person. Do not hesitate, whether you have an old man or a woman, a girl or a boy before you; kill! Thereby you will save your life, ensure the future of your family, and win eternal glory."

I have no doubt that the Russians will administer stern justice to the Nazi criminals and degenerates and their willing accessories, but I do not believe that they will ever visit upon the whole German people the same bestiality that was practiced by the Germans in Russia, simply because they are convinced that in the long run it does not pay as a military and political policy. Unlike a few noisy "total exterminators" among the Anglo-American populations (which suffered nothing faintly comparable to the crucifixion of Russia under Nazi invasion) the Soviet leaders kept their heads and, despite all their hatred of Nazism, they recognized that it could not be defeated by the same methods, taken out of Nazi ideology. Stalin early drew a distinction between Nazi war criminals and "the German people which is enslaved by Hitlerite misrulers." Russian strength, he pointed out, must be drawn from the consciousness of every Red Army man that he could "proudly say that he is waging a just war for liberation," inspired by "a noble and lofty aim." And after two years of war Stalin was still able to declare to wide applause:

> Sometimes the foreign press publishes twaddle to the effect that the Red Army's aim is to exterminate the German people and to destroy the German State. This is, of course, a silly fable and stupid calumny against the Red Army. The Red Army's aim is to drive the German invaders from our country and to clear Soviet soil of the German-Fascist aggressors. It is highly probable that the war for the liberation of Soviet soil will lead to the expulsion or destruction of Hitler's clique. We should welcome such an outcome. But it would be ludicrous to identify Hitler's clique with the German people, with the German State. The experience of history shows that Hitlers come and go, but the German people and the German State live on.
>
> The strength of the Red Army lies, finally, in the fact that it does not and cannot feel racial hatred for other peoples, including the German people; that it has been trained to recognize the equality of all peoples and races, and to respect the rights of other peoples. The German's racial theory and practice of racial hatred

187

have led all freedom-loving peoples to become enemies of Fascist Germany. The U.S.S.R.'s theory of racial equality and its practice of respecting the rights of other peoples have led all freedom-loving peoples to become friends of the Soviet Union.

Sometimes the foreign press publishes twaddle to the effect that the Soviet people hate the Germans as Germans, that the Red Army exterminates German soldiers as Germans out of hatred for everything German. . . . This is, of course, another silly fable and stupid calumny against the Red Army. It is free of such degrading sentiments because it has been trained in the spirit of racial equality and respect for the rights of other people. Nor should it be forgotten that in our country any manifestation of racial hatred is punishable by law.

This dignified pronouncement throws into most vivid relief the fundamental contrast between the two armies, and two systems, highlights the strength and weakness of each, and shows how even in their darkest hours the Russians never lost confidence in the superiority of their faith, nor in the conviction that in time they could reach behind the steel wall of Nazi ideology and beyond its concentration camps, and find in the German people allies whose courage and humanity Hitler had never succeeded in altogether crushing.

I did not find among the Russian people any phony psychologists trying to prove that German children are biological "Paranoids." The Russians could remember when under the Tsars they had had their own "Black Hundreds" preaching Hitlerite doctrines, and launching pogroms, too; and they knew why they now had them no more. I did not find any hysterics, even among the bereaved, demanding a life for a life. I remember being impressed at the reception a Russian crowd gave a column of German prisoners as they came in from Stalingrad. They marched down the snow-covered streets on trek to the rear, a forlorn lot, fantastically dressed in women's hats, shawls, skirts and other loot used to supplement inadequate uniforms in which they shivered at thirty below. Many of the Russian onlookers must have wondered what had happened to the women from whom the clothes had been stolen. You might think they would have tried to tear the garments from their backs and I am not sure Americans would not, under similar provocation, have done so. But the Russians did not even jeer or call names or spit at them.

And in the end all Hitler's terror, all his arson and murder, were of no avail and without military significance. It did not stop his machine from going into a total reverse, which we, who were in Russia in 1943, could already see was final and total. For between the months of September, 1942 and February, 1943, the possibility of a Nazi victory had been left behind forever on the wintry Russian steppe.

IV

Blitz in Reverse

THERE is no one moment or action which brings victory or defeat in a great war. Everything is cumulative. The victory at Stalingrad would have been impossible if the defensive battle of Moscow had been lost. The winter offensive would not have been launched on such a scale had Allied deliveries of Lend-Lease weapons not permitted the Russians to dig deep into their own reserves. None of those events could have transpired without countless other conditions; and so on. Yet there does come a time when one army knows beyond question that it is winning the war, while the adversary realizes that he has been mortally wounded. Such a moment certainly came for the Nazis at the end of 1942.

In its last great offensive the Nazi command was still held down to an advance at about one-fifth the pace of the invasion offensive in 1941. Long before this major effort had attained its objectives it was interrupted by the Russian counter-blow, which recovered all the Nazi gains of 1942 and drove far into the Ukraine itself, taking back over 500,000 square kilometers of territory.

As a result of the fighting in 1942 and the winter offensive of early 1943 the Russians inflicted over a million casualties on the Wehrmacht and captured and destroyed 5,000 planes and 7,000 tanks. They virtually liquidated the military power of the henchman countries, Rumania and Hungary. They took away from Hitler, above all, a priceless year, and in that year the Allied production overtook and passed Germany in the race for superiority in tanks and planes.

But there was something still worse for Berlin. I saw it in the faces and manners and speech of the German prisoners at the front. I saw it among the German generals near Stalingrad. Not only fear of ultimate defeat was there, but the bottomless despair of loss of faith. At Stalingrad the impossible had happened. Germany's religion of total war had broken into a thousand fragments before German eyes.

Even the most fanatical believers must now have begun to question the bible of German war doctrine, the Schlieffen Plan and the teachings of Ludendorff and his Nazi disciples. A terrible suspicion dawned in the Nazi skull that perhaps the whole scheme had been too grandiose to begin with, that perhaps Germany had never possessed the means to realize it at all.

As is well known, Schlieffen was a strategist who, after Moltke, had left the deepest impression on modern German military doctrine. His book *Cannae* envisaged German domination of Europe, and ultimately of the world, through a series of victories won by Hannibal's tactics of encirclement and annihilation, and again, encirclement and annihilation.

Schlieffen's plan for world mastery considered it essential for Germany to reduce Russia, the eastern menace and the major potential threat to German power. To achieve that he prescribed several fundamental conditions, one of which was the war of the single front. Another was complete organization for a mighty blow guaranteeing a short war and a decision won as in *Cannae*. "It is either Cannae for the enemy," he taught, "or death for Germany."

As early as 1919 General Ludendorff came out with reaffirmation of the Schlieffen Plan. At one time he actually proposed to the Allies that they should appoint him under Marshal Foch to destroy Soviet Russia and partition the western provinces. In his own volume Ludendorff modified Schlieffen's teachings in the doctrine of total war, which was later adopted as the Nazi strategy for world conquest. And to maximize the means for a quick decision the Nazi militarists perfected the tactics of blitzkrieg, the lightning war which could utilize all the political and social and economic, as well as the military, means of victory.

In June, 1941, the Hitlerites thought they saw the necessary prerequisites in ideal combination for use against Stalin. Only Russia stood between Hitler and total realization of the Schlieffen

Plan. Russia was militarily and politically "unstable," Hitler said. The bolshevik regime would disintegrate, once he delivered a "stunning blow" against the Red Army. Finally, he counted on dividing his other enemies politically by utilizing anti-Communist sentiment in America and Britain to prevent aid to Russia until it was far too late. All that remained was to give the order to the generals to encircle and cut up the main forces of the Red Army and to capture Moscow. Hitler promised to ride triumphantly into the Kremlin some time in 1941.

Happily the Hitlerites miscalculated in every respect. They gravely underestimated the Russian war potential, as Goering and Goebbels in 1943 weakly confessed to the nation. They misjudged what Russia called its "moral and political reserves." They underestimated the political sagacity of Messrs. Churchill and Roosevelt.

But few of the old-line Reichswehr generals were ever as enamored of the idea of "encircling" a giant of eight million square miles and nearly two hundred million people as were the Nazi leaders. Many remained frankly skeptical. Early in the war sharp differences of opinion arose over the assault on Moscow and leading generals already realized, before reaching the capital, that their tactical means were insufficient for the strategic tasks demanded of them.

After the Stalingrad battle, and at the end of the offensive, when the Russians had had ample time to question many of the enemy generals taken prisoner, an article appeared in the Russian press, throwing considerable light on inner divisions affecting the German Army. It was written by Professor E. Tarlé, a respected historian who had access to special data from the Red Army. According to Tarlé, the Russians had earlier learned that Marshal von Brauchitsch, Chief of the General Staff, was convinced by October, 1941, that Moscow could not be taken that year, that all the victories won up to that point would prove indecisive, and that none of them had anything in common with a Cannae or a Sedan. Brauchitsch and his staff were decidedly against the November drive on Moscow for which they predicted failure. And again in 1942 they asserted with greater vehemence that the capital could not be encircled in a roundabout movement from the East—through Stalingrad, Kuibyshev and Saratov.

Hitler and his immediate cohorts argued that the conquest of Moscow was essential for a Cannae, however. without which the war might drag on and Germany be doomed. Brauchitsch resigned and pursuit of the Hitlerian chimera continued. What was held doubtful in the first offensive was considered still more risky for generals entrusted with responsibility for the capture of Stalingrad, and again Hitler ignored the best advice of both his staff and commanding officers in the field, when he kept the army there with inadequate reserves on its flanks. In the end it was not the hunted but the hunter who was trapped, in a battle which did turn out to be one of the most brilliant of the Cannae type ever fought—only it was the Russians who won it.

Failure to conquer Moscow in 1941 established the wisdom of von Brauchitsch, who had advised that the Wehrmacht simply withdraw to the Polish border for the winter, and thereby release a couple of million men for intensified production of aircraft in preparation for a renewed drive in 1942. Again, in the autumn of 1942, General Franz Halder urged withdrawal from the dangerous salient at Stalingrad. Hitler refused for reasons of prestige and vanity, according to Tarlé. He too was replaced and General von Seidlitz became Chief of Staff. Every officer assigned to the Stalingrad operations realized the hazards involved, and after the debacle nearly every informed German understood the critical nature of the inner quarrel between the Potsdam tradition and the Nazi will, which underlay the tragedy of German arms.

Stalingrad, and the ghosts of the 240,000 dead Germans sacrificed there, undermined remaining confidence in the leadership, and surrounded with somber shadows of pessimism all future military plans of the Fuehrer. The supreme conception of victory, the Nazis knew, was the destruction of the Russian Army by encirclement strategy. They had exhaustively rehearsed themselves in its every detail. Given the perfect setting, success eluded the masters, while supposedly rank amateurs defeated them at their own game. What hope could remain?

The disaster left the Nazis strategically bankrupt, from then on men who never believed in victory by defensive operations were obliged to improvise a means of salvation. But they knew that defensive strategy meant the reality of a "long war," and that the same Schlieffen who had guaranteed victory in a lightning war had predicted "certain death for Germany" in a long one. The dream was lost.

I

News from Mongolia

I HAVE mentioned the visit to Moscow of Premier Choy Bolsan and a delegation of thirty-six men and women from ancient Khalka, the homeland of Genghis Khan, now known as the Mongolian People's Republic. Several such delegations, bearing gifts to the Red Army, made the long trip from Ulan Bator and back again, after the German invasion. But no one had been able to interview them about their country, which had been virtually cut off from the outside world for a whole generation. The reason for that isolation lay in Mongolia's unique political status.

Khalka became a Republic in 1921, when the Mongolian People's Revolutionary Party overthrew the old regime, with the help of the Russian bolsheviks, and declared its independence of remaining ties with the Peking government in China. In 1926 it abolished the last powers of the Lama Church and the princes. For the first time in centuries the Mongols were free from the domination of a corrupt and ignorant hierarchy which had almost destroyed this once great nation.

The Republic grew up under Moscow's tutelage and protection and, in 1936, this fact was formalized when the two governments signed a mutual defense pact. It is often supposed that Outer Mongolia has been annexed by Russia, but the Soviet Union does not so regard it, either *de jure* or *de facto*. Russia maintains a Legation in Ulan Bator and there is a Mongolian Legation in Moscow. Russia also recognized by treaty China's suzerainty over the State, although the Mongols themselves do not. At the outbreak of the war Mongolia was in fact Russia's only formal ally. The Red Army had already come to the Mongols' assistance when the Japanese invaded their country in 1939; and the Mongols now lived up to their obligations by helping Russia against Germany.

That was the external position. But what had been happening inside Mongolia? How did the people like the new government? What changes had been brought about? What did Mongols think about China and Japan? Was there any desire to return to Chinese protection or domination? As far as I know no one had talked to Mongols about such questions for years.

Soon after Marshal Choy Bolsan returned from the front I asked for an interview with him, through the Soviet Foreign Office. I was told that Mongolia was an independent country and the Russians did not handle their official contacts. Inquiries at the Mongolian Legation always brought the response that Choy Bolsan was not in town. It was the run-around.

Meanwhile the Metropole was overflowing with Mongols, picturesque in their yellow and orange and gold robes. Some were in uniform, wearing the high-peeked hats of the Far Eastern Red Banner armies. For weeks they stayed in the hotel waiting to see Stalin, but they gave the press a wide berth. At last I did manage to meet an even dozen of them. I was the first American any of them had talked to and they seemed as delighted as I was and were especially glad to meet someone from China.

From these interviews I did learn one or two quite startling facts which will have to keep for a while, but most of all I got a vivid impression of a nation going through swift revolutionary changes that may ultimately be of great significance in the Far East. What is happening there cannot fail directly to influence Inner Mongolia and Manchuria. And that is a pretty big slice of Northeastern Asia.

The Mongols to whom I spoke were not officials or administrators but workers and intellectual leaders chosen by their organizations as delegates to visit the Red Army. One of them, a well-educated man who knew Chinese as well as Russian, told me that "Outer Mongolia is a bourgeois-democratic state of a new type, not socialist and not capitalist, but with some features of each, and with a political system similar to that of the U.S.S.R. For instance, there is only one legal party, the Mongolian People's Party just as in Soviet Russia only the Communist Party is legal. We also have a government by representative councils, like Soviets.

"The country was divided into eighteen oblasts or provinces after the Revolution and these in turn were divided into counties and villages. Formerly we had tribal government and each prince

194

and lamasery shared power over certain herds and grazing lands. That system was entirely dissolved in 1924 and both the princes and Lamas were dispossessed and their herds were divided among the people."

Today the state owns all the land, which formerly was the property of Lamas and princes, but both farmland and pasture are given rent-free to the people for their own use. One of the women delegates I met wore a decoration awarded for animal husbandry and I asked her if she owned any cattle herself.

"I have thirty-eight horses, over 100 sheep and four cows and two steers," she replied.

"That would make you an outstanding kulak in Russia, wouldn't it?"

"Maybe so," she laughed, "but we are not a socialist state and our livelihood has to be earned from the pasture and we don't have the benefits a socialist worker gets. I own a little more cattle than most Mongols, but only because I worked harder in the early days. Before the Revolution I had nothing. When the cattle were first distributed I had only two horses, two cows and a few sheep, but when the final redistribution came I had done so well that I received nothing more."

The government's aim has been to transform Mongolia from a purely nomadic country into one with an agrarian-pastoral economy, which can broaden the basis of the Mongol's livelihood and culture. A few collective farms and state farms already exist, while many Mongol families now have small truck gardens of their own, a new thing to vary the Mongol diet with vegetables and greens. Every Mongol is entitled to the free use of a hectare of land for farming purposes, provided he cultivates it. Larger farms are taxed one-third of their crop. Herds are taxed above a figure which changes annually, in accordance with the total number of cattle.

"What incentive is there to increase your herds," I asked the Mongol cowgirl, "if the government taxes them all anyway?"

"The tax isn't a fixed figure; it changes in accordance with the total number of cattle in the country, and the tax is only a percentage of the increase. Today we have fifteen million head of cattle whereas we had only five million when the Republic was set up. So if every herd increases then the government needs less from each of us and the people keep getting richer."

These Mongols were enthusiastic about the cultural progress their country had made since the Revolution. Formerly what schools existed were under control of the Lamas and virtually no

Mongol outside the church could read or write. Today about three-fifths of the population is literate, they claimed. Education has been made easier through the use of a simplified alphabet for the Mongolian script; and more recently the Russian alphabet has been adopted. This made it easier for Mongols to secure access to a vast body of information hitherto denied them.

Damdin Surin, a rather good-looking Mongol of thirty-five, who was editor of the *Unen*, or "Truth," of Ulan Bator, told me that since the disappearance of the Lamas the Mongol race had had "nothing less than a spiritual and physical rebirth." Before the Revolution the Mongols were declining in numbers at a rapid rate, owing chiefly to sterility and death caused by syphilis, which infected nearly 90% of the population. The Bogdo Gegen-Khan, the last Grand Lama, who was both spiritual and temporal ruler, died of syphilis. One of the first effective acts of the government was to conquer this scourge and it is now fully under control.

"Lamaism was introduced among us by Genghis Khan," said Surin, "and in a few generations it ruined us. Before that all men respected Mongols; afterward they all spit on us. Lamaism taught us to fear death. Our people went about imagining that if they did not obey the Lamas they would in the future be reborn as dogs, pigs, asses and so on. Recently I studied some of the scriptures in our historical library at the Mongolian University, and I had to laugh again and again at what rubbish our fathers were taught to believe. I see now why our country made no progress for over 200 years. In Inner Mongolia they still believe in such things today. Under the Japanese Lamas go on preaching this poison to our people. I pity them."

It was interesting to discover that in one generation Mongolia had got rid of a religion which played the main role in Mongol society for centuries. "No youth today feels any need for Lamaism," Surin said. "We consider it a subject to be studied in the museum, along with the ancient bows and arrows of tribal times."

I found that these Mongols hoped eventually to see all their race once more united. They want a federation with the old Mongol banners of Inner Mongolia, which under the Chinese Kuomintang policy of attrition is to be "absorbed" as the "provinces" of Chahar, Jehol and Suiyuan. In other words, they would like a restoration of Mongol boundaries formerly recognized by the Manchu Dynasty. And if China would sanction such Mongol claims?

"Then we could co-operate as friendly neighboring states."

one of the delegates answered. "We have many cultural and historical ties with China and would like to have closer, direct relations with her. What we would like is to be an independent state on an equal footing with both Russia and China—but right now that is not possible."

As long as the Chinese government policy aims to "swallow up" Mongol pastures, however, there is no chance of closer ties between Ulan Bator and Chiang Kai-shek's regime, it was made clear. Such a policy is held to be a menace to Mongolian security and to justify the "alliance with" Soviet Russia.

"I hope after the war we shall be able to visit each other freely," one Mongol exclaimed. "You to visit Ulan Bator, and I to visit America!"

Such hopes were common among young Mongols who aspire to see their country emerge from its seclusion. What interested me was that the Russians had evidently not discouraged them from hoping for a broadened basis of national relationships. It seems likely that in the event Russia becomes involved in the Far Eastern war the people of Khalka may find a means of effecting the closer unity of which they speak.

Among the Mongols was one who had traveled in Inner Mongolia and North China fairly recently and had talked to Mongols from Pailingmiao to Peking. He said he had found little liking among any of them for the Japanese. He felt certain that Mongols throughout Inner Mongolia as well as Manchuria would join in with Outer Mongolia if it came to war with Japan.

II

The Mongols and Japan

IN A Russo-Japanese conflict the "new" Mongols of Khalka would be important not only as fighting allies but because of the strategic position occupied by their country. For about 2,500 miles it adjoins the Japanese-controlled frontiers of Manchuria and Inner Mongolia, while in the north its borders cover nearly 2,000

197

miles of the flank, or rather the belly, of Middle Siberia. Japanese militarists used to write quite frankly about how much easier it would be to invade Siberia through Mongolia than across the northern frontiers of Manchuria.

But times have changed since then, and it is now doubtful whether the Japanese would even be able to penetrate far inside Outer Mongolia, should they ever find themselves in the unhappy position of attempting it. The Mongolian Army itself is modern and well equipped and is said to contain several tank companies, with Mongol operators and mechanics. Some Mongol engineers and technicians have been trained in Russia, both for new industries set up in Ulan Bator and to work in the army. There is no separate Mongol air force, but a number of Mongol pilots have been trained in Russia. "An appointment to a flying school is much sought after by our Mongol youths," one of them told me. "We make good flyers for the same reason we are good horsemen—because we have excellent eyes!"

Conscription is enforced among men and women. The standing army is about 80,000, I was told, which seems quite large for a country allegedly holding only 900,000 people. Some units have seen service on the European front and are battle-tried and experienced in the use of modern arms. Since 1936 the Mongolian People's Army has been supported by Red Army Border Guard detachments and units of the Red Air Force. Modern airdromes have been built and a network of military highways connects them with Ulan Bator and Khatkhyl (on Lake Kosso-Gol) and with Chita, headquarters of the Red Army's Trans-Baikal command, and with the neighboring Tanna-Tuvan and Buryat-Mongolian Republics.

My Mongol friends told me that since their victory over the Japanese at Khalkhyn Gol, in 1939, they had not feared an attack from that quarter. "The Japanese learned a lesson they won't forget," they said. The significance of the quite large battle fought along the Khalkhyn River west of Lake Buir Nor, from May till September, was overshadowed shortly after its conclusion by the German invasion of Poland, but that four months' undeclared war undoubtedly was intended as a Japanese try-out of Soviet arms. It profoundly influenced their subsequent decision not to invade Russia. I met several Russian officers who participated in the Khalkhyn Gol fighting and their stories agreed with those of the Mongols.

It was in this battle that Marshal (then a general) Georgi Zhukov, later to become Stalin's Chief of Staff, made his reputation. By skilful maneuvering of flame-throwing tanks on the Mongolian steppe he encircled and virtually destroyed the Japanese-Manchukuoan invasion force of over 50,000 men. Even the Japanese official communiqué admitted 18,000 casualties, an acknowledgment almost unprecedented. In Moscow the then German Military Attaché, General Koestring, told Henry Shapiro, the able correspondent of the United Press, that in this battle Zhukov had proved himself a "master of tank warfare." Later on Koestring revealed that he had used his report on the Khalkhyn Gol fighting to try to convince Berlin that the Red Army was led by men fully at home with modern arms.

A healthy respect for the Red Army thus came over the Japanese, which no subsequent success made them forget. The lesson naturally was emphasized by the experiences the Wehrmacht later suffered in Russia. Border incidents miraculously ceased and Japan made a neutrality pact with Russia in 1940. It was mainly fear of Russia that kept Japan inactive against Britain and America till Hitler marched into the Ukraine.

Not many people realized it, but the fact was that the power of initiative on the Manchu-Siberian frontier decisively passed over to the Red Army in the autumn of 1942, and there was no likelihood of a Japanese attack after that date. Siberia and the Far East had by then become a self-sufficient nation, able to mobilize a mighty army independent of European Russia.

III

Is Siberia Ready?

THE number of Europeans and Americans who know much about wartime Siberia is hardly greater than those who have personally visited Mongolia. The best-informed American on both subjects may be Angus Ward, our Russian-wise Consul in Vladivostok and the only officer in the consular service who speaks and reads Mongolian. A heavily bearded man of fifty, who loves the Russian East, Ward is said to have passed up promotion in order to continue in Vladivostok.

Except for Mr. Ward and a few naval observers, I believe no American was allowed to travel east of Chita after the war began. My own request for permission to visit Siberia met with no more success than others had. Occasionally American airplanes carrying big-shots have flown across Siberia, with Russians navigating. The first of these was the *Gulliver*, which carried Wendell Willkie's party. But none of them saw much more than Yakutsk and the broadest expanse of snow that ever looked up at a B-24.

Nevertheless, no one can spend six months in Russia without meeting people who have been in Siberia; and nobody could fail to carry away an impression about the average Russian's attitude toward the Japanese. I never met a Russian officer who had anything good to say for them. Without exception, every Russian I knew well enough to ask for a frank opinion told me he wanted the Japs beaten and most of them added that they would take pleasure in helping.

Four decades and a change of regime did little to erase the humiliation every Russian felt over defeat at Japan's hands in 1905. The savagery of Japanese intervention still rankles in the memory of thousands of bolsheviks. In 1935 the Japanese made them eat humble pie again when they took advantage of Russia's unpreparedness in Siberia and of the internal conflicts which then weakened the government at the center, to compel Moscow to sell the Russian interest in the Chinese Eastern Railway at a fraction of its value. I happened to be in Manchuria at that time and talked to some Russians and know how bitterly they regretted this act of appeasement.

From that time on the Reds rapidly built up their military power in Siberia. Extremist right-wing younger officers in the Japanese (Kwantung) Army in Manchukuo fostered scores of border conflicts along the Amur River, hoping to provoke the Russians to large-scale retaliation which would enable them to stampede the Tokyo General Staff into major war. One of these incidents, at Changkufeng, came within an ace of succeeding; but the unexpectedly determined Russian resistance impressed Tokyo, and the pro-war party failed to override the opposition of the more cautious General Staff. Then in 1939 came the climax at Khalkhyn

Gol, in Outer Mongolia, when it was finally realized even by the Kwantung Army that the Russian Far East could be invaded only as a total effort.

The great change in Siberia's strategic security was brought about through the stabilization of the Soviet regime, the success of planned industrial development, improved communications, an increased population, and the strengthening of the Soviet defense forces in every respect. Much of this development took place before the German attack, for Russia had to be prepared for a two-front war—of which adherents to the Anti-Comintern Pact then talked very openly.

It was a tremendous task of organization. Russia's Far East is approximately twice as far from European Russia as England is from the United States, which was perhaps the chief reason for the defeat of 1905, when everything had to be hauled 6,000 miles across one single-tracked railway from Europe. Today new railways connect Vladivostok with the northern cities of Nikolaevsk and Soviet Harbor. Under construction, and scheduled for completion in 1944, is another railway which, leading from Soviet Harbor and Komsomolsk westward to Bodaibo, north of Lake Baikal, outflanks the trans-Siberian railway and furnishes a second major supply line from Europe.

The Red Army east of Lake Baikal is no longer dependent on Europe. It has three zones of industrial support behind it—not only the Urals and the Kusnetsk area, already described, but a young industry rapidly growing up in the Far Eastern territory itself. There are iron and coal mines in the Amur River valley, adjoining Manchukuo, and steel mills near Chita and Komsomolsk, while heavy industries in Kharbarovsk produce tanks, airplanes and machines. Evidently precision instruments are also made in the Kharbarovsk area, the most important industrial center of the Far East.*

Field command of the Far Eastern Red Banner armies continues to reside in a picked corps of officers backed up by panzer divisions known to be first rate in equipment and among the best in Russia. They are organized under two autonomous war areas, one with its headquarters at Kharbarovsk, the other at Chita. Nobody outside the Red Army could know how many troops are being diverted here away from the main front in Europe, but

* Recently I saw a fine Russian copy of a late-model Leica camera stamped with the name of a Kharbarovsk factory.

200,000 is one commonly accepted figure for the Red Border Guards,* aside from regular troops and militia. Many new landing fields and supply stations have been established, but first-line air strength is believed rather small. The Red Navy in this area in 1943 was thought to comprise about sixty submarines, and the Amur and Ussuri Rivers were patrolled by a large number of torpedo boats.

Behind the shock forces stood several hundred thousand trained workers of Siberian industry, and several million peasants organized as militia. Some of these were drawn into the European front, as we saw in the case of General Guriev's crack Guardist division at Stalingrad. Reserves were further strengthened by a more intensive training of women for service in the militia. Siberia's population may have trebled in the last twenty years, particularly since Soviet planning began. Today there are said to be seventeen million people living in the Siberian hinterland, a human reservoir which should be able to absorb any initial blows, without heavy reinforcement from the West. Russian officers I met who had served in that area, and some who participated in the battle of Changkufeng, were uniformly cocksure about the ability of Siberia and the Far East to take care of itself alone, if necessary.

Despite this general improvement, however, the Soviet government continued to maintain a formally correct neutrality toward Japan, although after 1942 there was a definite stiffening in attitude. Not till the Moscow Conference did Russia unmistakably serve notice that she considered Japan could not win the war. In signing the Four Nations Declaration, with China as one of the signatories, Russia for the first time recognized China as ultimate victor and the nation with which she would deal in settling postwar problems in that part of the world.

At Moscow, and later at Teheran, Allied diplomats probably broke the ice with which Russia had so long surrounded her attitude toward the Pacific War. The public cannot yet know what, if any, commitments Russia made on those occasions, but there is good reason for Japan to fear ultimate collaboration against her.

But it should be emphasized that neither the Soviet government nor Soviet citizens believe they are under any obligation to help us chastise the Japs for our own ends. They think they have done more than their share in fighting the Axis. In occupying the German Army virtually alone for nearly three years they gave us

* The Border Guards are under the N.K.V.D.

time to prepare not only against Hitler but also against Japan. The mere presence of the Red Army in Siberia immobilized large Japanese forces which might have been thrown against us elsewhere.

If Russia goes to war it will be for objectives of her own. Stalin himself is supposed to have said to an Allied diplomat, "There are issues between Japan and ourselves which can be settled only by war."

He probably had in mind more than prestige, for Russia has now got all the military prestige she needs. But not merely the memory of past humiliations remains; the physical symbols are there too. The Japanese still hold fishing concessions all along the coast from Vladivostok to Petropavlask and these are a painful belt of thorns in the side of the Russians. Half the island of Sakhalin is ruled by Japs and Sakhalin is East Asia's biggest oil producer north of Borneo. Farther east are the Kuriles, a chain of islands which lock in Russia's maritime provinces behind the sea of Okhotsk. In candid moments Red Navy officers have admitted a determination to get the Japs out of those places once and forever. They want this to be the last war in which any foreign naval power can close their harbors by mining and patrolling adjacent seas.

A young people pushing toward the Pacific as irresistibly as Americans migrated toward the same ocean a century ago, Soviet Siberia must naturally seek a warm water outlet and a short overland route to it. Vladivostok is not ice free but Dairen and Ryojun are. Half a century ago Russians first developed those ports (as Dalny and Port Arthur) but they had to sign them over to Japan in 1905. It was to reach those ports, via Manchuria, that the Tsar built the Chinese Eastern Railway, which cut a thousand miles from the long trip around the trans-Siberian line to Vladivostok. This feature of Manchuria is probably no less interesting to the Soviets than it was to old Russia.

Soviet Russia has not been in the habit of satisfying her needs through wars of conquest, and the recovery of the Baltic States and part of Poland, which were also lost after defeat in past wars, do not offer an exact parallel, as Manchuria was never actually incorporated in the Empire. There is perhaps a closer comparison in the case of Iran, which blocks Russia's access to the Persian Gulf much as a Japanese (or Chinese) Dairen cuts her off from the warm waters of the Pacific. Russia has guaranteed the territorial integrity of Iran, but it must be remembered that it was only after

203

physical occupation of the northern part of that country that she acquired rights which gave her entirely satisfactory access to the sea. One thing is certain: she would not long tolerate an anti-Soviet government in Manchuria.

Thus, Russia would not want the United States and Britain alone to decide the fate of a region of such vital importance to her. In this regard the realization of the Cairo communiqué may ultimately be qualified by the fact that Russia is destined to play a dynamic role in the concluding phases of the war against Japan. Her influence is likely to condition the character of any regime set up in Manchuria and Korea.

What form will Russian intervention take? Obviously Russia never intended to attack Japan—or let us "use her bases," which some people suggested she could do without going to war—until she had completely disposed of Germany. But afterward? Much would then depend on relations existing among the three big Powers and whether they would quarrel about the political control of post-war Europe or co-operate smoothly. If policies harmonize in the West there will also be a working coalition in Asia, and some of the possibilities suggested below would not then mature; but it is well to remind ourselves that for Russia, as well as for us, an alternative always exists.

Since Russia would not enter the Pacific War till after Germany is mopped up, this means that any estimates of her actual force in Siberia before that date is rather beside the point. For it is not that force, adequate as it might be to repel any invasion, but the main Red Army itself, some ten to fifteen million men, which would eventually face Japan across her long land frontier. What hope would Japan have to prevail against such an immensely superior machine, after it had smashed every system of fortifications devised by German ingenuity? None whatever. And for that very reason Russia may accomplish her major aims by "intervening" without becoming a belligerent against Japan.

In March, 1944, the Russians demonstrated clearly enough that they do intend to use their increased prestige and power to recover the territories and concessions yielded to Japan as a result of past weakness and defeat. They insisted upon the cancellation of the valuable Japanese oil and coal rights in the northern half of Sakhalin Island as a condition of renewal of the Japanese fishing concession. Acceptance of this demand was openly hailed in the

Soviet press as a defeat for those Japanese who had been gambling on a Hitlerite victory.

That Russia will, as her power becomes more flexible and Japan's position worsens, require the Japanese to make other adjustments, may be taken for granted. And the possibility that Japan may, toward the end, make very generous offers to Russia to take on the role of mediator, is also to be reckoned upon. Stalin is no amateur at power politics and he might not be completely satisfied to see Japan, one of Russia's most important neighbors, become entirely subservient to the United States, any more than we would necessarily welcome a Mexico dominated by Russia. While the Russians may consider it in their interest to have a Japan too weak to be a menace to Soviet frontiers, they may desire a Japan strong enough to constitute a frontier in the Western Pacific. All of which is a point to be kept in mind by those who on the one hand demand that we tell the Russians where to draw their frontier with Poland, and on the other demand that they enter the Pacific war on our side.

Two could play at the game of "preserving Japan as a buffer," if we tried to make the Son of Heaven the puppet of an anti-Soviet Japanese "Liberal" monarchy, as some "experts" desire, or to set up a *cordon sanitaire* in Manchuria. Moscow would not have much difficulty in finding a pro-Soviet group in Japan, or something comparable to the Free German movement. In that case Russia might not have to enter the war directly, but could merely support a Japanese "people's revolt." There is, of course, a Japanese Communist cadre which could take the leadership of it.

There are other ways Russia could make her influence felt, short of frontal attack on Manchukuo and Japan. She could greatly enlarge the flow of supplies to China, for one thing. She could send divisions of Red Army volunteers to China across Chinese Turkistan and Mongolia. She could open up for us a new air ferry route and supply line so that we could send planes, men and equipment via Siberia to North China. Or she could supply the Chinese Communist armies with weapons and encourage them to carry on heavy guerrilla warfare right into the enemy's rear in Manchuria and Korea.

The last point is a possibility that seems worth brief speculation in a section by itself.

IV

Russia and China

THERE is little love lost between Stalin and Chiang Kai-shek and between the Russian Communist Party and the Kuomintang. The Generalissimo was "made" with the help of Russian money, brains and arms, in the days when the Comintern was actively promoting revolutions. After he had gained power he turned on his benefactors, set up his own anti-Communist regime, and began his long attempt to "exterminate" the Chinese Reds.

Chiang thus "outsmarted" Stalin, who happened to be chairman of the Communist International at that time (1927) and responsible for its policy. Stalin was severely attacked by the Opposition (Trotsky and Zinoviev) as a result, and he did not fully establish his leadership of the Russian party till 1928. From that point on he became identified more and more with the policy of "building socialism in one country." "Revolution," he said, "is not for export."

It is improbable that Stalin has forgotten his unsettled score with the Generalissimo, but for many years before the complete abolition of the Comintern the Soviet government gave no material help to the Chinese Red Army. The Soviet peoples retained an especially warm interest in the Chinese movement, but Moscow was diplomatically correct in its relations with the Kuomintang government from the time it recognized Chiang Kai-shek's regime at Nanking, in 1933.

If China had not been estranged from Russia in 1931, the Japanese might never have dared invade Manchuria. Shortly after the restoration of Sino-Russian relations the Soviet government actually offered Chiang Kai-shek a mutual defense pact, such as it made with Outer Mongolia. Chiang rejected the proposal through his then Foreign Minister, Wang Ching-wei—now Japan's puppet ruler in Nanking. Neither the fact that the pact was offered, nor the reasons for its rejection, are generally known. Two members of the Soong family told me that it was turned down mainly because Wang Ching-wei convinced the Generalissimo that the Japanese were not going to invade China from their base in Manchuria, but planned to invade Siberia. Instead of a mutual defense pact with Russia, therefore, Chiang Kai-shek authorized his War Minister, General Ho Ying-chin, to sign the so-called "Ho-Umetsu Agreement," whereby China gave *de facto* recognition of Japan's occupation of Manchuria and part of Inner Mongolia.

Naturally the Russians did not renew their offer after the Japanese attack on North China. But in the difficult years when America, Britain and the Dutch Indies supplied Japan with the things she needed to conquer China, Russia supported the Chinese demand, at Geneva, for a "quarantine" against Japan. Russia herself virtually boycotted Japan and gave generous credits and military supplies to the Chinese. It is important to note that Moscow dealt solely with the Generalissimo's government and that not even the most rabidly anti-Soviet members of the Kuomintang ever suggested that Russian arms or any kind of help was being given to the Chinese Communist forces in the northern provinces.

The Russians also sent a military mission to aid the Generalissimo. That was after Hitler withdrew the German mission from China in 1938, following a speech in which he declared that the Chinese were "mentally incapable" of winning. This was a severe blow to the "nazified" staff officers in Chiang's army, who had for a decade been closely associated with the German advisors, headed by General von Falkenhausen. The Germans explained to them that this was a necessary preliminary to Hitler's invasion of Russia in co-operation with Japan, however. After June, 1941, these pro-Nazi elements in Chiang Kai-shek's army were convinced that Stalin was doomed.

So undisguised was that belief in Chungking that the position of the Russian military mission became untenable, and it was withdrawn early in 1942, as already mentioned. About this time the Generalissimo apparently was persuaded that it was an opportune moment to ask the Russians to "abolish" the Chinese Communist Party, in order to retain Chungking's good will. According to reliable diplomatic sources, the Generalissimo actually delegated Sun Fo, then his envoy in Russia, to raise this question with Stalin. The proposed formula was, however, flatly rejected by Molotov, who indignantly informed Sun that the Kremlin had no intention of interfering in China's domestic affairs. Relations between the two governments remain cool to this day, despite the assurances contained in the Moscow declaration of 1943.

There were two other significant developments in relations between Chungking and Moscow. At the beginning of the Stalingrad battle, when Russia's position seemed most precarious, the Generalissimo determined to put his troops into Sinkiang province, or Chinese Turkistan, which extends far into Central Asia, between Outer Mongolia and Soviet Kazakhstan. Kuomintang troops had never controlled that vast area of half a million square miles. For some years it had been ruled by an ex-Manchurian general, Sheng Shih-tsai, who carried out a pro-Soviet policy. After the Japanese invaded China the Russians had sent in a small force of combat and service troops to help police the area, and to maintain the overland supply line to the Generalissimo. They also wished to prevent Japanese penetration westward from Inner Mongolia —a development which otherwise almost certainly would have occurred, as the Generalissimo was as powerless to defend the region as he was to protect Outer Mongolia. All these activities, including Russian help in developing some oil wells and other industry in Turkistan, had the Generalissimo's tacit consent.

Now, during the Stalingrad battle, and after the withdrawal of the Russian military mission, and during the rise in Chungking's optimism about an early American defeat of Japan, the Generalissimo's envoys descended on the Sinkiang governor, Sheng Shih-tsai. They made demands that he invite the Russians to leave and permit Kuomintang troops to take over policing duties. After cajoling and threats, General Sheng agreed. The Russians, apparently feeling the Japanese menace to their Mongolian flank had passed, promptly concurred in Sheng's wishes. But to the consternation of General Sheng, as well as of Chungking, they withdrew not only their gendarmes, but all their machinery, including the oil-drilling equipment, all their trucks, and a good deal of the arms, which they had brought into the big province.

This development indicated that the Russians are not interested in acquiring frontier territory just for the sake of expansion. Although Sinkiang has never been incorporated inside Russian boundaries, it has frequently been under Russian influence and Russian occupation. It happens that the largest elements in the population are Turks and Kazakhs, racially the kin of peoples in the neighboring Soviet states of Kazakhstan and Kirghistan. Only five per cent of the population of so-called Chinese Turkistan is

208

actually Chinese. A case could be made out for an autonomous Turkistan, guaranteeing the rights of various nationalities.

Evidently the Kuomintang authorities feared just such a possibility. Soon after they got power, therefore, they began forcibly transplanting the Kazakh people from their historic homeland in the fertile Altai Mountains (between Mongolia and Kazakhstan) to the semi-desert southern plain. Thousands of Kazakhs resisted this by force of arms; breaking away from Chinese troops they fled across the border into Outer Mongolia. This dramatic episode was revealed only on April 1, 1944, when a *Tass* dispatch from Ulan Bator, capital of Outer Mongolia, sharply reminded Chungking that the Soviet Union had a mutual-defense pact with the Mongols and would fully enforce it.

"Chinese troops in the northeastern part of Sinkiang," said the *Tass* report, "pursuing the Kazakhs, broke into the territory of the Mongolian People's Republic and from airplanes fired on the refugees and on inhabited localities. The government repulsed these invading Sinkiang troops . . . Leading government circles (here) are firmly convinced that in the event such violations recur the Soviet government will be forced, in the interests of ensuring the safety of the territory of the Mongolian People's Republic, to give every necessary help and support."

There was another interesting event in 1943, when in August an article appeared in Moscow's *War and the Working Class* (which more or less replaced the *Communist International* after it ceased publication). This article did much to clarify Moscow's attitude toward policies pursued by Chungking. It was written by Vladimir Rogov, former chief of the *Tass* Bureau in Shanghai, and it severely criticized the Chinese government's failure to mobilize manpower and resources against Japan. It pointed out that official personalities were engaged in hoarding, speculation, and trading in enemy goods, on the economic front, while military leaders were preoccupied with preparations to destroy the Eighth Route and New Fourth (Communist) armies. Chungking's best troops were used to blockade the Communists rather than fight the Japanese.

Rogov concluded that victory for China depended upon whether Chiang Kai-shek "understood the need to avert further internal struggle" which, he declared, "might well be the consequence of measures being taken against the Chinese Communists." It was an unprecedentedly candid pronouncement and as nothing appears by accident in the Russian press it must be assumed to reflect the attitude of the Kremlin.

Reading between the lines of Rogov's article and of the *Tass* story about Outer Mongolia it was clear that the Generalissimo had been skating on rather thin ice in his relations with Russia. It was also plain that the Russians regarded Chungking not only as congenitally anti-Soviet but as of doubtful use in a military sense. While this opinion remained passive as long as Russia was not involved in the Pacific War, it might find active expression in broader policy later on.

The Chinese Communist-controlled armies are likely to be the most effective forces in North China and Manchuria for some time to come, and the ones with which Russians could most readily make contact. If the Generalissimo continued to treat them as "rebels," and to withhold all supplies from them, it would not be very surprising if the Russians, once they entered the war against Japan, began to work directly with them. Out of that combination and out of an independence movement in Korea and an eventual Free Japan movement, the framework of a new political structure might arise in Northeastern Asia.

What if Anglo-American policy were at that time still gambling solely on the Generalissimo and the Kuomintang party dictatorship in China? Would not Soviet intervention then raise questions which our policy had not considered? An attempt to answer this question will be made farther on, against the background of China.

Meanwhile, it is useful to emphasize again that Russian policy in the East depends directly on the results of Anglo-American-Soviet co-operation in the West. The real key to it therefore must be sought in the larger objectives of Soviet peace-time as well as wartime objectives, in the more decisive arenas of domestic and international politics. What are those objectives? To estimate them it is necessary to understand what the U.S.S.R. is and why it works.

A good beginning can be made by attempting to state more precisely the reasons for Soviet victory.

I

Why Russian Victory?

VERY few Americans could be called experts on the Red Army, which has turned out to be the greatest army Europe ever saw. When Germany invaded Russia in 1941 our General Staff agreed with the British that it would likely be over in six weeks. At that time it was reported that Brigadier-General Philip Faymonville, who later became head of our Lend-Lease Mission in Moscow,* was about the only American in the War Department who expressed the opinion that the Reds might destroy the Nazi Army.

Remembering that, we must recognize how little we knew about Russia and how much there was for us to learn. Both our information and our method of analysis were inadequate to the task of understanding Russia; and that is still true today. If it were otherwise I would not presume to speak from my own limited experiences and knowledge of a military force which has profoundly altered the future history of mankind.

If the Red Army had collapsed as anticipated it is highly possible that most of us would not have lived to see the end of this war. We were spared enormous sacrifices of life only as an incidental to the Russians' struggle for their own salvation, of course, but the objective result of their decision to fight Nazism to the apocalyptical finish was that it saved Africa and it saved the Near East and the Middle East. It prevented Germany from linking hands with Japan and giving our enemy the help she needed to hold her conquests in Asia and the Pacific. Of course nobody gets anything for nothing in this world; and in one way or another history will exact its price from us for Russia's services.

When Hitler invaded Russia he had behind him the greatest

* But was withdrawn in 1944, for undisclosed reasons.

211

resources ever mobilized for war by any conqueror. He was master of virtually all Europe and in excess of 200 million people. Britain was knocked out of the war in so far as any offensive threat was concerned and the United States was not yet in it. Hitler had looted the arsenals of Europe to equip his Wehrmacht. He began his assault with superiority in tanks and airplanes, though possibly not in guns, and he was able to concentrate nearly all his striking power against Russia for nearly three years in a single-front war.

Those were the odds which the Red Army knew in advance would face it. And that is the measure of Russia's triumph in halting the Nazis and turning them back in their own tracks. But what has this resistance cost the Soviet peoples?

What the Russians have recovered is for the most part a desert of worthless rubble. Only the soil is still intact and Hitler would have poisoned that if he could. Some idea of what this means can be suggested by comparisons in geographical terms of the United States. Take a dozen large towns and cities which have been devastated by the Nazis—Sevastopol, Rzhev, Kursk, Kharkov, Kiev, Odessa, Leningrad, Stalingrad, Smolensk, and Dniepropetrovsk. In population they formerly about corresponded to the American cities of Trenton, Atlantic City, Nashville, Boston, Baltimore, San Francisco, Chicago, Milwaukee, Peoria, Washington, Des Moines and Cincinnati, respectively.

Leningrad was never fully occupied by the Nazis, but they shelled it for more than two years. It will have to be largely rebuilt. All the rest are from 30% to 90% destroyed. Stalingrad was a city nearly the size of Washington, D. C. before the war, but it is now about 95% obliterated. Most of the others still resemble cities when you see them from afar but on closer examination they are only shells hardly less useful than stage properties.

Just conceive of all that would lie buried in such a man-made desert if this country had gone through the same thing; or think simply of Kharkov, which was as big as Boston and is now 70% ruined. Think of the tens of thousands of buildings lost; the countless factories, power plants and other public works, the wrecked or stolen agricultural machinery, the demolished railways and bridges, the administration buildings, schools, libraries, shops and office buildings, the churches, homes and apartments, the tens of billions of man-hours of honest toil that have gone up in dust and fire.

In this way we get an idea of the price Russians have paid for victory. And do not forget the biggest item of all. The Red Army had by late spring in 1944 suffered around six millions of its young manhood in killed and missing, plus three millions incapacitated, and another six to seven millions wounded.

What explains the ability of the Red Army to sustain such enormous losses and recover to win victory? No doubt the wise man could sum it up in an epigram about General Winter, or about Hordes and Spaces. But ought we to stop thinking about it there?

Did weather beat the Germans? Yes, to some extent; undoubtedly their equipment and training were not as well suited to winter warfare as the Russians' equipment. But it was a relatively minor factor and in any case a superficial explanation. It only leads to another question: why were the Germans weaker in these respects?

Again, some say it was Russia's great masses. An officer high up in the Allied command told me quite seriously that Germany was licked by "the Asiatic Hordes." She was overthrown because the Germans are not a "Horde" and could not compete with Russia in the sacrifice of manpower. What is the fact? Hitler had more manpower at his disposal than the Red Army. After the first year, the war cut off a third of Russia's population and, in effect, put it at Hitler's disposal, in addition to what he had in Europe. And anyway what makes the "Horde" die like that? Why didn't the "Horde" overwhelm the Kaiser in the first war, when they had a second front to help them? Why did not China's "Horde" defeat Japan? Why could not Britain's colonial "Horde" of half a billion men defeat the Axis?

Others think it was space that frustrated Germany. The Nazis lost themselves in the immensity of Russia. They spread out too far until they could no longer concentrate for a decisive breakthrough. There is something in that, but not very much. Why not? Simply because as the Germans extended their lines the Russians had to do the same thing. They had to rely on bases in the Urals, much farther from the front than those with which they began their defense. People have also compared Hitler's debacle with the retreat of Napoleon. But Napoleon retreated without ever being defeated by General Kutuzov. The reasons for the destruction of his army were quite different from those which sent Hitler into a reverse blitzkrieg.

Foreign aid, chiefly American help with planes and tanks, also affected the outcome. "Without American production," Stalin

213

said, "victory would not have been possible." But the Russians know that our weapons did not begin to arrive in decisive numbers until after the turning point of the war. Up to Stalingrad we and the British combined had delivered to Russia roughly less than 10% as many planes and tanks as the Germans had when they began the invasion. Similarly the Allied bombing of Europe, which beyond question speeded up the retreat and break-up of the Nazi Army, did not impair German military efficiency in time to affect the decision.

It is also said that the Russian is fighting simply because his fatherland has been violated. He is motivated by good old-fashioned patriotism. There is nothing like having an enemy in your own back yard to make you fight, and love of Russia plays a very big role in the average soldier's heroism. But did the Frenchman love France less than the Russian loves the fatherland? Why did the Germans fail to find a Marshal Pétain in Russia, after the Russians lost over a million men in the first three months of war? Russian patriotism alone does not explain that.

More of the answer perhaps lies in some unusual features of the Russian Army. First, there is only one party and one leadership and all high officers belong to it; it is a unified army and there are apparently no contradictions between its political and military aims. Second, conscription applies to everyone equally and promotion is open to all. As it is a democratic army and there is no basic discrimination, it is not hard to maintain the rigid discipline insisted upon. Most of the dozen generals I interviewed at various fronts in Russia were the sons of illiterate parents; the Red Army had taught them everything they knew. Virtually without exception all officers of the Red Army are of working-class origin.

Third, Russian officers and civilians alike have no economic investments which could conflict with their single-minded devotion to the interests of the nation as a whole. They are not troubled by personal losses of property involved in the "scorched-earth" policy or the suppression of hoarding, speculation or profiteering. Fourth, this is an international army. Russians, Ukrainians, Uzbeks, Mongols, Jews, Georgians and so on, men of scores of races, are found among its high officers. Racial barriers are not permitted to block individual advancement. As this principle also applies in Soviet society, the conscripts are highly literate and intelligent.

Fifth, the Red Army had the advantage of combat experience acquired in an undeclared war with Japan and a war with Finland

and some of its officers also served in Spain and China. It was a young army, aware of its weakness; it was not ashamed to incorporate into its methods the lessons of those preliminaries to Russia's war with Germany.

Otherwise, the Red Army did not differ greatly in the physical material, training and weapons from all modern military forces. What finally made it a winning organization perhaps lay beyond any of those external conditions. As I saw it in Russia what decided the outcome was what in final analysis decides all wars between nearly evenly matched contestants. It was morale. Morale and all it includes in the broadest meaning of that term: the way it influences and determines the mobilization of the human and technical resources of a nation to overcome the crisis of its existence.

The Russians had greater morale in the battle for Moscow and they had it again at Stalingrad, the two battles which determined the fate of the Nazi Army. At Stalingrad the Russians did not call it morale, as we have seen, but "stability."* And all the sacrifices through which this "stability" was achieved at the front would have availed little if they had not been matched by similar performance in the rear and if the Soviet peoples had not concentrated everything on the organization of production to achieve maximum military striking power at the point needed.

The evacuation of industry from the occupied areas, the transfer eastward of millions of workers, the development of new industry in the Urals and in Central Asia are feats of Russian energy now well known abroad. But with all that effort, the total Russian production did not exceed just the percentage of *increased* production in the United States since the war began. What then enabled the Russians to make so much of what they had? I have stressed the answer: that everything went for war purposes except the barest minimum of goods required for the social and physical life of the Soviet Union.

Winston Churchill was quite right when he said, "No government ever formed among men has been capable of surviving injury so grave and cruel as that inflicted by Hitler on Russia." And in Mr. Churchill's statement lies another part, a key part, of the answer to the phenomenon of the Red Army. For inside the fighting front and behind it was the leadership and direction of the Soviet Government and the Communist Party. Some of us may not like either one, but only the blind can now deny that the triumph of

* See p. 129

the Red Army is the triumph of Soviet socialism and, above all, Soviet planning. Had they failed, Russia would have failed. In the most critical battles, at Moscow, at Stalingrad, at Kharkov and Leningrad, at Novorossiisk, everywhere Communists and Young Communists were in the vanguard of organization and leadership. They died by hundreds of thousands.

Is it then to be supposed that after weathering this storm the Soviet regime could now be overthrown, or would voluntarily change its domestic or foreign policies?

There are other questions akin to these and in the next chapter I am rash enough to ask and even attempt to answer some of them.

II

Is Russia "Abandoning Communism"?

IS RUSSIA going nationalist? What about the sharp differentiations in pay, quarters and privileges among workers and intellectuals, peasants and commissars, officers and soldiers? What of the adoption by the army and navy of epaulettes, once considered hated Tsarist symbols of class distinction? Why the more tolerant attitude toward the Church? Why the segregation of boys and girls in the school system? Is this a betrayal of socialism? Is Russia swinging back toward "private enterprise"?

Generally speaking, there seem to be two rather prevalent schools of answer-men at the moment. From the first school you learn that Stalin is adulterating or abandoning "Communism" and moving toward the right. Some people in this school seek to disarm bankers and other right-wing elements by proving that since the bolsheviks are becoming more conservative and more like us we can live peacefully with them. Anti-Stalinists in the same school use that thesis to prove that Stalin has betrayed their Marxist ideals and is a menace to progressive man. The second school takes the view that Soviet Russia is a sinister Oriental enigma or anyway a dictatorship little different from Nazi Germany. Stalin is a dictator; Hitler and Mussolini were dictators; ergo, Communism and Nazism are the same thing. Democracy is equally menaced by them.

Both those views are false. It is just as misleading to say that Fascism or Nazism and the Soviet system are one and the same as it is to contend that Russia is a liberal democracy. Some people who realize that, intellectually, nevertheless are emotionally or psychologically incapable of reconciling themselves to the fact. Aside from such special groups, however, the vast majority of men and women who are bewildered about the Soviet Union apparently lack elementary information concerning its make-up and purposes. At the risk of seeming pedantic, I wish to repeat some of that information here.

Some people jumped to wrong conclusions because of external resemblances between Soviet Communist and Nazi methods, or because they employed similar tools. In both cases there were one-party rule, secret police, "liquidation" of opposition elements, and strict control of the press. But although surgery and murder both employ a knife, society does not regard them as synonymous. Under the Soviet system the victim was held to be a privileged class, which had to be liquidated in so far as it obstructed realization of socialist society in the U.S.S.R. and the elimination of "exploitation of man by man through private ownership of the means of production." Under the Nazi system the victims were frankly stated to be whole peoples, not only the Jews and the Slavs but ultimately all who opposed "Aryan" mastery of the earth and a system of maximum exploitation of man by man, through the ownership of the means of production confined to one "race," and for the private benefit of the owning class.

The simple truth seems to be that the U.S.S.R. is unique. Sidney and Beatrice Webb called it "a new civilization" and there is apparently nothing harder for man to accept than the idea of something new in social organization. Back in the eighteenth and nineteenth centuries the United States of America was also unique, but historians in England and Europe asserted that it could not "last." Men were not "equal" and you could not build a stable powerful state without a hereditary ruling class and an aristocracy and a king.

Today there are still plenty of people who are convinced that socialism will not work; and they are continually discovering, in every change announced in the Soviet Union, indications to prove it. If there is weakness and failure, it proves that socialism is not practicable; but if there is success, then it is because Russia is abandoning Communism. Ideological dissenters on the other hand establish just the opposite conclusions: if there is failure it is because "true" socialism has been murdered by Stalin; if there is success it is because even Stalinism has not yet been able to destroy everything good in the one and only religion.

No attempt could be made here to examine the countless ideological differences with the Soviet application of Marxist principles, or to what extent it properly honors the essential content of the teachings of Marx, Engels and Lenin. All I am interested to show is whether or not wartime changes represent fundamental departures from that economic, social and political form of state which in the Soviet Union is called socialism, and which evolved there after the overthrow of capitalism. The most authoritative definitions of that state, and the aims and functions of its government, are to be found in the Soviet Constitution, which was adopted in 1936. In what way have its principles lately been revised or abandoned?

It is not my purpose to read a brief for or against the Soviet Constitution. Personally I like being an American and I prefer taking my chances with America for better or worse, perhaps because for me it has always been better. I wouldn't change places with anybody in Russia in my generation. I don't think we could establish a Soviet Russian type of state here unless we could duplicate Russian society and Russian history; and I don't think we could do that. But that has nothing to do with whether socialism works in Russia, and if you wish to know the answer to that you cannot afford to ignore its Constitution. To do so is to make as foolish a mistake as a Russian would make if he came to this country and tried to understand us without studying the American Constitution. Let us examine its fundamentals.

Article 1 of the Constitution declares, "The Union of Soviet Socialist Republics is a *socialist* state of workers and peasants," and Article 2 defines "the political foundation of the U.S.S.R." as "the Soviets of Toilers' Deputies . . . and the achievement of the dictatorship of the proletariat." Nowhere in the Constitution is the state defined as a democracy; it is a socialist "dictatorship of the proletariat." Also, strictly speaking, the Constitution does not claim to establish "Communism." Communism is something that

218

may or may not be realized before that millennium when, according to Karl Marx's vaguest prophecy, "the state will wither away," after the attainment of plenty under the principle, "from each according to his ability, to each according to his need."

The U.S.S.R. concentrates instead on working for more practical goals which are defined in Article 12 of the Constitution as follows: "In the U.S.S.R. work is the obligation and a matter of honor of every able-bodied citizen, in accordance with the principle, 'He who does not work, neither shall he eat.' In the U.S.S.R. the principle of socialism is realized, 'From each according to his ability, to each *according to the work performed*.'" Thus, the practice of gradation of reward for services performed is clearly recognized. Differences in pay, housing, clothing and social benefits and special forms of recognition (including epaulettes and aiguillettes) whether in the armed forces or in civilian life, are in no sense a betrayal of Constitutional principles, or any innovation suggesting a "return to capitalism."

Article 4 of the Constitution states that, "The economic foundation of the U.S.S.R. is the socialist ownership of the implements and means of production firmly established as a result of the liquidation of the capitalist system of economy, the abolition of private property in the implements and means of production and the abolition of the exploitation of man by man." And Article 4 defines "socialist property" in the U.S.S.R. as either state-owned (the possession of the whole people) or co-operative and collective farm property. Have these fundamentals been affected by recent changes? They have not.

Article 9 states that, "Alongside the socialist system of economy, the law permits small private economy of individual peasants and handicraftsmen based on their personal labor and precluding the exploitation of the labor of others," while Article 10 guarantees citizens the right to personal property in their income, savings, dwelling houses and household economy and personal possession, "as well as the right of inheritance" of such personal property. These basic principles have not been changed.

Finally, in Article 11: "The economic life of the U.S.S.R. is determined and directed by the state plan of national economy for the purpose of increasing the public wealth, of steadily raising the material and cultural level of the toilers, and of strengthening the independence of the U.S.S.R. and its power of defense."

We do not have to look far to discover that the realization

219

of planning has been the foundation of Soviet success, and not only in terms of production and defense. A little-noticed fact outside Soviet Russia is that despite its total war against Hitler the state budget of 1944 actually planned for a greater expenditure for educational purposes than for "power of defense." As far as I know, this was true of no other country at war.

So much for the economic organization of society. Until there is a sharp reversal of policy in at least one of the foregoing respects, there can be no ground for supposing that Russia is "going capitalistic."

I cannot here enter into detailed analysis of the whole Constitution, but readers should know that it defines the U.S.S.R. as a "voluntary association of Union Republics," each with its territories, autonomous regions, and autonomous Soviet Republics. In some ways it resembles the United States of America, but one very important difference is that the U.S.S.R. is not limited, by name or by implication, to any one or even two continents. Another difference is that member Republics of this Union can now enjoy separate diplomatic and military organizations and representations at home and abroad, a very significant fact which is discussed elsewhere.*

According to the Constitution, the highest organ of state power is the Supreme Soviet, which is elected by popular ballot throughout the Union. It exercises the legislative power and consists of two chambers, the Soviet of the Union and the Soviet of Nationalities, which correspond somewhat to the American Senate and House of Representatives. The Supreme Soviet meets twice a year, or at its own discretion. It elects the Supreme Court, which is the highest judicial organ; it elects the Procurator of the U.S.S.R., potentially a very important gentleman; and it elects its own Presidium of the Supreme Soviet.

The Presidium dismisses and appoints the members of the Council of People's Commissars of the Soviet Union, acting on the recommendation of the Chairman of the Council, who is Josef Stalin. The Council of Commissars is, in effect, Russia's Cabinet, and the highest executive and administrative organ of the state power. Similar organs in each Union Republic, autonomous Republic, territory, region and locality, are responsible to their own Soviets elected by popular vote.

Such is the Constitutional system and such is the system which

* See p. 252.

in fact exists and functions. Inside it and beyond and above and around it at every point there is, of course, the Communist Party. But it is only when you get down to definitions of the "fundamental rights and duties," of citizens, and examine the electoral system, that you see how control of the Communist Party is secured and how the system departs from democracy or dictatorship elsewhere. I shall come to that.

Meanwhile it should be noted that in some fundamentals the Soviet Constitution promises more than our own Constitution. It guarantees citizens (regardless of class or racial origin) the right to work and fair compensation, to rest and play and a seven-hour working day, to maintenance in sickness and old age, and to free primary and higher education.* On the whole those securities were steadily being realized before the war. Constitutional guarantees also include the right to freedom of speech, press and assembly, "in conformity with the interests of the toilers and in order to strengthen the socialist system." But we shall see the severe limitation on that right, in examining the role of the party dictatorship.

Citizens of the U.S.S.R. are "guaranteed inviolability of person," but this is qualified to mean that "No person may be placed under arrest except by decision of court or with the sanction of the procurator." Since procurators are "independent of any local organs whatsoever," and are in effect subservient to the will of the secret police of the N.K.V.D. (or People's Commissariat of Internal Affairs) this guarantee is of little value to anyone found in opposition to the state. The same qualification also applies in practice to the guarantee of rights of inviolability of the home and "secrecy of correspondence." Both articles lack the solemn dignity and reality of our own Constitutional guarantees against unreasonable seizure and search.

There are five other important differences between the Soviet citizen's rights and our own. First, we have seen that the state is frankly founded on the socialist ownership of property. Our Bill of Rights prohibits the use of private property of all kinds without just compensation by law. The Soviet Constitution defends just the opposite principle, the socialization of all property, with the exceptions already noted. It condemns as "enemies

* Tuition was required in secondary schools after 1940 for students whose scholarship fell below certain standards entitling them to government subsidy.

221

of the people" persons who in any way encroach on the system of socialist property.

Secondly, the Soviet Constitution guarantees "the equality of the rights of citizens of the U.S.S.R., irrespective of their nationality or race, in all spheres of economic, state, cultural, social and political life." It makes discrimination of all kinds, "on account of nationality, as well as the advocacy of racial or national exclusiveness or hatred and contempt, punishable by law." This Article, 123, is strictly enforced. Our own 15th Amendment contains no such explicit guarantee, nor can we Constitutionally punish people for preaching doctrines of racial hatred and contempt. The war has been a vindication of the wisdom of Article 123 and a demonstration of the unity and strength which realization of it has brought to the Soviet Union.

"Women in the U.S.S.R. are accorded equal rights with men in all spheres of economic, state, cultural, social and political life. The possibility of exercising these rights of women is ensured by affording women equally with men the right to work, payment for work, rest and leisure, social insurance and education, and by state protection of the interests of mother and child, maternity leave with pay, and the provision of a wide network of maternity homes, nurseries and kindergartens" (Article 122). There is no such explicit guarantee in the American Constitution.

Are the Soviets "abandoning" that principle of sex equality? Allowing for physiological differences, Soviet women are today doing everything that men do. They have the same opportunities for work in the fields or factories, and the same chance to compete for scholarships in the higher schools where co-education continues. The decision to separate boys from girls in the primary schools does not abridge women's rights. Obviously the guarantee of *equality* of rights cannot in every sphere and at every stage of life mean the guarantee of identity of rights, unless socialism is expected to produce men with wombs, or women without them. The decision to abandon co-education in the lower grades had nothing to do with Soviet socialism, one way or another.

A fourth basic difference is that our Bill of Rights forbids Congress to make any law "respecting any establishment of religion, or prohibiting the free exercise thereof," while the Constitution of the U.S.S.R. guarantees that "the Church is separated from the state and *the school from the Church.* Freedom of *religious worship* and freedom of anti-religious propaganda are

222

recognized for all citizens." My italics indicate the degree of religious freedom in the Soviet Union as distinguished from the United States, where the right to "free exercise" of faith permits the Church to intervene in many temporal affairs, including education, the press, business and politics. Note that there is no promise in the U.S.S.R. of any rights to the Church or the clergy, not even the freedom to conduct "religious propaganda" to counteract the "freedom of anti-religious propaganda."

Has this attitude toward the Church been fundamentally changed? Was the restoration of the Patriarchate of the Orthodox Church at Moscow in any sense a restoration of the old alliance between the clergy and the state which existed in Tsarist times and such as exists in Spain today?

While I was in Russia not only the Metropolitan of the Orthodox Church invoked the aid of the Lord in the "holy crusade" against Nazism, but the head of the Jewish and Mohammedan Churches did likewise and called upon the faithful to slaughter the "bestial invaders." Each one of them, in separate encyclical notices, was careful to describe Stalin as "the chosen of God." The Soviet press gave wide publicity to these statements, thereby recognizing their value in promoting loyalty and patriotism. At the same time public attacks on religion virtually ceased.

Even before the war the Communists began to relax their anti-religious drive. A canvass of the population had astonished them when it was revealed that nearly half the population still believed in God. Now the promise of a hereafter was for millions of bereaved people a faith which made bearable the desolation of present grief. The government recognized the moral value of this assurance and in demanding full co-operation from the older people it further softened its attitude toward the Church.

It should be understood that this concession came only after the successful "liquidation" of Church power in secular affairs. Atheism is still taught in the schools and, as far as I could learn, the younger generations seemed nearly 100% atheist. I cannot say how far the reality here conforms to the appearance. But the Church certainly is no longer an economic power; it can in no way control or influence the people's livelihood or threaten the socialist system. So if the Kremlin now looks upon the Church more benignly, it may be because it can without fear employ it as an organization amenable to its political will. The Kremlin is not unmindful of the value of the good will of the Patriarch

223

in Moscow, and of his usefulness in reconciling Slav-orthodox elements in neighbor countries—Greece, Turkey, Rumania, Bulgaria, Yugoslavia and, to a lesser extent, in Czecho-Slovakia, Poland and the Baltic States—to Soviet leadership in Europe.

We come now to the fifth and perhaps the most basic difference between the Soviet Union and this country. Our Federal Constitution does not recognize any political party, it does not even determine the qualifications of voters. These matters are decided by individual states. But the Soviet Constitution, while ensuring the right of the people to unite in various public organizations, recognizes only one political party. "The most active and politically conscious citizens in the ranks of the working class and other strata of the toilers unite," states Article 126, "in the Communist Party of the Soviet Union (Bolsheviks), which is the vanguard of the toilers in their struggle to strengthen and develop the socialist system and which represents the leading core in all organizations of the toilers, both public and state."

The Constitution furthermore provides that candidates for election to the Soviets can only be nominated by Communist Party organizations, and by "public organizations and societies of toilers: trade unions, co-operatives, youth organizations and cultural societies." Membership in the latter totals many millions, probably a generous majority of the population, and many minor and even some highly responsible positions in the Soviets are held by non-Party electees. But since the Party "represents the leading core" in all such recognized "public organizations," no candidate of whom the Communists disapprove would in practice be elected to office.

Thus the directive power of the state rests with some 4,300,-000 Communist Party members and candidates, and, to a lesser extent, with about fifteen million Komsomol members,* who now include youths up to the age of twenty-nine. Thus the Constitution, both explicitly and implicitly, establishes the Communist Party as the super-power. And thus it can and does control the State from the bottom right through to the Central Committee of the Communist Party, and to its own "leading core," the Political Bureau.

Among responsible Communists there is no attempt to disguise that fact. The Webbs in their own monumental work**

* Membership in the C.P. greatly increased during the war. The estimate of Komsomols was given me by Olga Mishakova, one of its secretaries.
** *Soviet Communism: A New Civilization.*

quote Stalin as follows: "In the Soviet Union, in the land where the dictatorship of the proletariat is in force, no important political or organizational problem is ever decided by our Soviets and other mass organizations without directives from our Party. In this sense we may say that the dictatorship of the proletariat is, substantially, the dictatorship of the Party as the force which effectively guides the proletariat."

As the supreme leadership of the socialist state, then, the Politburo naturally also directs not only the economic and social life of the nation, but also the armed forces, which are at the moment greatest of all Soviet "mass organizations." Some people suppose that the war has created or will create an "army leadership" as separate and rival to "party leadership." What is the actual fact? "There have been changes in the army command during the war," wrote Walter Kerr, the *Herald Tribune's* Moscow correspondent, in his brilliant book, *The Russian Army,* but "not only has the army failed to move in on the political leadership but the political leadership has moved in on the army. At the start of the war only one of the fourteen (members of the Politburo) held military rank. Now five of them wear uniform." And all down the line you find leaders in the Party organs similarly identified in rank with the staff and combat command.

All the foregoing seems to answer questions about whether Soviet Russia is adhering to its constitutional promise of a "socialist state." In the main it is. Nor do the "revival of Russian nationalism," the glorification of symbols and institutions of historic Russia, mean the abandonment of the basic principle of a union of many nations. It is natural that in this war the press and propaganda should not overlook the emotional enthusiasm which can be aroused by appeals invoking *Russian* history and culture. After all, the R.S.F.S.R. (Russian Soviet Federative Socialist Republic) itself accounts for about four-fifths of the area and nearly three-fifths of the total population of the Soviet Union.

What many people failed to note, however, was that all the other "nationalisms" of the various Union Republics were being similarly glorified in their own territories, to identify patriotism with the defense of the Soviet Fatherland. Because they did overlook that fact, those who had convinced themselves that "Russian nationalism" was somehow displacing Communism (or Sovietism, Stalinism, or constitutional socialism) in the Soviet Union, were caught off balance in February, 1944. In that month the Supreme

Soviet, meeting in Moscow, adopted the changes which gave increased powers of autonomy to all the sixteen Republics of the Union—changes which opened up broad perspectives for expanded relationships of the U.S.S.R. with the rest of the world in general and its neighbors in particular.

What will that decision mean in terms of Soviet Russia's foreign policy and our ability to co-operate with it? To answer that we must first know a little more about Soviet domestic policy and the new and old needs which determine it. More precisely, let us have a closer look at the staggering tasks of reconstruction that face Russia, and how she proposes to face them.

III

Rebuilding a Continent

ALTHOUGH Russia covers a sixth of the surface of the earth, few Americans in the past thought of it as a great market for our products. Perhaps this was because too many of us were looking at maps on which Russia was labeled "Enigma." But now it seems that the "Enigmamen" who live over there are *homo sapiens* too, with the normal appetites of customers. And they are going to need everything from washers to washing machines after Hitler, on his way home, has destroyed most of what remains.

It is not my purpose here to argue how many angels can dance on a socialist needle, nor to minimize Russia as a factor in our post-war economy. Obviously America can and will "do business with Stalin," as the cliché goes, as long as we have something essential to a Soviet scheme of things, a scheme laid down in the master plan of development drawn up by the big nation's rulers. But note this carefully: not what the individual Russian consumer or particular region or group may want to buy from us, but what the State plan requires for its fulfillment, will determine the size and nature of the Soviet market.

In that respect, and it is fundamental, there has been no

change whatsoever in Soviet policy. The complex needs of the whole nation as seen by the Soviet State Planning Commission, then, govern the role of foreign trade in Soviet reconstruction. On the face of it, those needs are prodigious; but the Russians intend to answer them in ways which will most quickly secure "the techno-economic independence of the country building socialism in a capitalist environment"—which was and remains a basic Soviet principle.

In addition to the extensive destruction in its Western territory, which I have already described, the Soviet Union's pre-war industrial needs have been aggravated. Maintenance and normal replacement have been neglected. All machinery has carried excess loads and is rapidly becoming obsolete or worthless. Harbors and ports under construction have been ruined or work on them is halted. And the Red Navy and the merchant fleet require speedy rehabilitation, for Russia is determined to become a maritime power commensurate with her size and length of coastline.

Public buildings everywhere have fallen into disrepair. All new housing construction, except that essential to the war effort, ceased in July, 1941. Repairs are needed on a vast scale to make habitable even many of the buildings now standing and thousands of new homes must be built for people literally living in holes in the ground. Everybody's clothes are worn out or wearing out. For over two years practically no garments but uniforms have been produced. Many thousands of people are now walking on paper soles stuffed in their only shoes.

Against the broad canvas of devastation which Russia will present at the end of the cataclysm, how do people there feel about the forbidding outlook? For millions of men and women now middle-aged, who for two decades worked prodigiously to build up a land of socialist plenty, and for millions of old people who were bent to the yoke of collectivism with the promise of economic freedom, the prospect now means resignation to many more years of the bitterest kind of drudgery and toil. The reward of their labor which otherwise should have brought them the "rich life" has instead burned up in the smoke of war. For older Russians the future must appear somber with the knowledge that the great abundances will not come in their lifetime. But among Russian youth, at least, and it is chiefly a job of youth that lies ahead, there is little defeatism and plenty of enthusiasm and high hope. Their Communist elders have convinced them it's

227

going to be wonderful to tackle something on just as big a scale as confronted their revolutionary paters.

"There can be giants among us, too!" exclaim the Komsomols, with blazing eyes.

Foreign observers in Moscow often speculated on the time needed to get Russia back to its pre-war condition. Estimates among us varied from fifteen to thirty years. But the natives I talked to on the subject were more optimistic. They considered it would be an easier job than reconstruction after the First World War. Some Russian Communists told me that as far as getting back to the level of *pre-war industrial production* they could fully recover within five years!

"Our problems won't be nearly as difficult as they were at the end of the last war and the Civil War," a Russian pointed out to me. "At that time we had almost complete paralysis of production and complete disorganization of distribution. We had little industrial plant and only a small percentage of it was heavy industry. We had few technicians and skilled workers. The war had penetrated everywhere and there was widespread famine. Battles had been fought in the Caucasus, the Ukraine, the Donbas, the Urals, in Siberia, and along the Volga. No part of the country was untouched. It took us about seven years to create order out of the chaos."

Viewed from that angle, things could be a lot worse. By far the larger area of the country has been physically unaffected and several mighty bases of production remain intact. In some of them, as the reader has noticed, construction has out-distanced all enemy efforts at destruction elsewhere and real net gains have already been registered in production. Another point: the three Five-Year Plans placed great emphasis on the development of reproductive industry. Production of the means of production was over 60% of the total industrial output—which was twelve times greater, incidentally, than during World War I. By 1941 machine-making accounted for about 25% of all Soviet industrial production. This last was enormously important in the battle against Germany and will be likewise in the battle of reconstruction.

New mineral and agricultural resources have been opened up and when the lost lands are won back Russia will be richer in those respects also than in 1941. The mechanization of agriculture in some backward areas has been completed. Though war wrecked thousands of railway buildings, installations, and rolling stock, elsewhere it hastened their construction. As the battle line moved westward, much of the damage to transport was of necessity speedily repaired. Here American aid was of first importance. Instead of facing foreign intervention and blockade, the Soviet Government now gets billions of dollars worth of Lend-Lease materials from us—a good percentage of which is of permanent reconstructive value.

"Don't forget, also," said a Russian economist I know, "that we shall be the victors this time, and a country can rebuild a lot faster with victory than it can against a background of defeat. The Germans have used slave labor in Europe to tear down the Soviet Union in war. We shall have plenty of jobs for them when it comes to building up our country in peace."

No one could foresee how much German labor would be left to mobilize for the tasks of Soviet reconstruction, but Moscow made clear its intention of utilizing it. The well-known Soviet economist, Eugene Varga, who frequently speaks for the Kremlin, estimated that it would take a decade for ten million Germans, working twenty-four hours a day, to repair the damage Hitler has done to Russia. Varga recommended the widespread employment of German labor in payment of reparations, which he thinks may run into the neighborhood of 260 billion dollars when all the Allied claims are entered. In addition to the use of "war criminal" and ex-Nazi (and possibly some Rumanian, Hungarian and Finnish) labor, the Russians may transport certain German industries to Soviet soil, although they have disavowed any intention of "annihilating" German industry. Very probably the Soviet Planning Commission has already decided upon the amount of reparations to be demanded of Germany and the methods whereby their demands can and must be met.

Which leads us to the last and most dramatic differences between Russia's preparedness and ability to recover today, and her position after World War I—the results of Soviet planning.

IV

Russia's Next Plan

··◦〗[〖◦··

THE richest inheritance of this post-war generation of Russians is the existence of a stable administration, politically experienced, technically skilful, and sure of its objectives and of the methods of achieving them. Today there are no more classes to be liquidated, no more internal battles to be fought on the grand scale. There is no organized internal opposition.

Despite severe losses on the battlefield and in the Nazi terror behind the lines, the Soviet Union will be able to mobilize a far greater number of skilled workers and technicians than Lenin commanded in 1923. The fact that there are more skilled industrial workers in Russia now than before the present war, as officials claimed, was made possible, basically, because of a system of education which reduced illiteracy from about 60% in Lenin's time to less than 5% today.

Even before the war, 40% of the students in Russian universities were women. Since large numbers of males went into the Red Army, women in the higher and secondary schools are said to account for well over half the total. Many of these girls and women are learning to become technicians. It was officially stated that 80% of the doctors graduated in 1943 were women. The percentage of women was also high among scientists and engineers.

I have already explained how Soviet education is turning the whole of the nation's youth into skilled technicians. About 75,000 new industrial, transport and communication engineers, physicians, agronomists and other specialists were graduated from Soviet schools in 1942, according to Sergei Ogoltsov, head of higher education in the U.S.S.R. The number increased in 1943. So the Russians do not expect to need any post-war outside engineering assistance, or at any rate nothing comparable to the early days.

"We shall want only a little help from the foremost specialists in the very latest techniques developed in America during the war," I was authoritatively told. But even here the Russians propose to do the job themselves. They now prepare hundreds of selected students to send to this country for advanced study. The vanguard began to arrive as early as 1942.

A Komsomol girl was my guide to some of the schools I visited. She was Vera Smirnova, a charming girl of twenty-two, blonde, very feminine and very competent. But I had known her some time before I discovered that Vera was the daughter of illiterate peasants and had won her way through the higher schooling system entirely on scholarships. She was a graduate engineer, had designed subway cars for the new Metro, and helped build the defense works which stopped German tanks outside the capital.

I questioned Vera and some young technical students for hours. From these talks I got two powerful impressions about modern Russia. One is that the average intelligent youth today is almost totally unconscious of any barriers other than his own ability which could prevent him from learning to do any job for which scientific knowledge could prepare him. He is also sure of his ability to assume responsibility. These Russian youths cry for responsibility! The other impression is that just because it thus draws upon the widest masses of youths for its professional people of tomorrow, the Soviet government has no fear that this war will "drain off its best blood" or "kill off irreplaceable leaders."

In tackling its tasks the Soviet government will follow general principles laid down in the Five-Year Plans of the past. Housing and other human needs cannot be wholly ignored, but replacement and further development of heavy industry of all types will come first—restoration of the oil and mining enterprises, the erection of power plants and new iron and steel works, construction of basic reproductive industries and factories for making the means of transportation and mechanized farm machinery.

A. Shcherbakov, of the Politburo, told me that "machines to make machines" would have priority over everything else in Russia's imports from the United States, though she would need some commodity goods, too, in the first year or two.

But once the war ends, Russians state, existing light industry can fairly quickly satisfy the more urgent needs for processed foods, wearing apparel, household goods and articles of personal use. Industrial co-operatives are to be encouraged on a much wider scale, Mr. Shcherbakov said. New fields of light industry apparently will be opened to organizations of that type, particularly for returned soldiers, and there will be permitted a fairly large open market. To that extent, private initiative may get a new lease of life; though, of course, industrial co-operatives in Russia are fundamentally like everything else—state enterprise.

Despite the war, a great part of the Third Five-Year Plan was realized, and the fact that it was designed to meet strategic defense needs made it possible to adhere to its basic principles. The latter were summarized for me in Moscow in this order: (1) the utmost possible distribution of productive forces over the wide territory of the Soviet Union, with industry located near sources of raw materials and consumption wherever possible, to level out the national economy and eliminate unnecessary haulage; and (2) emphasis on the development of economically backward sections and national regions of the U.S.S.R.

In practice, that meant concentration of new capital construction in the Eastern and Southern parts of the U.S.S.R. For example, three-quarters of the total new blast furnaces were to be built in the Urals and Siberia. A comprehensive new metallurgical base was to arise in the Far East, fully capable of meeting the needs of the entire area. A second Baku was to be opened up between the Volga and the Urals. And those aims were, in fact, accomplished.

One day I asked a middle-aged Russian Communist who had spent several years in our country, "In what way do you consider the Soviet Union better prepared for the future than America?"

He answered instantly, "The unquestioned acceptance here of national economic planning. This is the main factor which will help us recover from the war in a few years. One must stress that again and again, because it means there are no contradictory interests which can interfere with the logical development of post-war economy."

There are no contradictory interests, simply because the principle of opposition is denied by the whole Communist Party dictatorship. It is the same whether it involves an individual Ukrainian worker who might want to build a house for himself rather than apply his labor on the erection of a new turbine in accordance with the plan, or the case of a political group which might want to restore private trade and capitalism, rather than support state monopolies.

Such is the price the individual pays for whatever benefits he or his children may get from Soviet planning. In fairness, it must be admitted that it is not so high a price in Russia as it would be

232

here. Many Russians actually are unaware of being deprived of such rights, since they never enjoyed them in our sense in the past. Many are on the contrary genuinely grateful for immensely greater equality of opportunity than Russians ever had before.

It cannot be stressed too often that, the important thing to remember is that the Soviet Union is a nation inhabited by peoples who were Russians long before Socialism was even a theory, and that these men and women are the product of only twenty-five years of Socialism—and it is Russian Socialism—as against centuries of Tsarist political absolutism following centuries of Mongolian despotism. It is only in that perspective that we can get an objective understanding of present Soviet methods and how and why they work.

In America and Britain we have evolved our own methods out of our own political history, different in so many respects from that of Russia. It is hardly necessary to emphasize that here the rights of political opposition are a fundamental tenet of a democratic faith, jealously guarded and improved for more than 160 years. We could not abandon that principle without scrapping our political heritage. But to keep it also means enormously complicating the difficulties of economic planning without which no state in the future can long survive. It is just that necessity always to reconcile an opposition, which is the price we in our turn pay for our form of political democracy, that the Russian Communist I quoted meant by the term "contradictory interests."

In other words, under the Soviet system they have a small all-powerful group which can decide how many locomotives to make; how many power plants to build, and where; how many sewing machines to produce, and how many needles. They can decide how many engineers are needed at Sverdlovsk and how many doctors in Tashkent and how many reindeer in Yakutsk and put them there, just as they can decide what factory machinery to take out of Germany and how many German prisoners are needed to rebuild the cities, and who is to manage both.

Also, Russia does not have competing interests seeking foreign markets and there is no need to reconcile different pressure groups to a particular trade policy. There is but one vested interest: the state trade monopoly. Stalin calls it "one of the unshakable foundations of the Soviet government." Russia possesses within its boundaries virtually everything needed to build a powerful modern state. No individual makes any profits out of trade and the state monopoly is not after large exports and imports, or small, *per se.* What it seeks is simply to export enough goods to balance the imports required to strengthen Russia's economic independence in accordance with objectives planned for a particular period.

That peculiar feature of Soviet foreign trade was dramatically demonstrated during the depression years, 1929 to 1932. World trade then declined by 25.5%, but exports and imports of the Soviet Union increased by 26.6%, simply because the state plan required them to. Thereafter the general volume of world trade increased, but Russia's exports and imports declined by about two-thirds.

During the early period, which coincided with the First Five-Year Plan, Russia imported large amounts of machine-building machines and equipment for chemical and electro-technical industries. She had to export to acquire exchange. In the later period, Soviet heavy industry was already able to make most of its needs in machines. Just before the war the Soviet Union was thus able to stop exporting raw materials and agricultural products and instead sell industrial goods and machinery abroad. Some of those Soviet exports were for the first time used to balance imports of "luxuries." This indicated that the achievement of self-sufficiency and "techno-economic independence" of industry need not exhaust the Soviet Union as a market for foreign goods.

Even before the war the United States sold more to Russia than she bought from any other nation. It was not then a very large item in America's total trade; in the best year, 1938, Russian purchases amounted to only $69,691,000, which was less than the Philippines, or China, or ten other countries, imported from the United States. Compare it with our exports of Lend-Lease goods to Russia since 1941. By January 1, 1944, we had shipped Russia $4,243,804,000 worth of war equipment, food, industrial machinery and other necessities.

The conclusion to be drawn is not that war is the only means of stimulating Soviet-American trade, however, according to *War and the Working Class.* In February, 1944, that Kremlin mouthpiece declared that future "trade with the Soviet Union can without doubt be profitable for England, the United States, Canada and other countries. Our country can be for them—if sane attitudes are taken toward business—a voluminous and stable market such as most likely no other customer would ever be . . . [but] it is plain the size and structure of our imports will depend considerably upon the size and condition of credits allowed to the Soviet Union."

Russians in Moscow insisted to me that the Soviet Union could provide a large and profitable market for the United States, if we extended to them long-term low-interest credits and made it possible for Russia to export goods to us sufficient at least to meet interest payments. They were, of course, speaking of peace-time arrangements. No official pronouncement has yet been made concerning Russia's position nor anybody else's with respect to Lend-Lease repayments, and the report that Stalin told Donald Nelson that the United States would be reimbursed in goods as well as on the battlefield was a canard. I asked Mr. Nelson about that and he gave me these facts:

"When I talked with Marshal Stalin in Moscow about possible post-war transactions between the United States and Russia he made the point that any obligations contracted by Russia in connection with post-war rehabilitation would be repaid in full. This statement was later misinterpreted by the American press to cover wartime Lend-Lease as well as post-war transactions. I have since been at pains several times to make it clear that Marshal Stalin's statement was specifically aimed at the question of post-war trade."

There is no doubt that this huge state, owning vast industrial and natural resources, could find plenty of things to export in exchange for her needs from the United States. It must be remembered also that Russia's State Bank is now believed to have very considerable reserves of gold. While the man who thinks of the Soviet Union as a permanent high-profit "panacea market" is simply listening to his own Charlie McCarthy, there is no reason to ignore its first-rate importance in planning a "way out" for American industry in the critical post-war years.

Josef Stalin will probably make the final decision in future trade arrangements with us, but he will lean heavily on the advice of a scintillating little Armenian who may soon become better known in Britain and America. He is Antastas Inavonvich Mikoyan, who heads the Soviet Foreign Trade Monopoly. Mikoyan is immensely popular in Russia as the man who organized the pre-war Soviet food industry so well that rationing was abolished. He is the only member of the Politburo, other than Molotov, who has visited the United States. Others stand higher in the Politburo, historically, and momentarily he is somewhat obscured by military stars, but many consider Mikoyan a likely successor to Stalin, if his fellow Caucasian were for any reason to leave the scene.

Mikoyan is said to have furnished much of the brains behind the Soviet Fifteen-Year Plan which was projected just before the war. It envisaged very widespread reorganization and technical improvements in Soviet production, with more generous reward to the most skilled performances in every field. This plan is probably the basis of the long-view blueprints of reconstruction which Russia is already putting into effect. Among other things, it promised that Soviet Russia would equal and surpass the United States in every line of production, before 1960. Very likely the goal —and the date—remain the same in spite of the war.

Such is the "logic of things," to use Stalin's phrase, which should breathe economic life into the body of a "long peace" and furnish a basis for the close Soviet-American co-operation necessary to maintain it. But what about the logic of feeling? Does the emotional climate in Russia favor Americans? What do they think of us?

V

What Russians Think of Us

IN THE winter of 1943 William Harrison Standley, then American Ambassador in Moscow, startled us out of our comfortable enjoyment of a log fire in his study. He said the Russian people were being "bamboozled" about the importance of American participation in the war and "were not being given the facts about American aid to Russia," and he said it for publication.

Some people interpreted this outburst to mean that the Soviet government was hostile to Americans, while others looked for sinister American anti-Soviet purposes behind it. The fact was simpler. Standley is convinced that the world can enjoy a long spell of peace provided there is co-operation between the United States and Russia, based on mutually improved knowledge between us. He just decided it was time to widen the breach in the dam through which such knowledge ought to pour. Usually a mild-mannered and gentle soul, he has his old-seadog moments and this was one of them. He chose the direct method of blasting open a passage. Contrary to the impression in America, Russian officials weren't particularly annoyed. No one likes a blunt attack better than Stalin. The Kremlin knew the Ambassador had a good case and must have believed he had no ulterior motives. After his outburst the trickle of ideas and information between us perceptibly improved.

But it was not simply an exchange of news the Admiral was after. He and our Military Attachés had been trying to get some military information out of Russia for months, without success. He thought we at least ought to know how our planes and tanks performed, in token of the gift of them. But in that respect his protest earned no dividends, as far as I know. The reasons for the Russians' reluctance to impart any useful military information to us lay in their long tradition of distrust and suspicion of foreigners, which was noted even in Tsarist times, and was accentuated after establishment of the Soviets. The attitude could not be changed overnight by Lend-Lease supplies. But I think Standley was essentially right in believing that it could, with patient persistence, eventually be improved.

Anti-Soviet newspapers in America undoubtedly still contribute to this mistrust and suspicion, and continue to exacerbate Russian feeling. The Russians are not sure how many Americans agree with them. All anti-Soviet comments are cabled back by *Tass* and every important Communist reads them, even though they are seldom published in the open press. In fact since we became allies little (if you except early second-front propaganda) has appeared in Russian newspapers which could arouse bad feeling against us. If the Russians reprinted some of the attacks made on them in this country the masses would be astonished at our ignorance. They would not suppose such views could be expressed in war without official support. But Standley's complaint was not that the Russian press was unfavorable but that little appeared about America at all.

Soviet news policy emphasized domestic events almost to the exclusion of everything else. Four or five papers of national circulation gave the people nearly all the news they got. They were only of four pages each, the paper shortage was severe, and only the last page carried foreign news. It was usually confined to one or two columns and was practically identical in all papers. Yet it was understandable that the government wanted to keep national thinking focused on the problem beside which all else paled to insignificance: the defeat of the enemy on Russian soil.

President Roosevelt's speeches appeared in full and were avidly read by the Russian public. Stettinius' reports on the operation of Lend-Lease, some official communiqués, and very important political events were also widely reported. But that was about all the Russians heard of us on our war effort, before the Moscow and Teheran Conferences. The British published their own newspaper in Russia, but we did not. Our O.W.I. was non-operative in the U.S.S.R. until Ambassador Harriman went over. At this writing Mr. Davis' organization is still without effective methods of reaching the Russian public.

Some American movies are more popular with the Russians than their own and provide perhaps the most vivid impression they get of America. Russians are tremendously impressed with the technical brilliance of American cinema productions and it is the ambition of Russian movie stars to get to Hollywood. The choice of films seems rather odd. *The Great Waltz, Merry Widow, The Four Musketeers* and a few other musical comedies and extravaganzas seemed to be the main diet, mixed with old Chaplin films, Mickey Mouse, Donald Duck and other Disney creations. Ideological considerations cause the rejection of many of our films. Even Disney's deer, *Bambi*, came in for heated criticism from Olga Mishakova. "Technically it is a superb film," she told me, "but the content is all wrong. It teaches youth that animals are man's enemies. We believe animals are man's friends."

"But I thought you Communists were realists," I replied. "After all, men do hunt animals, don't they?"

"Men hunt men, for that matter," she came back. "But we don't think it is right, normal or moral. We don't glorify it in our teachings. This is where we believe the educational policy of government should take control."

Theodore Dreiser is highly regarded as an artist and Hemingway has had a big influence on Russian writers. Neither one is as popular as Upton Sinclair. Translations of Mark Twain are now in their fourth million and Jack London's books have sold nearly seven million copies. It can hardly be said that Russians are permitted to read "nothing but propaganda" about America, when these and many other American classics are available. Since 1918 the Soviet publishing houses have published translations of more than 800 American books, in addition to the complete works of thirteen American authors, in all editions totalling more than thirty-six million volumes.

Talking to an electrical mechanic of sixteen one day I discovered he had read *The Valley of the Moon, The Sea Wolf,* and *Martin Eden* and had consumed three Dreiser books, three by Mark Twain and a volume of Hemingway. But he thought *Popular Physics,* a translation of an obscure American textbook, more interesting than any of them. How many American mechanics have read Tolstoy, Chekhov and Pushkin? I continually encountered among adolescents a better familiarity with American life acquired through reading American fiction than most American adults have of the U.S.S.R.

A wide selection of American technical journals was available in the Lenin Library. The Russians worship modern technique and regard America as the teacher of the world in industrial science. The ambition of any factory manager is to have it said that his plant is run with American efficiency—which might be called one of the chief goals of the whole Soviet industrialization program. Technical schools I visited were leaning heavily on American textbooks. Because the Soviet regime frankly expects to borrow from our industrial experience and to use the latest American machinery, the study of English now begins in the primary grades.

There was a great demand for a general book on America and one finally came out in the spring of 1943. It was called *The United States of America.* It sold out everywhere in one day and waiting thousands were turned away. "At the Sixteenth Party Congress," says this book, "Stalin characterized America as 'the main capitalist country.'" Throughout it speaks of the world as divided between capitalism and the U.S.S.R., and it is evident from this book that Russians still think of themselves as dwellers in a quite different universe. The book gives a Marxist interpretation of American economy, but its statistics seem correct and it is a work of objective scholarship which does not minimize the technological brilliance or the social and economic achievements of American capitalism. The same thing is true of a recently published book called *The Pacific Ocean.* Since no book may be published about a foreign country without the Kremlin's approval, such little straws are significant.

Russians admire American products of all kinds and dream

of the day when they can buy them, or Russian copies just as good. Give a Russian a slick-paper magazine and he immediately becomes lost in the advertisements picturing goods on sale. He cannot believe we take war seriously after he sees what Americans still buy and sell. I often wondered what their reaction to a "Monkyward" catalogue would be.

Many Russians daydream of a trip to America. There is sharp competition for scholarships offering a year or two of study here. Any Russian returning from America is questioned in the closest detail by his fellow workers or villagers. Hundreds of thousands of Russians have relatives in America who write back descriptions of life there. At the front Russian soldiers come up to ask you to look up their relatives. There are many thousands of American-born Finns in Karelia, and they talk a great deal about their former homeland. Millions read Ilf and Petrov's satirical but good-humored stories of *Little Golden America* and laughed and cried with us through them.

All the different sources of information about America I have mentioned probably tell the Russians more about American life than is generally supposed; but the government certainly does not give a complete picture of the American working man's life. If the average Russian could fully visualize the material comfort in which the American worker lives and the political freedom he enjoys, it would probably be a difficult thing to keep his mind on the stern goals set by the Soviet system, and to reconcile him to the tremendous hardships which still lie ahead for the next ten to twenty years.

Soviet youth at least can still look forward to reaping the rewards. But many of the older people who made such heavy sacrifices to build up the country must now feel heartbroken at the ruin around them, and at the realization that it must all be done over again, and that they cannot in their lifetime enjoy the peace and comforts of success. In Russia I often wondered how even some of the younger Communists would react to an exposure to life in prosperous war-time America, where those "classical contradictions of capitalism" appeared to be wiped out. These youths have never lived under a capitalist system and cannot know the deep personal hatred of it that animated the early bolsheviks. Their renunciation of its evils is purely theoretical.

Victor A. Kravchenko, a middle-aged Soviet Russian official in Washington, recently decided to remain in America, rather than

240

to return to Russia. "I confirmed my long suspicion," Kravchenko said, "that capitalist democracy as presented in propaganda at home, has no relation to the reality I found in the United States." Kravchenko denounced the Communist dictatorship and its denial of civil liberties and placed himself "under the protection of American public opinion." When you think of the years of dreary toil and self-denial awaiting them at home, the surprising thing is that hundreds of other Russians now abroad do not follow his example and "make the most of what we yet may spend."

Actually there is now going on a revision of official Marxist interpretation of the capitalist system as it functions in the United States. Whereas a decade ago it was considered that American capitalism was on the verge of collapse, Soviet economists now concede that it may yet have a long life ahead of it. One Moscow Communist astounded me by saying that Russian Marxists now speak of the possibility of "fifty years more of American capitalism." The main reason for this revision of opinion apparently lies in what Stalin called "the logic of things" (or the "logic of facts") as seen in the practical demonstration of a capitalist state co-operating with a socialist state in the most critical test, the test of a general war against the socialist state. Marxism and even Leninism did not foresee that possibility. Today it would seem utterly silly to go on adhering to the doctrine that the two systems of economy could not long co-exist, after this proof to the contrary.

One day when I was talking to A. Shcherbakov about the future of Soviet-American co-operation, I asked him, "Is not the fact that the greatest capitalist power, the United States, has supported the great socialist power, the Soviet Union, in a war against fascist imperialism, the most important historic event in a Marxist sense since the Russian Revolution? Does not this event in itself constitute a profound deviation from the development of history as foreseen in Lenin's work, *Imperialism?*" His response was prompt and unqualified in the affirmative.

On another occasion I spent an afternoon with P. F. Yudin, head of the Soviet State Publishing House, a prominent Russian economist, and one of the authors of the official Soviet history of Marxism. "It is proved," he told me, "that there is nothing in Marxism which need prevent progressive capitalist countries from co-operating closely with the Soviet Union in the economic and cultural spheres."

It is true that Marxism never denied that "bourgeois democracy" is a progressive system as compared to feudalism, but formerly it was contended that capitalism had exhausted its possibilities with the advent of "imperialism"—in the Leninist sense of that word. But candid facing of the fact that capitalism cannot be entirely "reactionary" since it has sided with the Soviet Union against fascism, was bound to find its reflection in official Marxist teaching. As the Communists also look forward to a long period of peacetime collaboration with the United States, it is necessary to place new emphasis on the progressive role of capitalist democracy —and this is exactly what is now happening in Soviet education.

At the same time the Russians adhere to their own system, and contend that Soviet socialism is the "highest" type of economic organization yet developed. They anticipate recurring economic crises in the capitalist countries in the form of unemployment and depressions. They still recognize that reactionary forces may again get the upper hand in Britain and America and may interfere with the economic co-operation needed to help rebuild Russia. They will still see any such anti-Soviet activity abroad as the work of "class enemies" of the "proletarian state."

"While there is no law of Marxism which prevents Russia from co-operating with capitalism," Yudin said to me, "we are not at all convinced that the American government is ready for any such thing or has the apparatus which can enforce it. Just consider, for example, the news in today's paper. Have you not read it? I refer to the news that the United States Congress has again rejected the President's proposal that a ceiling of $25,000 a year be placed on personal income. How far can a Congress which refuses to pass such a reasonable law as that during wartime be expected to give the President the authority needed for world planning in peacetime?"

However much they may dislike the regime and what it is trying to do, few Americans who have been to the U.S.S.R. do not pay tribute to Russian genius and like and admire Russians as people. Even Eddie Rickenbacker came out telling me, "The Russians are our kind of people. They are more like Americans than any other people in Europe." Russians generally like Americans, too; at least they seem less suspicious of us than other "people of the capitalist world." We have never fought against Russia except during the Allied intervention against Bolshevism and the Russians seem prepared to forget our part in that. In a book recently published by the government called *The Army of the Soviet*

Union, the Anglo-American role in the intervention is not mentioned.

Fortunately we are not connected in the Russian mind with the Munich period, the grievance of which still overcasts Anglo-Russian relations with suspicion. On the whole, the Russians are inclined to regard us as less devious diplomats, more frank and sincere, but also more naïve and inclined to be led by the British. They do still fear an Anglo-American bloc against them. President Roosevelt evidently went a long way to correct that impression in his meeting at Teheran, where he served in the role of mediator between the goading Stalin and the irascible Churchill, but more than one Teheran will be necessary to dispel deeply ingrained Russian suspicions.

Whenever you meet Russians in a setting free from distrust and with politics put aside, they do indeed seem more like Americans than almost any other European race. We both like the direct approach. We are expansive peoples, given to exaggeration and boasting, but also given to accomplishments on a stupendous scale, a similarity doubtless influenced by geography which in both America and Russia is one of wide limitless spaces full of challenge and possibilities. There is something else about the Russians, a generosity of spirit, an absence of that meanness and pettiness of soul you find in some Europeans, a mercurial temperament in minor matters but a wholehearted readiness to stake absolutely everything on a greatly felt issue. All of which strikes a response in most Americans.

In these paragraphs I have been speaking rather abstractly about what might loosely be called the "extra-political" sentiments of some Russians I know, and how we appear to them as peace-loving human beings pretty much as they see themselves. The convinced Communists among the Soviet population—who probably now include most people under thirty-five—think they have a better social system than we have, it is true. But no one now dreams of overthrowing the American system by force. Russian Communists are satisfied with the Stalinist principle that the best way of proving the superiority of socialism over capitalism is by making a triumphant success of it within the borders of the Soviet Union.

I believe the last thing on earth the average Russian wants, and here I would include Communists, is a war with the United States. Aside from ideological differences, there do not seem to exist between us any of the traditional causes of war. There are no vital territories in dispute between us. Both countries are virtually self-sufficient in raw materials and resources. There is little trade rivalry for the world market. Russia does not seek exports on a large scale, as we have seen, but on the contrary needs our machinery and has the means to pay for it.

In Russia the feeling against the idea of war with the United States is so manifest that even if, for some now inconceivable reason the Soviet government attempted to lead the people into some kind of aggression against us, it would most certainly end in fiasco. The Russian people would fight America only if our troops were demonstrably engaged in aggression against the continental territory of the Soviet Union, or in border regions of utmost strategic importance to it.

If that is correct then the only way a war could arise between us now would be as a result of an American denial by force of Russian strategic needs, rather than a Russian denial of the United States' needs in the Americas or on the world's highways. What are these Russian "needs"?

VI

What Russia Wants

FOR the accomplishment of Russia's main post-war task, which is reconstruction, a long peace is indispensable, and experience has taught Russians that another word for peace is security. They are determined to rid their frontiers of any menace of invasion—today and tomorrow and "for at least fifty years," some have told me. That is the first objective of all Soviet foreign policy, in Europe as well as in Asia.

Just as we want pro-American governments near us, and do not want hostile regimes, so the Soviets want friendly governments on their frontiers. But they fear insecurity more intensely than we do because they have not got two oceans nor even an English Channel protecting them from the Continent, and because their neighbors are not potentially incapable of invading them. If wars had been bred on our frontiers for generations, and if the last two of these wars had cost us over twenty million casualties, as they have Russia, we would doubtless take very decisive measures to immunize ourselves against a recurrence of the disease. It is improbable that we would permit Russia to tell us what measures were or were not justified.

Yet I do not see any reason to doubt that the Soviet leaders believe that a system of collective security would offer them the best possible environment for peaceful development. Long before this war Russia sought to establish the principle that "peace is indivisible." Soviet Foreign Commissar Litvinov tried for years to give the League of Nations a blood transfusion by proposing formation of an anti-aggressor front, not only for Europe but also for Asia, and the enforcement of a program of collective security. The world knows that the Anglo-French answer was the appeasement policy toward fascism, which led to this war. It is likewise not forgotten that the U.S. Congress refused to legitimatize Wilson's brain child, which was the League, refused to take part in enforcing peace on the new map of Europe which Wilson had helped to draw, and retreated into isolationism.

Soviet leaders today remain skeptical of the willingness and ability of Anglo-American governments to devise and support measures to eliminate war in Europe and to control its causes. Until there are convincing demonstrations to the contrary, Russia will remain in a position to safeguard herself by her own means, against a third war and against another interruption in her internal growth. Much as the Russians need our co-operation, they say, in effect, that they do not intend to wait for Congress to make up its mind whether and how it will preserve peace on the Soviet Union's frontiers. But in so far as concrete measures are proposed for establishing world security the Soviet leaders say they are eager to join in enforcing them. It must be admitted that thus far they have assumed every responsibility that we have offered to share with them.

After Russia was invaded she subscribed to the terms of the Atlantic Charter, renounced any intention of territorial aggrandizement and promised the right of self-determination to countries liberated from Axis control. In October, 1943, the Tripartite Conference at Moscow affirmed the will of Britain, Russia and the

245

United States to continue wartime collaboration into the peace and it also discussed "economic co-operation and the assurance of general peace." It envisaged a post-war "system of general security" and pledged that the Allied armies would not occupy the territories of other states, except for aims commonly agreed upon in the declaration "and after joint consultation," and it promised to confer later to secure post-war disarmament.

At Teheran the meeting of Stalin, Churchill and Roosevelt "shaped and confirmed our common policy," at the end of 1943, not only in war but in peace. "We recognize fully," said these three men to whom the earth looked for guidance and promises, "the supreme responsibility resting upon us and all the United Nations to make a peace which will command the good will of the overwhelming mass of the peoples of the world and banish the scourge and terror of war for many generations." They also surveyed the "problems of the future," and announced their determination to organize the world as a "family of Democratic Nations," dedicated "to the elimination of tyranny and slavery, oppression and intolerance."

In addition to such declarations the head of the Soviet government, Josef Stalin, on various occasions reiterated Russia's firm resolution not to seek territorial advantages. As early as November, 1941, he declared: "We have not nor can we have such war aims as the seizure of foreign territories or the conquest of other peoples, irrespective of whether European peoples or territories, or Asiatic peoples or territories, including Iran . . . We have not nor can we have such war aims as the imposition of our will and our regime on Slavic and other enslaved peoples of Europe who are waiting for our help. Our aim is to help these peoples in their struggle for liberation from Hitler's tyranny and then to accord them the possibility of arranging their own lives on their own land as they see fit, with absolute freedom."

And in April, 1944, Foreign Commissar Molotov reaffirmed this principle when the first concrete case arose as the Red Army surged across the frontier of Rumania: "The Soviet government declares it does not pursue the aim of acquiring Rumanian territory or of altering the existing social structure of Rumania."

As for the rest, it cannot yet be stated in more concrete terms what was decided at Moscow and Teheran. Very likely understandings were reached which would render academic some of the questions which exercised American commentators between Cassino and the major invasion of the Continent. It seems certain, for instance, that it was conceded all around the table that, while national boundaries of the three powers would not be expanded through aggression in this war, neither would any power be expected to give up sovereignty in territories where it was established before the power acceded to the Atlantic Charter.

Churchill had much earlier categorically stated this principle, when he declared that the Charter did not apply to India or any of the extensive colonial possessions of the Crown acquired prior to the enunciation of the Charter. And the Russians were equally emphatic about the immutability of their own frontiers as they existed prior to June, 1941.

The actual wording of the Charter recognizes "the right of all peoples to choose the form of government under which they will live," and expresses the "wish to see sovereign rights of self-government restored to those who have been forcibly deprived of them." That is rather loosely said, but unless all the nations are to submit to partitioning, it must be held to assume the validity of their pre-Charter boundaries. But many Americans apparently felt that Moscow was violating the spirit of the Atlantic Charter by retaining strips of frontier territory which she had repossessed between the time of Hitler's invasion of Poland and his attack on Russia. These critics thought that Russia should reconstitute the independent Baltic states, restore part of the Ukraine to Poland and return Bessarabia to Rumania.

Here I cannot examine in any detail the pros and cons of conflicting historical claims to these frontier regions. They are small in relation to the total area of the Soviet Union, but admittedly are of strategic importance to her as great as Panama, Puerto Rico, or the Hawaiian Islands are to us. It must be recognized that frontiers have nowhere yet been decided on the basis of ideal justice. In this case it is contendable that Russia has as strong a historical claim to her frontier areas as the United States would have to Texas, New Mexico and California in a hypothetical dispute with Mexico, and perhaps somewhat stronger than the British have to some parts of their Empire, or the Chinese have to Manchuria or Inner Mongolia.

Bessarabia was part of Russia for a century before Rumania grabbed it from a weakened Bolshevik regime which had to suffer many humiliations in order to gain what Lenin called "a breathing space." The Baltic area was torn from Russia by Germany under similar conditions and then taken over by the Allies after defeat of the Kaiser. It was divided at the Versailles Conference, which revived the long defunct state of Lithuania and created two new states entirely new to the map of Europe—Latvia and Estonia. This elaborate device was adopted pretty deliberately to create an "anti-Red buffer." They were freely recognized to block Russia from her access to the Baltic Sea, which Peter the Great had secured, after centuries of struggle. They all fell under anti-Soviet semi-fascist regimes which no more gave their people self-determination than Rumania did.

The same thing was true of Polish rule, but Poland did not go to war against Russia and the territorial issue is more complicated. In fact the "Polish question" agitated such a wide section of American opinion that its partisans really constituted a separate group of anti-Soviet opinion.

Before the last war Poland had been a vassal state of Tsarist Russia for generations, as had Finland also. Before that the frontier power had been now in Polish or German hands, now in Russian. Centuries ago the Poles invaded Russia as far as Moscow and for a short time ruled there. Finns and Swedes were once the lords of the whole Dnieper Valley. Before the Revolution the Russian bolsheviks promised self-determination to both Poles and Finns. Actually Poland was constituted as the result of the defeat of Tsarist Russia and then of Germany, and the subsequent victory of an anti-Red Polish army organized with Allied support, and under the guidance of Marshal Pétain.

Faced with both civil war and Allied intervention, the bolsheviks bought another "breathing spell" with a treaty which gave "White" Poland control over parts of Byelorussia and the Ukraine. This area lay far east of the line which an Allied commission had earlier determined as the limit of Polish ethnical influence—a division known as the Curzon Line after Lord Curzon became its chief advocate. Poles were admittedly a small minority* in that conquered area, where Byelorussians, Ukrainians and Jews predominated. But Russia continued to respect this frontier, until Hitler's invasion of Poland finally put on the Versailles Treaty structure the finishing touch of that destruction

* "Hardly 10% of the population," according to Sir Bernard Pares, in his *History of Russia*, N.Y., 1939. Other estimates place it somewhat higher; the Russians put it at still less.

which Anglo-French appeasement and American isolationism had already so far advanced.

It is significant to note that the Premiers of the British Cabinets in both world wars justified and approved of Russia's action in Poland. Churchill has described the Curzon Line as "clearly necessary for the safety of Russia" and Lloyd George even more vigorously supported it. "The German invasion," he said, "was designed to annex to the Reich provinces where a decided majority of the population was Polish by race, language and tradition. Russian armies marched into territories which were not Polish and which were forcibly annexed to Poland after the Great War despite fierce protests and armed resistance by the inhabitants. Inhabitants of the Polish Ukraine are of the same race and speak the same language as their neighbors in the Ukraine Republic of the Soviet Union . . . White Russia was originally annexed by Poland as a result of a victorious war against Russia."

Churchill and Lloyd George should know far more about the matter than I do, and I am prepared to accept their opinion. With such commitments behind him it was hardly possible for Churchill to quibble over Russia's frontier and there is no reason to suppose he did not concur in Stalin's position at Teheran. While Roosevelt expressed his partiality toward deciding the sovereignties of disputed territories by means of plebiscites conducted under an international authority, it is known he did not press Stalin when the Russian indicated that the frontier of 1941 was not open to re-examination.

What was anyway evident to us who were in Moscow when Russia broke off relations with the Polish government-in-exile in 1943, after a series of provocative articles in its press appeared in London, was the curious ineptitude of Polish diplomacy. It never seemed to realize that only Russian victory and the spilling of Russian blood could restore Poland as a state. The Red Army quite obviously would be in physical possession of all Poland at the end of the war and Soviet good will might be necessary even to permit the exiles to re-enter Warsaw. In spite of that fact the London Poles officially expressed their credence of Goebbels' story that the Nazis had discovered the corpses of hundreds of Polish officers allegedly executed by the Russians, and demanded an International Red Cross investigation.

In their continued attacks on Russia and insistence upon reclaiming part of the Ukraine the London Poles overlooked the

249

fact that they had originally taken that area from Russia by force of victory and that now the shoe was on the other foot. They ignored two other important facts. First, after the Soviet occupation of this region in 1939, the great estates of the imported Polish land barons, which Lloyd George called "the worst feudal system in Europe," were broken up and the land was redistributed to the peasants. This change alone made impracticable if not impossible the return of any regime which represented the interests of the exiled land barons. Secondly, since the regime-in-exile was never democratically elected by the Polish people, Russia might decide to recognize another regime set up on Polish soil. There was no commitment which would prevent Britain and the United States from eventually following suit and entrusting such a regime with the conduct of a plebiscite. That such a possibility occurred to Churchill was evident when in March, 1944, he publicly urged upon the Poles the wisdom of accepting Russia's offer to recognize the Curzon Line as a frontier.

As for Finland, it seems probable at this writing that a peace agreement may be reached which will enable her to keep most of her territory and sovereignty intact, despite her anti-Soviet alliance with Hitler—a fact which prevented Russia's allies from interceding on Finland's behalf.

But many people who recognize Soviet Russia's right to her pre-war frontier point out that it still excludes much former Tsarist Russian territory which the Red Army could permanently occupy. Despite the pronouncements by Stalin and Molotov, despite Moscow's adherence to the Atlantic Charter, despite sixteen years of Stalinist doctrine based upon the renunciation of "exporting world revolution," many people still distrust Russia's aims. What else does Russia want for "security"? She says she wants "friendly regimes" around her. What does she mean by friendly regimes?

I have no inside track to this, but Czecho-Slovakia seems worth studying as a place that seems to have the answer. Here is one country—which had the only truly democratic government in Eastern Europe—whose rights Russia consistently respected and with whom her relations were and remain cordial. The Czechs never permitted their land to become an anti-Soviet base and they never complained that Russia violated her pacts or tried to "bolshevize" them by force. So evidently small nations can live side by side with Russia if they observe the same rules of propriety.

Unfortunately there are not many people in Eastern Europe who have the political unity and economic experience and wisdom of the Czechs. The Balkan countries were before the war ruled by reactionary governments or *opera-bouffe* monarchs like King Carol, and their social systems were backward and semi-feudal. These non-democratic regimes led their people into disaster and there is little possibility that they will recover their power intact. Anti-fascist movements like Marshal Tito's in Yugoslavia are growing up in the fires of this war and will produce a new leadership at its end. In Rumania, Greece and Yugoslavia the underground has a strong native Communist background. It may be expected that the Red Army, when it comes into contact with such movements, will rely most upon this Communist element, and will directly support it during its military occupation.

It is obvious that the dissolution of the Comintern did not abolish the international character of the Communist movement, nor its adherence to doctrines enunciated at Moscow. Despite the absence of any central authority over other parties, the prestige of the Russian Communist Party and the Red Army is now so immense, and the associations of many years exercise such a powerful centrifugal pull, that Soviet policy as expressed through its public press in effect still serves as an international directive. It would be naïve to suppose that all diplomats are not aware of this. They also realize that various national liberation movements represented in Moscow are more or less rivals of the regimes-in-exile sponsored in London and Washington.

Such movements are not mere puppet organizations, or instruments of Soviet power, to be called into use to enforce an "alternative policy," in case of Soviet disagreement with the capitalist powers, or suppressed and ignored in the event of harmonious relations. They are, on the contrary, at all times integral with Russia's main policy and play a role in it directly in relation to the real mass following which they command in each particular case.

It is just as "natural" to expect the Russians to rely upon pro-socialist elements in extirpating fascism in territories entered by the Red Army as it is for us to expect Anglo-American armies entering France or Italy to rely upon elements there which believe in capitalist democracy. Everywhere in Europe there is, beneath the surface of the national war against fascism, a certain amount of struggle for dominance going on between adherents of two dif-

ferent systems. The Red Army could no more set up a pure capitalist system and make it work than General Eisenhower could be
expected to set up a Communist system in France or Germany.
It is all very well to say that neither army will interfere in the
internal politics of the occupied countries, but in practice such a
thing as a political vacuum can never long exist. What actually
happens is that during the period of military occupation the
authorities favor one element or the other element to assist it, and
naturally they tend to encourage adherents of the system most
familiar to them and which signifies stability to them.

The test of Russia's pledge not to seek territorial aggrandizement, and to give other states the freedom to choose their own
form of government, will not come during the period of occupation but after the war, when the Red Army withdraws to within
its own national boundaries. The test will be whether Russia uses
any form of coercion to include the states of Eastern Europe
inside her national boundaries, or whether, having disarmed the
fascists in the Balkans, Austria, Poland and Germany, she con-
fers with Britain and America on the methods whereby political
power is to be transferred to the inhabitants, as she has promised
to do, and abides by decisions secured through such consultations.

Aside from that, anyone with a sense of *realpolitik* can see,
however, that Russia's actual power position in Eastern Europe
may give her the main influence and responsibility there for at
least a generation ahead. Perhaps Russia could not avoid that position even if she wished to, any more than, say, the United States
could avoid enforcing the Monroe Doctrine. Small nations wedged
in between big neighbors have to lean one way or the other, and
just as the Low Countries fall into the British orbit, so Eastern
Europe is Russia's special concern. The community of interests
which exists cannot be altered by creation of a larger federation
of nations, although it can be stabilized by it.

The Soviets recognized that fact when they enacted the constitutional change granting the Union Republics "autonomy" in
foreign relations with other states. Essentially what this measure
accomplished was an increased flexibility in the machinery of
Soviet diplomatic policy as it affects frontier relationships. Among
other things it may in practice mean that the Communists in
Soviet Karelia may handle matters affecting Finland, that the
Soviet Baltics and the Ukraine and White Russia may seek close
direct ties with Poland and Prussia, that the Ukraine may do

similarly in the case of Rumania, Hungary, Austria, Bulgaria and Yugoslavia. Very wide explorations could take place in this way without embarrassing Moscow's relations with Britain and the United States. Mutual-defense pacts and economic pacts might be made; cultural, scientific and military missions exchanged; political bodies organized. Eventually these neighbor states might voluntarily and democratically merge into some new regional grouping of their own, or simply into a larger federation of democratic nations in Europe, if one is organized, or into the U.S.S.R. itself, if no international structure proves practicable.

But the key to Russian security in Eastern and middle Europe is not seen by the Russians to lie in control of any of the smaller countries, but in the industrial heart of the region, which is Germany. Historically every great invasion of Russia since the Middle Ages has come from Germany or has had its support. Russian Communists repeatedly told me that when Nazism and its roots are plucked out, fear of aggression will vanish from the map. We may take it for granted that the Soviets will do the job of extirpation at least as far as Berlin, which the Red Army intends to enter.

Obviously no agreement could have been reached at Teheran on concrete measures to be employed in Germany, since neither the Americans nor British at that time had forces on the Continent to compare with Russia's. But it is probable that Stalin made his own minimum conditions clear. He and other Russians have not attempted to make a secret of their main wishes about Germany. They want the country reduced in size to correspond roughly to the old state of Prussia. They will want the great capitalists who supported Hitler punished as war criminals and their heavy industry and other machinery, or what is left of it, given to Russia in the form of reparations.

Large numbers of German war criminals will be needed in Russia to help rebuild the cities they destroyed, but German children will not be penalized. The Russians will want them to attend schools where anti-Nazi teachings prevail. The Russians may favor permitting Germany to rebuild, in time, sufficient heavy industry to balance a simple self-sufficient industrial-agrarian economy, and to make machines for her own use; but no luxuries of any kind, and no armament, for at least a generation. Beyond that, Stalin has promised the Germans that their national entity and culture will not be destroyed and that they may have an army. From there on it will be up to the German people to find its own way out of the wreckage left by Hitler. What particular group in Germany Russia may favor for post-war leadership will naturally depend on the conditions of surrender, but it is obvious that the Free German Committee will be at least a factor in that leadership.

That is approximately what Russia wants in the way of regional security. As for Western Europe, Asia, the Americas and elsewhere, she expects us to create a structure of regional security satisfactory to ourselves and our neighbors. She has made no attempt to interfere in those areas. Her newspapers do not advise us what to do with the Pacific Islands we are recovering nor how to dispose of Japan or China which are more vital to her than the Ukraine is to us. They also have refrained from pointing out that the Atlantic Charter nowhere applies in the vast colonial world, or in Libya or the Near East.

All this means that Russian foreign policy works according to a plan with concrete objectives and consisting of two parts. One part concerns her vital near-interests, in the regions adjacent to her national territory. There she seeks to build up a wide belt of friendly states prepared to co-operate with her in every field of diplomacy. The other part concerns her broad international interests. There she concedes to other powers the same rights of regional security as she demands for herself. At the same time she subscribes to the endorsement of such practical proposals as promise to maintain general peace and international co-operation.

As far as I can see these two sides of Soviet diplomacy are part of the same coin. The Russians admit no contradiction between them and do not regard one as an "alternative" to the other, but see them as the essential parts of an organic whole. Each is dependent upon and influenced by the other and neither is considered adequate without the other.

There are several good reasons why the United States and Britain will co-operate with this Russian policy. One is that we both carry out in our own ways similar foreign policies, which combine regional doctrines unilaterally enforcing stability where our vital interests are concerned, with broad international doctrines of peaceful working-together. Another is that Russia's regional organization of security does not collide with our own vital needs sufficiently to create serious contradictions. A third is that we desire Russia's support for our war against Japan and for enforcement of security in Asia. A fourth is that the great mass of the Russian, British and American peoples want, more than they want anything else, an enduring international peace, and the co-operation of their government in maintaining it.

Finally, and the most important of all, the only alternative we have to seeking to win Russia's confidence by recognizing her regional organization of security, as she recognizes ours, and on this basis to bring her into the family of nations, is likewise the only alternative Russia has to co-operating in an international structure with us. That alternative is the pursuit of a policy of imposing our will by force; it is the policy of preparing for the Third World War, the war of the continents. It is the renunciation of the Teheran promise to "banish the scourge and terror of war for many generations." It is the alternative to which all the internal needs of Russia are opposed.

Book Three

RETURN TO THE EAST

China

U. S. S. R.

LAKE BAIKAL

Irkutsk

NIKOLAIEVSK

SAKHALIN I.

MONGOLIA

MANCHURIA

Harbin

Kirin

Vladivostok

SEA OF JAPAN

JAPAN

Mukden

Tokyo

KOREA

Peiping

Tientsin

Pt. Arthur

Seoul

Kyoto

Yulin

GREAT WALL

Lanchow

Sian

Honan

YELLOW SEA

CHINA

Hankow

Shanghai

Hangchow

Chungking

Changsha

Hengchow

Foochow

FORMOSA

INDIA

BURMA ROAD

Kunming

Lashio

Mandalay

BURMA

FRENCH

Canton

Macao

CHINA

SEA

PHILIPPINE ISLANDS

THAILAND

INDO

Bang Kok

CHINA

Saigon

BORNEO

Main Guerrilla Bases
Border Region

I

Moscow to Delhi: Snafu

A<small>T</small> THE end of April, 1943, I flew out of Moscow and Russia in the *Gulliver II*, a B-24 loaned to Admiral Standley for his use, which he now sent back to America. Major Serge Klotz, who had earlier piloted Wendell Willkie's *Gulliver I*, and his able co-pilot Arch Steele, brought us over the jagged snow-peaks that rim in Teheran, but they couldn't find a hole in the soup anywhere.

"Go down there," said the Russian navigator, pointing into a blank wall of white. Klotz nosed the ship over and held his breath. We came out, just as in the movies, clean and neat, right above the airfield.

"That's the worst flight I ever had!" Klotz said, when he got down, pale and sweating, and he wasn't kidding. "This Russian never looked at his instruments, he just kept pointing his finger at trees and mountains all the way down!" It was then we noticed that the big ship had stopped with one of its wheels a couple of inches away from a foot-deep fault in the field, enough to have wrecked our starboard prop if we had hit it. Klotz swore he was never going back to Russia, but a few months later he was in Moscow again, carrying Cordell Hull.

From the general conversation I gathered I was the only man on the plane who was sorry to be leaving Russia. One reason was that it was pleasant spring in Moscow now, and I was going to

259

India, in the middle of its worst heat; another was that I was still convalescing from influenza; furthermore, I had an abscessed tooth. I couldn't do anything about that tooth in Teheran, so in Cairo I tried to find an American dentist; but it was a week-end and Cairo was fresh out of dentists. I flew on then to Khartoum, hoping to see an army dentist; from Khartoum I could get a plane across the Red Sea to Karachi. At the hospital I found only a sergeant; the dentist was in town and wouldn't be back for two days, and the town was out-of-bounds to air freight such as myself. The sarge took a look at my bicuspids, though, and wiggled them back and forth speculatively.

"You've got trench-mouth, chum," he comforted me, "and will probably lose most of those teeth." But he wasn't authorized to pull an abscessed tooth, himself; besides, he wasn't sure which tooth it was. So I left him, with the molar still shooting lightning into my jaw.

After that I thought I might as well go on home and get myself some store porcelain. Walter Kerr was along and he was afraid he had a case of advanced pyhorrea, also, from two years of de-vita-minized Moscow diet. When Klotz flew on to the West Coast that night I went along; the pain increased with the altitude. We landed a little after dawn and I went to the airport hospital and there at last found an American dentist. In half an hour he had X-rayed me, removed the offending tooth, and assured me I did not have trench-mouth. So at the last minute I pulled my bag off the *Gulliver* and turned back for India.

It was not till I reached Karachi, two days later, that I realized I had flown from Persia to the South Atlantic, and back again, to have a tooth pulled, and that the whole trip had taken less than three days.

"How's the war going?" I asked the first American I met after I returned to India.

"Which particular war do you mean, sir? There are several going on around here. If it's the war against the Jap you have in mind, the answer is *Snafu!*" An economical expression it is, too, a convenient conversational time-saver in the hot countries, and the piece of war neology most likely to stick. Snafu means "situation normal, all fouled up." Only for "fouled" read the most eloquent word in Elizabethan language, and the most often used in any English-speaking army. How's the weather? Snafu. How's the food? Snafu. How's the front? Snafu. And now if you asked an Indian or a Chinese coolie on an American airfield about his health, you found his vocabulary has doubled. He was as likely to answer "snafu" as "okay."

On the surface the "situation" a year after the loss of Burma did seem to be "normal." The Japs had been fully occupied with war in the Southwest Pacific and India had not yet been invaded. Business was booming and the hill-stations were full of sahibs and memsahibs again enjoying their customary summer siesta, away from the heat of the plains. Gandhi and Nehru were still imprisoned and the tenant farmers and city poor were getting less to eat and wear than ever.

The tall, thin, chilly man in the viceregal mansion had won his battle for Britain against the saint of Wardha. Order—the old order—had been restored throughout this paradise of princes and purgatory of the pauper. Gandhi's public life was now confined to writing letters, which the Viceroy invariably read with "close care and attention." But in spite of his interest, it seemed from the published correspondence that he could not do a thing for Mr. Gandhi in the latter's predicament. Neither fasting nor letter writing had brought the Mahatma any nearer a re-entry into Indian political life.

The Viceroy was determined to leave India's *enfant terrible* interned, unless his friend publicly renounced the resolution he had persuaded the National Congress to adopt the previous August. For Gandhi, the alternative of cooling his heels in the Agha Khan's palace had so far seemed preferable. He had gambled that under British leadership India was bound to go the way of Malaya and Burma, and so far, it seemed, he had lost. But the war was not yet won.

On the other hand, the wind which blew Gandhi ill had been steadily blowing good to his chief political opponent, Mohammed Ali Jinnah. The Qaid-e-Azam, the Grand Mogul of the Moslem League, had apparently put his bets on the right horse. By taking up a nominal pro-Ally stand and staying out of rebellions the Mussulman leader had kept his freedom to talk. And he had made exceedingly good use of it by blanketing India with propaganda for his pet scheme of Pakistan.

"Jinnah is sitting on the finest velvet of the land," one of the Viceroy's officials said to me. "The field is his. The longer Gandhi is kept under a lid, the better Jinnah prospers. But the thing is

261

beginning to worry us. Pakistan is gaining headway like a rolling snowball. It may soon be too late to stop it."

How seriously was that danger actually exercising the servants of Messrs. Churchill and Amery? The bigger the snowball the less chance there was that India would ever break off in one hunk from the Empire. That the ball was growing, however, was impressed on me during a trip to Northwestern India. I found representative Moslems there were pretty solidly behind Jinnah's doctrine. Men who a decade ago were quite content to be plain Indians now prided themselves on being "members of the Muslim Nation" and "quite separate people" from the Hindus, with whom they were actually the same flesh and blood.

While Congressmen continued to boycott the government, and its elected officials resigned, Jinnah moved in and put his followers in areas where Moslems predominated. Meanwhile the League pounded away at its thesis in the schools and the press and in the training of youth stressed loyalty to Pakistan first, with India coming off a poor second best.

The Qaid-e-Azam got some reinforcement from an unexpected quarter—the Communist Party in India. Its youthful secretary, P. C. Joshi, told me that Pakistan agreed with the Communist principle of "self-determination" for national minorities, so that the Party could wholeheartedly back it up. Jinnah had said publicly that he would unite with the devil himself if it would bring him Pakistan. Could a Red be worse than the devil? Evidently not. He now invited Communists to join the League and help him organize Moslem youth.

Naturally the marriage had its benefits for the Communists too. Like Jinnah, they made hay while Gandhi's star was down. As old-time Congressmen sat immobilized and frustrated, an army of young Communists captured many new streets of power. Their national following now cut across racial, religious and even party lines, with Hindu, Sikh, Moslem, Bengali, Parsi and Christian boys and some hundreds of girls and young adults making up the network. It included more full-time paid workers than the Congress and the League combined.

Paid? Yes, they got six dollars a month each. On that they slept five to ten in one room in the cities, ate coolie curry and garlic, and otherwise lived on hope. Actually they put little stock in either Gandhi or Jinnah. Not for them did they dedicate themselves to the privations of life on a party worker's wage.

Communists agitated for the release of Gandhi, but they never backed up his last call for civil disobedience, and thus they retained legality and freedom of action, as did Jinnah. They echoed Gandhi's demand for immediate independence, but also called for maximum co-operation with the national-defense effort. In June, 1943, they went the limit when they resolved to work against all strikes for the duration of the "patriotic war," and launched a campaign glorifying Indian troops as "defenders of the motherland." It was the first time any Congress leaders had recognized the Indian Army as anything but a "tool of British imperialism."

But though revolt in India was thus again confined to carpings of the press—heavily subsidized by government advertising, ironically enough—there was one thing for which tear gas and tommyguns offered no solution. It was the steady deterioration of India's wartime economy along lines predictable many months earlier. There was as yet little in the press about that; but I began to smell oncreeping famine when I went to visit some workers in Delhi and found that even among them, relatively well paid, the rise in food prices was causing serious deprivations.

It was a suffocating night and long after sunset the stone walks were uncomfortably hot. I sat talking to Tulsi Ram, a middle-aged worker in the Birla mills. Tulsi and his family of six lived in one of the Birla tenements in a little cell of a room no bigger than a good-sized closet.

The Rams' total income was about thirty dollars a month, which represented the combined wages of Ram and his two sons. In this family, as among a dozen neighbors who joined in the conversation, nobody had eaten vegetables or meat of any kind for many months. Their diet was down to corn or millet cakes, and potatoes, consumed twice a day, day after day. No fruit, milk, butter, tea, coffee, sugar, eggs—nothing like that. Not one of them had ever owned a pair of shoes or a pair of stockings. In the chill winters of Delhi they covered themselves with rags and their three thin blankets. They owned only a few sticks of rickety furniture. When I asked them if they had ever seen an American movie, the whole tenement laughed.

"What's the joke?"

"Do you see any rich men among us? Where would we get money to see American moving pictures?"

It was people like these, and they were most of India, whom

our O.W.I. propaganda never reached. They could not read it in the press, and they could not afford to buy admission to it in the cinema. Their information came from gossip in the bazaar, where Axis propaganda was circulated. Ram and his friends told me, when I asked why food was scarce, that it was because American troops were eating up all the cows in the country. It seemed the Americans tempted the peasants with great hunks of gold. After they had sold their cattle the peasants had no way to till the fields. Hence the scarcity!

About this time (May, 1943) I heard the first rumors of food riots in Bengal and Bombay, but in the Secretariat these were branded as false. Up in Kashmir, later, I heard of other riots in the neighboring Jammu state. The price of rice was doubling and trebling. Results of Delhi's sins of omission were catching up with us.

The Indian famine, which shortly afterward broke out on a national scale and in an acute form, was caused by the war crisis and the lack of measures to cope with it. When India was cut off from normal imports there was an obvious urgent need to stimulate new production of both agricultural and industrial goods. No national plan or leadership appeared for either project. Nothing was done, either through rationing and control of stocks, or by priming native industry, to maintain a market in essential manufactured goods, and scarcities speedily developed. Price rises on this market were accompanied by hoarding of commodities and grain. As no faintly adequate measures of rationing or control were introduced, speculation in the necessities of life rapidly attained the widest scale.

What the outside world did not realize was that the "sudden" famine in India did not result primarily from any abnormal food shortage, but almost entirely as a result of absence of measures of control adopted by virtually every other country at war. Remember that India had not even been invaded. The main effect of the war on the food situation was to deprive the country of its normal import of Burma and Siam rice, which amounted to only two million tons annually. This was but six percent of India's own average rice-wheat crop of thirty-four million long tons. But even before the war India's combined production plus imports of grain were far inadequate to feed its people. If you had divided the total grain equally among all Indians the share would have been only about two-fifths of a pound per person per day, or less than the nominal daily ration of bread in the lowest category (non-producing dependents) of workers in the Soviet Union, after that country had lost its best wheatlands and faced the worst crisis of the invasion.

There was, however, nothing even approaching an equality of distribution in India. Studies* have shown that 4,000,000 Indians get one-third of the total annual national income, while 240,000,000 live on only 30% of that income. Since purchasing power determines food consumption in an uncontrolled market, it is obvious that millions of Indians were obliged to reduce their consumption below the minimum subsistence level, after grain prices rose by 40%, and in special cases rose very much higher.

The Indian population increased by seventy millions between 1930 and 1940, but the area under cultivation remained stationary at 197 million acres. There are about 150 million acres of cultivable but uncultivated land in India, and this excludes some millions of acres of princely estates and game preserves. Indian agriculture is still on the wooden-plow level and the use of modern fertilizers is almost unknown. No one expected Delhi to begin collectivizing and mechanizing agriculture in the midst of the war, but clearly a government which could have commanded the support of the people could most certainly have succeeded, by mobilizing and settlement of the plentiful labor available, in increasing agricultural production sufficiently to feed the nation during the war.

The famine began to assume grave military significance when its worst effects were manifested in the provinces of Bengal, Bihar and Assam, adjacent to Japanese-held Burma and the center of Indian war industry. Arch Steele of the *Chicago Daily News* estimated, after he returned from a tour of the afflicted areas, that roughly 50% of the total population of sixty million was affected, and some 15% in the provinces of Bihar and Orrisa. K. Santhanam, a former member of the Ben Legislative Assembly, publicly declared that over the whole province of Bengal as many as 100,000 persons a week were dying of starvation, at the height of the catastrophe, and this statement was passed by the Delhi censors.

"If non-officials and the Press, by the summer of 1942," wrote the British editor of the conservative *Statesman* of Calcutta,** "could clearly foresee a food shortage in India's rice-growing provinces, Government in New Delhi with their greater

* *Wealth and Taxable Capacity of India*, Shah and Khambata, 1924.
** Associated Press dispatch, New Delhi, Oct. 27, 1943.

265

knowledge must have done so, yet they acted not. . . . That so important a province as Bengal, lying conspicuously in the war zone of hostilities, should have been allowed to slide into the present hideous economic mess, is a disgrace not only to Indian public life but to the traditions of British rule."

Snafu!

II

Something About Wingate

OUT on the Delhi airport I sat one day for an hour talking to the man who, a year before, had told us when he came out of the Burma jungle, "The Japs ran us out and we ought to find out why. We got licked, but we are going back again."

Lieutenant-General Joseph F. Stilwell was back from London and Washington and conferences with Roosevelt and Churchill. The old gleam in his eye was fiercer than ever. Unfortunately it cannot be said even now all that lay behind that gleam. I can only repeat what I cabled home at the time:

If by chance anyone is expecting Uncle Joe to administer to the Japs, in the near future, that licking which he will surely one day return to them with interest, he had better haul out his map again and consider such matters as distance, available shipping, our promises to another Joe up Moscow way, and the reluctant ways of our Allies in this part of the world.

Stilwell was frankly worried about Japanese plans to anticipate his own efforts to reopen the Burma Road and he was worried about his persisting "lack of means" to thwart them. He saw that the enemy could still invade Yunnan and cut off our airline to China. And he was by no means so complacent as New Delhi was about the Japanese inability to invade India by land. The Japs had missed the boat all right; they did not have the naval and air power to protect an invasion by sea. "But they could still catch the bus, Snow, they could still catch the bus," said Stilwell. And so they would, before the next monsoon.

Our Commanding General was in a curious position out here. Although we called this the "C.B.I.," or China-Burma-India, theater of war, and it was the largest land area included under any combat command, Stilwell had not as yet been given any ground combat troops. We had two air forces—the 10th in India and the 14th in China—but they were both small affairs compared to their tasks. For fighting forces Stilwell had to rely on the Fifth Chinese Army which had retreated from Burma with him, and which Americans had re-equipped and re-trained and reinforced in India.

General Stilwell had plenty of responsibilities in spite of his scarcity of means. He was Generalissimo Chiang Kai-shek's Chief-of-Staff. As head of our supply mission to China he was accountable to the Lend-Lease administration. After the formation of the East Asia Command he was, in theory, subordinate to Lord Louis Mountbatten also; yet Mountbatten had no authority over the Chinese troops. Many critics abroad had no idea of the complicated nature of command relationships in this part of the world, nor of the difficulties which faced the Americans sent there to do a job, without troops of their own. But at this writing the situation has been somewhat altered, by the appearance in upper Burma of a few thousand American "Ranger" troops under Brigadier-General Frank Merrill.

In the summer of 1943 there was one English commander in India who seemed to agree with Stilwell about the importance of hitting the enemy in Northern Burma before they increased their forces there. He, too, thought that there were enough troops already in India to do the job, without waiting for the clean-up of Hitler in Europe. This man was Brigadier (later Major-General) Orde Charles Wingate, whom I met not long after he came out of Burma with the survivors of a mixed raiding party of British, Indian and Burmese troops. He had led them in as far as the Irrawaddy River and had learned many lessons about jungle warfare. The most important one was that the Japs could be licked by their own methods.

Wingate was a short, compact figure, but wiry and tough; he went in for various exercises and was said to be good at jujitsu. Though he was forty when I met him he looked years younger after getting rid of his jungle-grown beard. There was a sharp, at times almost a fierce, look in his eye when he was defending one of his passionately held beliefs. He was a Scripture-quoting soldier who hated the army, he said, because it was an orthodoxy and he hated orthodoxy. You sensed that the chief pleasure he got out of being in it was the occasional chance to prove his superiors mistaken.

"Of course I'm not the type of fellow who would ever get anywhere in the army under normal circumstances. I was never cut out to be a general at all; it's just an accident I happened to be called in to do this job because they think I know something about fighting in unorthodox ways."

One of Wingate's convictions, and the secret of his success before he came to India, was his belief that he could make fighters out of brown or black men as well as white troops. There is no doubt he had tact and ingenuity in handling men, in an extraordinary degree: and he had the human respect for them which must have been common among early British empire-builders.

Wingate was a Greek scholar and he knew Sanskrit and Arabic. In this, as in other ways, he naturally reminded one of "Lawrence of Arabia," who, he told me, was actually a cousin of his. But he much resented the comparison and was quick to deny any suggestion that Lawrence's career had influenced him.

"I became convinced quite early that the Germans would rebuild their army and we would have to fight them," he told me. "It was in 1927, during a push-bike ride through Germany, that I learned the Germans thought they had not been defeated in the First World War and meant to have another try at us. From that time on I was preparing for it."

Wingate's first foreign assignment was in the Sudan, where he continued his studies of Arabic. Then he walked across the Sand Sea in Libya, looking for a lost oasis called Zina. "I had a number of theories about sand formations," he said, "and I was the first desert traveler to discover that the great sand dunes— some of them are seventy miles long—were moving to the west. I came to this conclusion very simply, by observing that the dunes were steeper on the east side than on the west." Wingate was tremendously excited about those sand dunes—as he was about all his experiences.

His interest in Arabic naturally led to an army job in Palestine, where he learned Hebrew and got along with the Jews better than any English officer ever sent there. He organized squads of

Jewish peasants and taught them how to beat the Arab raiders at their own game. As head of the Arab police he succeeded in putting down the Arab terrorists with the help of these Jewish guerrillas and won the D.S.O.

Wavell sent for him after the war began and ordered him to "mobilize the Abyssinians" to fight Mussolini. "I am a great lover of the Abyssinians," Wingate told me, "and this was a job I liked. They are a very civilized people—much more so than we are, you know—civilized since the days of Menelik, who was the son of Solomon. I remember saying to my friends when Mussolini invaded Abyssinia—it was all very well to say we ought to have acted in the case of Manchuria, but Abyssinia was different, we had the forces here—I said to my friends, 'We have saved 50,000 men by refusing to stop the Italians; we shall lose 5,000,000 men later.'"

With the help of a small force of Ethiopians, Wingate went into Abyssinia with Haile Selassie and fought a mobile war against the fascists. He killed or disarmed some 40,000 Italians and marched triumphantly into Addis Ababa. "The value of the Ethiopians' help to us in that campaign was greater than we ever admitted. It shortened the war by many months. In that sense it was the main factor, because if Rommel had had a few more months to get into Africa we might never have won in Abyssinia at all."

Wavell brought Wingate out to Burma to organize "irregular warfare," but he arrived too late to do anything. "The Japanese type of warfare was irresistible. They had thought about how they were going to fight for many years; we had not. We did not know the potential of new weapons in the forest, we didn't know that a modern army could be destroyed by infiltration, and we didn't know that a modern army could be cut up by those means alone.

"The only way to answer infiltration is with infiltration, just as the only answer to guns are guns. We hadn't been taught what that kind of war meant and that the answer is to go forward like hellcats. This is high-speed war and to be successful at it you have to keep the pace by using air power—bringing up your infantry by air to the place it is needed, and supplying it by air too."

Wingate persuaded Wavell to let him try out his ideas about jungle warfare. He maintained that the best way to learn to fight the Japs was to fight them—then a sensational idea in those parts.

269

Under Wavell he organized a raiding expedition and put it through rigorous pre-invasion morale and combat training exercises much like the program adopted by Colonel Evans Fordyce Carlson with the American Marine Raiders. In fact these two men had many similar ideas, particularly in the importance they attached to leadership, and concerning fellowship between officers and men. They would have made a magnificent team in Asia if they had been brought together before Wingate was killed.

Wingate's "Chindits," as they called themselves (after the Burmese temple guardian), were a spectacular success. For three months early in 1943 they ranged through the Burma jungles and river valleys, reconnoitered, wrecked bridges and railways, and completely outfought the Japanese in an area where they were outnumbered ten to one. Some of the party went right across upper Burma and came out in China. A much larger British column down on the Arakan coast attempted to take the Burmese port of Akyab, by orthodox methods, and in the same period. It was roundly trounced by an enemy force which the British outnumbered ten to one. Wingate felt he had proved the correctness of his doctrines.

"The Jap is no more a born jungle fighter than we are," he told me, "and he has several weaknesses. He is not a good shot and he does not have the physical endurance we have. He is not an imaginative fighter and he loses his head when confronted by the unexpected. Inability to respond to an unusual situation—that's his main weakness. We took full advantage of it. We always did the unexpected against him."

Wingate's troops in Burma had been supplied entirely by air. This kind of supply line—"invulnerable to attack"—was so successful that Wingate became convinced a much larger operation could be carried out along similar lines. Like Stilwell, he felt North Burma could be taken back and held, by a determined force striking swiftly and in surprise, and fully supported by air. Not long after I saw him he was called to the Quebec Conference and there evidently convinced the big shots that a large-scale airborne invasion was worth making. It would be the "most unexpected" thing feasible against the Japs.

I met Wingate again in London when he was on his way back to India and he put me through a long interrogation about Chinese guerrilla tactics. His mind was already running ahead of the Burma campaign. He did not subscribe at all to a widespread

270

belief that "the Chinese won't fight." He believed the Chinese soldier was fundamentally sound stuff; the trouble was only with the leadership. He was convinced that we could organize large commando units from Chinese troops and that after some re-training and re-arming they could alone drive the Japs out of most of Southeastern Asia.

Back in India Wingate gave a special course in Japanese jungle tactics to Merrill's "Marauders." He also organized the British air-borne troops who were to support the main column of Chinese troops coming down the Ledo Road—an operation in which he was to meet his death.

Nothing could be written about these plans at the time, but I decided to go up and see for myself Stilwell's "road to nowhere," as some skeptics in Delhi then called it—behind the "old man's" back.

III

The Road to Tokyo

UP IN the pervasive wet of Assam, where a thousand streams empty the melted snows of the Himalayas into the erratic serpen-tine of the Brahmaputra, and the jungled hills of Burma crowd upon white-flowered gardens of green tea, I found American Negro boys completing the first motor road in history to link India and China.

Army engineers directing the work called it the Ledo Road but the markers were just an arrow, "To Tokyo." Some of our men had such hazy ideas of geography that they literally believed that beyond the mud and undergrowth lay Japan. And so it did— a little over 3,000 miles beyond.

Work on this project began in December, 1942, when we had no other way to get at the enemy by land except by building some 200 miles of road at him, through malarious swamp and jungle. It was war of a very different pace from Russia, where on a vast front the Nazis were seldom out of sight. It gave a rough idea too of the trouble we were taking to aid China. Supplying China was our sole mission in India, or so we were told, as part of our main mission of "improving the combat efficiency of the Chinese Army." It was just incidental that we had to help Britain re-establish her empire in Burma to accomplish that mission.

Our supply line to China, via India, was the longest in the history of warfare. It was 25,000 miles from point of origin to farthest point of delivery, before the opening of the Mediter-ranean improved matters. By the most commonly used route our Lend-Lease goods had to travel thirty-six days before they reached Assam and the air gate into Yunnan.

When I first went up there in May, 1942, we were still haul-ing people out of the jungle, in flight from Burma. We had only one squat-tag airfield and in heavy rains it was a lake. But it was our remaining link with China. Only the incredibly bad weather of Assam saved us from being bombed out of it, for the field was a few minutes' flight from Japanese bases in upper Burma and it had no protection.

At that time a few battalions of Japanese troops might have taken Assam for a bargain price, by infiltrating across the Manipur trail. But apparently they were convinced we could never establish a base of any importance there anyway. When they finally saw that they were mistaken, and that both the airline and the "into-Burma road" were becoming serious military factors, they would launch a blow at Imphal. But by that time Stilwell's boys would already be far into the Japanese rear in Burma, by way of that road that "should never have been built," according to the gen-eral's critics.

Local reasons for early opposition to the Ledo project were not unconnected with the history of the "blind frontier" of India and Burma in the past. The big British-controlled steamship com-panies had always objected that establishment of land communica-tions between the two countries would ruin their business; the monopoly of Indo-Burmese water transport was very profitable in-deed. And the British Army which never had expected an attack on India to come from Burma, was perfectly satisfied to depend solely on a sea-route of supply. Hence, when they once lost Ran-goon to the Japs, they lost communication with India. They were lucky to withdraw as many men as they did across that unknown frontier.

Despite the experience, however, opposition to Stilwell's road-building project continued for some time. Had it not been for our obligation to supply China, it might never have been begun. But Stilwell was convinced it was more than a political gesture, or a way of making land contact with China. He saw it as the opening wedge in a successful campaign to drive the Japs out of all Southern Asia.

From the air I saw the road stand out against the Naga Hills like a white tape on a tennis green. Enemy reconnaissance planes, flying over, saw the same thing. And the Nipponese began building, too; roads intended to outflank ours. Increasing suspense hung over the work, like the two-way construction of the Union Pacific nearly a century ago. Only in this case the workers on both sides were not carrying any golden spike to mark their meeting place. On a trip over the worst of the jeep-deep mud I managed to get into former no-man's land myself. Anti-aircraft guns pointed up from well-camouflaged positions, manned by our men. Ahead of us and around us were Chinese troops, part of the divisions armed and trained in India. Under the command of young, tough and able Brigadier-General Haydon K. Boatner, of Stilwell's staff, they were already meeting the Japanese and winning every argument.

Despite almost constant work with wet feet in a region infested with malaria and dengue fever, and despite the food, which was steady corned beef and rice for three months, the morale of the American Negro boys up here was praised by every officer I met. General Wheeler said they were as good as any engineering troops he ever had on a job, and Wheeler had had plenty. With stunts, wisecracks, and kidding, our dusky sergeants got more work out of the slow-moving Assamese work gangs than any white master ever did. One reason was because they did not mind doing the job with the laborers. The strength of the black Americans was becoming legendary.

One story that spread through Assam told how an American Negro watched four underfed Indian coolies trying to move a huge log from one side of the road to another. Presently he interrupted their struggle, spit on his hands, pushed them aside, lifted the log on his shoulders and tossed it over their heads. Then he grinned and said, "Rest yo'self, brothers, you-all jes' done four days' work."

IV

The Hump

THERE never was anything like this winged transport line Americans built into China from India, which began as a Toonerville trolley of the air and ended up carrying more cargo than the Burma Road ever handled and more than the combined air freight delivered by all the airlines of the United States.

The whole miracle was made possible, basically, by a wonderful cluster of airfields built in one of the wettest spots on earth by the hand labor of women and children. They made an unforgettable sight: long lines of barefoot, bangled women, with heavy silver and gold anklets and bracelets, and some with rings of gold in their noses, stretching as far as you could see, coming from rock piles in the distance. Gay saris seemed weird costumes for the work, with their dragging skirts and with mantles draped round their heads, but graceful and colorful against the dark Indian skin. There were young women with babes clinging to their breasts; others, advanced in pregnancy, plodded along with expressionless faces. There were older women with white hair. Their lips moved incessantly, as naked infants solemnly wheeled along beside them.

On they came, and each woman, reaching the appointed spot, repeated the same act. A brief pause in the stately walk, a nod of the head, and off rolled the single stone balanced on top of her head. Beyond them I could see 400 million Chinese patiently watching as those stones fell one by one, to pave the way for promised help. It was slow going, for these people had no interest in the outcome of the war. Weakened and undernourished, they would not work in the rain, and it rains about half the time in Assam; and they would not work on religious holidays, which may or may not coincide with the rain. Nearly all the airfields and military buildings we have in India grew up in the same way, rising literally from millions of nodding Indian heads.

Lack of modern construction machinery was not the only handicap overcome by our engineers trying to help China. It often took months to pry loose needed sites for the airfields from tea-planters for whose protection they were constructed. In one case we had to build a wide detour taxiway because an obdurate planter, who apparently preferred to have the Japs in rather than his tea bushes out, refused to lease his land. Everywhere our engineers encountered red tape and bureaucratic obstruction as well as labor peculiarities. In the end many of the barracks stood on low swampy ground, often flooded and always full of malaria, while choicer spots were reserved for tea. But Americans got the freight flying.

Down at a huge new airport I again saw Colonel Joplin, who had been up on the Hump since the beginning, when we had had only four Douglas planes to maintain it. What a job he had had, sweating in pilots flying unarmed cargo planes over this route which crosses unmapped mountain peaks and jungles and enemy-held territory! As far as I am concerned, nothing is too good to say about "Jop" and the boys with him—most of them youngsters with only a few hours' flying time behind them—who made this the world's greatest air-transport line. As a month-to-month proposition it was one of the worst spots an airman could be sunk in. Most of them eventually got dengue or malaria and dysentery, if no worse. The odds pile up with the number of trips a pilot makes over the 17,000-foot passes that lead into Yunnan. We lost more planes in transport service here than in combat with the Japs. Yet the outside world knew little of the work they were doing. They got few ribbons, and promotions were slow.

In Assam I met Captain Eddie Rickenbacker on his way over to inspect our airfields in China and at his invitation flew into Yunnan with him, for my third trip over the Hump. On the other side we found a dozen new airfields had been partly or wholly completed, with many new barracks built for Major-General Claire Chennault's 14th Air Force, scattered all over Southwest China. In Yunnan I visited several fields and landing strips in towns through which, a dozen years ago, I traveled by caravan down into Burma. On one trip we left Kunming for a certain point which it had taken me ten days to reach on my earlier trek across the roadless province. This time we got there and back in the smaller part of an afternoon. Once it took me two months, by caravan and steamer, to go from Kunming to Calcutta. Today it is a routine one-day flight.

Construction of airfields and of new roads on both sides of the Hump, under Lend-Lease arrangements, is already an achievement of far-reaching permanent importance. But in China, as in India, we shall have no post-war claim to these fields which were all made by hand labor, under American engineering supervision. Chinese work a lot faster than Indians, incidentally. One great field I saw was completed in six weeks after 40,000 farmers— mostly women and children who had never seen an airplane— were mobilized for the task. Farther east a force of 250,000 people was at work on a field from which our heavy bombers would soon bomb Formosa and Japan.

In many Southern provinces now our engineers were building advance headquarters and locating supply bases. New fields were being laid out and new means of communication. New sources of supply were being organized inside China, too. Some day soon Americans would unroll a noisy parade of trucks and airplanes, tanks and cars down the highways and skyways. For the first time in history white men would come into Eastern Asia not to conquer men but to liberate them.

More lasting perhaps than the defeat of Japan will be the economic, social and political effects of new communications opened up by the necessity of supplying forces for war in these hitherto inaccessible regions. It amounts to adding a good-sized nation to world intercourse. By the time Japan is pushed out of Eastern Asia, highways and railways will exist connecting Siberia to China, India and the Persian Gulf. Using the new Alaska-Canadian Highway, a man ought to be able to drive from anywhere in America right through to Delhi, India, with the short ferry ride at Bering Strait the only water gap over the whole distance.

India and China inevitably will be thrown closer together by these dramatic developments. Tribal peoples lying in between them will be quickly brought into the fold of modern society. Indians may turn their eyes more toward the East and toward the Pacific, rather than toward Europe. It is significant that at a 1943 conference of Indian educators changes were discussed which would introduce into the curriculum of Indian schools the compulsory study of Chinese history, geography and culture and put Chinese language study on a par with English.

276

Enough post-war tasks are growing out of all the possibilities created by war, to keep men busy for a long time to come. Immense power resources all over lower Asia need to be harnessed to the service of man; drainage projects and irrigation works ought to be built, new land cleared, new roads and railways constructed, and after them modern cities and factories laid down as the foundation of a free and democratic Asia. . . .

"That's all very well, chum," remarked an American engineer in Kunming when I enthused on the rosy prospects, "but first we gotta drive the Japs out and next we'll find out who is going to do all that construction and development. It's got to come, yes. But where do you see anybody wanting a free and democratic Asia? In China? Take a look around, and then tell me what signs you see of it here today!"

So I looked around in China, once more.

PART-II-CHINA'S DESTINY: 1944

I

Book Review

THE Sino-Japanese war may be divided into three periods: Japanese conquest of North China, 1937-39; consolidation and pacification of Japanese conquest, 1939-42; stabilization of frontiers of conquest in South and West China, and intensification of Chinese partisan warfare in North China, 1942.

Contrary to popular impression in Britain and America, the Japanese forays made in China after the outbreak of war in Europe were not seriously intended to annex large additional territories in the South and West. Japanese operations after September, 1939, were primarily intended to stabilize the perimeter of the occupied areas, and were also troop-training maneuvers and reconnaissance and foraging expeditions. Once Japan had secured her main objectives in China—control of the coastline, a protected flank, and possession of the economically developed areas—she concentrated on preparations for the coming Pacific war and tried to reduce her commitment in China to a mere policing force. But it was impossible to realize that plan fully because of the steady development of partisan warfare behind the North China front, which is dealt with in the next chapter. By late 1943 another factor began to rob Japan of the security she had enjoyed on the China flank for five years. This factor was the rise to supremacy of American air power in the China skies, under Major-General Claire Chennault's famed 14th Air Force.

When I had revisited Chungking early in 1942 I had found an interesting psychological change in the capital. There was naturally a feeling of immense relief at the lightening of the war load. It was our turn now; the ruling Kuomintang (Nationalist) Party understood that we had inherited the major task of defeating Japan. There was also an illusion of early victory. After Pearl Harbor there was never any possibility that the Chungking government would make a collaborationist peace with Japan, despite rumors to the contrary circulated in Washington by those opposed to the beat-Hitler-first strategy.

This "psychology of victory," in the face of what remained regional defeat, accelerated two developments already incipient under the Chungking regime before America entered the war. First, earlier tendencies toward some modification in the one-party structure of the Kuomintang dictatorship now came to a halt. What was the need for "representative popular government" now? Was not America going to send to Chungking all the airplanes, tanks and guns necessary to build a great army? What internal opposition could then challenge Kuomintang rule?

Second, with the half-billion dollar American loan given unqualifiedly to Chungking, plus promises of Lend-Lease aid on an unlimited scale, efforts to develop China's own resources as a means of waging war against Japan began to wane. In economics as well as politics the conservative ruling circle seemed to lose interest in the latent strength of the 300 million people in unoccupied China and the partisan areas. The early spectacular success of Chinese Industrial Co-operatives had proved that the people's productive capacities could, if mobilized in a democratic way, have answered most of the civilian and many of the military

278

requirements of China. But now Chungking need not rely on such efforts any more—and anyway the rise of new economic power in the people had unpleasant implications. Kuomintang bankers spent their time drawing up grandiose schemes for post-war industrialization of the Eastern provinces, with the help of American capital. Some dreamed of seizing Japan's lost markets with cheap goods to be produced by American machinery and coolie-level Chinese labor.

When I came back to China again from Russia in the middle of 1943 I found that the country's economy had become chaotic, its political life more reactionary than at any time since 1936, and its military efficiency was at the lowest level since the war began. Hoarding of commodities and speculation in grain and land were the chief occupations of landlords, pawnbrokers, merchants and native banks. Many industrialists had lost interest in production; there was more money to be made in hoarding raw materials and waiting for price rises which averaged better than 10% monthly. The cost of living had risen some 200 times above the pre-war level. Planes that should have carried in guns or machines were filled with American-made banknotes flown in at the rate of billions of dollars monthly.

The principal cause of China's runaway inflation was the failure to enforce measures, more than the lack of means, to meet the economic emergency imposed by the war. The fundamental reason for the failure to mobilize "the means" lay in the government's commitment to a semi-feudal economy of landlordism, peasant debt-bondage and usury. It was the gentry class representing that economy in a political sense, which was the foundation of the Kuomintang power.

It is true that early in the war Japan seized over 90% of China's modern industry. But for six years thereafter the government continued to have at its disposal greater natural wealth than Japan proper, and unlimited labor power. It failed to combine these assets to replace lost production and it never devised a rational scheme of distribution. The Kuomintang imposed no adequate controls over capital, raw materials, commodities or food, the market became dominated by hoarding and speculative influences and the highest officials and their offspring were numbered among the foremost profiteers. The government increasingly resorted to the printing press for a solution rather than to production.

Foreign imports were needed to prop up this economy and the blockade finally cut those off entirely in 1942. The result was vicious uncontrolled inflation and vastly increased burdens passed on to the principal producers in the country—the debt-carrying peasants who till the land but as a rule do not own it. Widespread famine often resulted not from genuine overall shortages but from speculative hoarding. By 1944 probably as many people had died of famine in Free China as in India. Even the army was gravely undernourished; nutritional diseases accounted for about 70% of the incapacitated, and wounded for only 30%.

It was in this scene, which demanded vigorous leadership and concrete measures to avert further disintegration, that Generalissimo Chiang Kai-shek published *China's Destiny*. It was at first intended to make this a textbook in every Chinese school, but in deference to adverse foreign reaction Chiang had it withdrawn from public circulation after the sale of half a million copies. Foreign embassies were requested to prevent publication of the original edition abroad until "revisions and improvements" were made. But it remains the Bible of the Kuomintang.

Some foreign missionaries in Chungking were shocked by Chiang's book because they had long believed him devoted to Christian reformism and to the solution of China's economic and political problems by democratic means. More realistic diplomatic and military observers were disappointed mainly because it offered no serious proposals for mobilizing Chinese resources in an all-out effort to help win the war, and to avert economic catastrophe.

China's Destiny actually dismisses the war in a dozen pages. The remaining 200 pages are devoted to the distinguished leader's plans to build up a powerful post-war China. Much of the book seems unexceptionable common sense. No one should object to its proposals to industrialize China on a large scale, nor even to the Generalissimo's insistence upon what has been called "militarization" of the nation's youth. But in this connection many were perhaps legitimately disturbed by Chiang's proposal to "recover" all those territories that were "deeply influenced" by Chinese civilization "a hundred years ago."

There are some interesting revelations in *China's Destiny*. It contains a somewhat inaccurate interpretation of Chinese history, in support of a racist theory of Pan-Sinism. Some critics think this little different from Hitler's Pan-Aryanism. Chiang is bluntly outspoken in blaming foreigners for most of China's troubles during the past century, and his facts are not always correct. Elsewhere he insists that there can be only one leader and one party in China—apparently a blow to those hoping for a two-party democracy. All intellectuals should join the "one party," says Chiang and opposition to that monolithic conception of the State is branded as "new warlordism." The Generalissimo also praises the conception of rule preserved under the Manchu conquerors (the Ch'ing Dynasty). In Chiang's peculiar nostalgia for institutions of feudal times some Chinese critics* discern alarming fascist intonations.

In advocating "Pan-Sinism," it seems, to such critics, the Generalissimo gives strong reasons for apprehension to the tribal peoples, and the Tibetans, Mongols, Moslems and the peoples of Turkestan. "If only the Manchus could have done away with the boundaries that separated the Chinese, Manchus, Mongols, Mohammedans and Tibetans," Chiang writes in one place, "and recognized that our five branches are in fact one unified body it would have been hard to find fault with them." Such a pronouncement sharply conflicts with the Mongols' aspirations for independent nationhood and a "Mongolian destiny" of their own, which I reported earlier.**

In foreign countries the Generalissimo is sometimes regarded as an individual "above party lines" and some people think that the Chungking government is not just an organ of the Kuomintang —which in fact appoints every member of it. But in this definitive book the Generalissimo clears up any doubts that he considers his role primarily that of the Kuomintang party leader. "If China today had no Kuomintang," he says, "there would be no China. If the Kuomintang fails it means the failure of the whole Chinese nation. *To put it briefly: The destiny of China depends solely on the Kuomintang.*" (Italics mine.)† On the one hand he insists there can be but one party and one leader and on the other he demands that the Communists, whom he calls "the new warlords," surrender all their military forces to him.

* See especially, *Critique of China's Destiny*, by Chen Pei-ta, *sub rosa* but widely circulated in China in 1943.
** See "News from Mongolia," p. 193-7.
† *China's Destiny*, a digest translated in English by A. Lutley
West China Missionary News, 1943 see p. 196 of original Chinese edition.

In effect, the Generalissimo states that he means at all costs to preserve the present political framework. This is a government which has been described by American observers as a "police state," because three of the Four Freedoms do not exist.* It is a dictatorship of a small clique of Kuomintang members, of whom the Generalissimo is the point of focus and the figurehead.

In form Kuomintang methods and rule in many ways resemble the Communist Party of Russia; in content they are radically different. The Kuomintang borrowed the apparatus of the Russian party in 1924 and kept it even after it adopted an anti-Communist program. Here the party *is* the government and there are no elected councils or organs like soviets. The peculiar composition of this party-government represents primarily the great landlord class and the compradore group of neo-capitalists with their heavy banking and industrial investments in Eastern China and America. The Generalissimo himself now officially ranks as the foremost banker of China. With his immensely rich brother-in-law and sister-in-law, Dr. and Mme. H. H. Kung, and their children, and the wealthy Mme. Chiang Soong Mei-ling, and her brothers, he holds today the key positions in all private and government finance groups. Incidentally, as far as is publicly known, no member of the Chiang-Kung-Soong family has ever filed a personal income tax report.

Here it suffices to state that few political changes have occurred since 1939, except for a gradual deepening of the gulf between the bureaucracy and the progressive social forces fermenting among the essentially democratic Chinese people. One development is the great increase in the repressive power of the secret police, and of special service regiments of the army.

On the other hand it would be a mistake to conclude that the Chungking government has become an outright fascist dictatorship; the loosely integrated character and semi-colonial economy would not permit the organization of a true fascist state. There are still many "gaps" in the realization of absolute party dictatorship in China—the most obvious being the continued existence of a large army in one part of the country under an opposition party, the Communists. In the interstices between these two leaderships also it is still possible for several minor parties, with an important following of liberals, to continue to exist and occasionally to express their views, although they enjoy no legality and no power. They are banded together in a Democratic Federation which in-

* e.g., Vide *They Shall Not Sleep*, by Leland Stowe, p. 45f. N.Y., 1944

cludes the Socialist Party, the Social Democratic (or "Third") Party, the National Salvationists and the Reconstruction Association.

Early in the war the Kuomintang authorized, as a concession to democratic opinion, the formation of a People's Political Council, which was supposed to be a kind of public forum. It meets for a few days once a year and debates national issues. It has no power of legislation or referendum—in fact no political power whatever —but here at least the various political parties are able to combine their representatives for brief periods of restricted discussion.

In 1943 a resolution was passed by the Kuomintang Central Committee which again promised that a convention would be summoned after the war, to introduce constitutional government. But two facts, besides the Generalissimo's book, render this pledge of dubious value. First, such a convention has been promised many times in the previous decade, but reasons were always found to postpone its fulfillment. Second, the rules laid down by the Kuomintang for organization of the convention were such that there could be no question that the overwhelming majority of delegates would be Kuomintang party members or appointees. If ever the meeting took place, therefore, it would merely confer "constitutional" status on a regime already in power.

Just before the outbreak of the Pacific War, the Democratic Federation of China issued a ten-point manifesto calling upon the government to end one-party rule, stop forcing students and teachers to join the Kuomintang, abolish concentration camps, eliminate one-party control of the National Army, restrict war profiteering, and permit some freedom of expression, press and organization in the mobilization of the people for the struggle against Japan. These demands were suppressed and some of the petitioners fled to exile in Kwangsi. Little was again heard from the Federation until September, 1943, when its chairman, Chang Piao-fang, issued a long statement to the nation under his own name. It sharply criticized the dictator and his party and called for an immediate end to the so-called "tutelage period," which the Kuomintang has been enforcing since it came into power in 1927.

Chiang Piao-fang, a distinguished scholar, seventy-two years old, was formerly governor of Szechuan and later president of Chengtu University. He was an early rebel against the Manchu Dynasty and has a long record of service in the State, and his great age and prestige make him somewhat immune from the retaliation that otherwise would have been taken against his outspoken criticism. Even so, his very scholarly review of the history of attempts to establish democracy in China had to be issued *sub rosa*. It concludes with these paragraphs:

"Unless there is an immediate suspension of single-party dictatorship, abandonment of one-party rule, and an end to 'partyizing,' true democracy cannot even be talked about. . . . For the past several years the officers of the government have been openly corrupt. Juniors have imitated their seniors. Laws and decrees have become scraps of paper. This is the political scene.

"Economically, the organs of monopoly and taxation have proliferated and have become burdensome and complicated. The government is hated on every side, the people are harassed and the gains flow into the pockets of middlemen. People have no grain and yet they are still made to pay grain (in taxes). True democracy should be established to empower the people to supervise the government, to check officials, and to help manage the nation's affairs. . . .

"Since the party dictatorship was established, able men outside the party have been wasted and all other political parties are severely repressed. No open activities are permitted. A particular case in point is the Communist Party, with several hundred thousand troops in seven or eight provinces under the continual threat of civil war. . . ."

Today the Chinese Communists and Nationalists seem to have drawn as far apart as they were a decade ago. Every proposal made to re-establish the "united front" between them has met with failure. Is the Chinese people's patient struggle after all to end, not in a blaze of glory and united national triumph over Japan, but in another savage fight between brothers for physical possession of an earth already scorched by decades of war? What is it about the Chinese partisans that makes them so intolerable to the Generalissimo as bedfellows? And how would a renewal of civil war now affect our own strategy against Japan?

To get the answers to such questions the reader is invited to raise his eyes on the map some 500 air miles north of Chungking, to the little town of Yenan. Here are the headquarters of the 18th Group Army. Here is the gateway to a part of fighting China little known abroad, the partisan districts waging war behind the Japanese lines.

Partisan China

HITLER is an awful liar, but even he could not avoid making a truthful observation once in a while. Somewhere in *Mein Kampf* he wrote, "The people's memory is unbelievably short." I am reminded of that nowadays when I hear American and British critics disparage China and its contribution to the war effort. How quickly they have forgotten those heroic years when China stood alone, in a sense no other nation in this war ever stood alone. From 1937 till the end of 1940 China not only received no help from the United Nations but had to fight against an enemy who was getting all the help she could buy from the United States and the British Empire as well as from her Axis allies.

Who could have blamed China then if she had accepted Japan's tempting offers of peaceful collaboration and turned against us? And how very different a picture the Far East would present today if she had done so! Whatever one may think of the predicament of China's armies or their ineffectiveness at present, no American or Englishman should forget the profound obligation we owe to the Chinese people. I say the Chinese people because it was the fighting democratic will of the people, and not any one leader of this or that party, which enforced the no-surrender policy through those dark years of solitary struggle.

How much greater a debt we owe, therefore, to a sector in China's ordeal which, after seven years, is still fighting the enemy, despite the fact that even today it is in a worse position than all China was before December 7, 1941. I am speaking of the partisan areas of China, which are still blockaded from all aid or promise of aid from any one of the United Nations. They are not only cut off from American Lend-Lease and military supplies which now go to China, but are also blockaded by the Chungking government itself. This is part of the internal problem of China, but we ought to take note of it and be grateful that the heroic Chinese partisan leaders behind the Japanese lines continue loyal to the democratic cause and do not join in with our enemies. In fact, the existence of just these forces in China have, as much as anything else, made it impossible for the Chungking government to capitulate to fascism.

The situation in China in some respects resembled that in Yugoslavia. The Chinese partisans led by Generals Chu Teh and Mao Tse-tung somewhat corresponded to Marshal Tito and his following, and the policy of Chungking toward them was about the same as that which Mikhailovich and King Peter tried to enforce toward the Yugoslav guerrillas. In Yugoslavia we and the British and Russians now actively aid Tito simply because his forces actively fight the Axis, but in Asia, up to the late spring of 1944, we gave no official recognition to the partisan armies which offered virtually the only armed opposition to the Japanese in North China. The Chinese partisan movement actually has much the largest guerrilla organization in the world. What makes it of special interest to us is the changing strategy of the Pacific War implied by the rapid westward advance of our naval and air forces.

In February, 1944, Admiral Nimitz revealed that the Navy intends to capture bases on the China coast from which it may attack Formosa and Japan. Hongkong and Canton might be the first China ports recovered, but from there it would still be a long bomber flight to Tokyo and Osaka. It is farther north, on the Shantung coast, that China lies closest to Japan; and the Chinese partisans there are thus potentially very important to us. Yet at this writing we do not even have an intelligence officer stationed in the vast areas which they control.

Stretching from the Yangtze Valley to the Mongolian steppe, and to the mountains and rivers of Southern Manchuria, thousands of villages make up the pattern of this "people's war." Its organizers are enterprising youths chiefly inspired and trained by the 18th Group Army—the combined Eighth Route and New Fourth armies. These forces are led by veterans of the former Red Army of China, who have behind them an amazing record of survival and growth through seventeen years of continuous civil and national war.

Foreign observers who visited the guerrilla districts in 1943 estimated that behind the Japanese lines they had organized and given crude training to militia numbering about seven million

286

people. These were the reserves of the main fighting units. In addition, there were said to be some twelve million members of various anti-Japanese associations which helped to clothe, feed, house, equip and transport the regular troops, and were their eyes and ears. Official data* showed partisan penetration in 455 *hsien* (or counties) of North China and in 52,800 villages, with a population of more than sixty million people. From three-fifths to two-thirds of the so-called "conquered territory" was asserted to be in guerrilla hands most of the time.

For nearly seven years the Japanese have been trying to exterminate these tireless enemies. Eighth Route regulars numbered hardly 50,000 men in 1937, and diverted only a few divisions of Japanese troops. But that vanguard multiplied in every direction. In 1944 more than half of Japan's 350,000 troops in China proper (excluding Manchuria) and some 200,000 puppet troops, were occupied in defending fortified areas against the 18th Group Army and in fighting punitive actions against it. Japanese military reports put its strength at from 500,000 to 600,000. Foreign military information gave a more conservative estimate of a total of about 200,000 rifles.

What is certain is that in every one of the provinces occupied by the Japanese, which cover an area three times the size of France, partisans have set up village and county councils. They have established four "border" governments in bases held throughout the war, except for brief intervals; and each of these regional governments represents liberated areas of several neighboring provinces. Wherever practicable there are elections by direct and secret ballot, and this is almost invariably the case in the village and county councils.

These behind-the-lines regimes perform nearly all the functions of normal administration. They have their own postal system and radio communications. They publish their own newspapers, magazines and books. They maintain an extensive system of schools and enforce a reformed legal code recognizing sex equality and adult suffrage. They regulate rents, collect taxes, control trade and issue currency, operate industries, maintain a number of experimental farms, extend agricultural credit, have a grain-rationing system, and in several places undertake fairly large afforestation projects.

If the world has recently heard little of these achievements it

* Vide *North China Front*, Chungking, 1943.

is not entirely the fault of the foreign press. In addition to military and economic blockade there has been a strict and highly effective news blockade at Chungking. Since 1939 virtually all news of activities of the 18th Group Army has been under ban by the Kuomintang's Ministry of Information, which monopolizes China's overseas publicity.

Nevertheless, the facts are well known to millions of Chinese, and are available to anybody who cares to run the risk of getting them. Among that small band of inquirers who have been in the guerrilla areas none was more impressed, and certainly none learned more, than one American Marine officer. I saw him in Shanghai during the fighting there, not long after returning from my first visit to Yenan; and when he expressed interest in the guerrilla areas and wanted to visit them, I told him what I knew of them. Later he got permission from his chief, Rear-Admiral Harry E. Yarnell, to make a study of the partisans. He spent many months with units of the Eighth Route Army, crossed and recrossed the Japanese lines, and finally emerged to write a valuable book about it.

Not long afterward we were at war and he was given a chance to apply what he had learned. Assigned to organize and train battalions of picked American youths for special tactical tasks, he incorporated many ideas avowedly borrowed from the Chinese guerrillas. Marine Raiders led by this son of a Connecticut clergyman are now carrying the Chinese cry of "Kung Ho!" ("work together") back across the Pacific. He is Colonel Evans Fordyce Carlson.

Since Carlson's trip, no other foreign military observer has been permitted by the Generalissimo to visit our partisan allies. But a few foreigners escaped from Japanese-held Peking, with the guerrillas' aid, and perforce became observers of life in this nation within a nation. I have talked to most of the foreigners who have traveled with the partisans—"returned students" as one of them called himself—and found that their impressions tally, in major respects, with my own. They include, besides Carlson, a British Army officer, an American bank manager, an American doctor, several American and British professors, a Belgian business man, a few missionaries, and half a dozen journalists. Their politics differ widely, but it is remarkable that they agree on these central facts:

Guerrilla China has become the scene of the broadest effort

of mass mobilization and mass education in Chinese history. The partisan regimes carrying out that effort have been able to survive and flourish because they have won the devoted support of the farmers, and particularly of youths, tens of thousands of whom have died in this little-publicized struggle. This fighting nation constitutes the closest approach to political, economic and social democracy that the Chinese have ever known. It has a system of government in which squeeze and corruption are so rare that it may be said to refute effectively the widespread belief among "Old China Hands" that the Chinese are incapable of running an honest government.

How did all this begin? It is a very long story going back to the civil-war period in China. Along with some others I have told that story rather exhaustively in the past and it is much too involved a period to recall now in any detail. But a quick synopsis of that phase of Chinese history is necessary to bring us up to date —to the approaching date of our invasion of Japan.

III

The People's War

THE defense perimeter held by Japanese troops in China in 1944 was, as we have seen, already stabilized before the end of 1939. When the enemy originally moved into the conquered provinces, most of the old officials of the Kuomintang government, as well as its troops, withdrew to the West and South. Behind them the administrative bureaucracy collapsed. In the cities it was replaced by Japanese and puppets, but a kind of political vacuum existed in the hinterland towns and villages, the interstices between enemy garrisons. Into that temporary vacuum moved the former Red Army of China—with arms, with teachers, and with faith in the people's strength.

This movement began with the Generalissimo's acquiescence. It was made possible first of all by Marshal Chang Hsueh-liang's earlier "detention" of the Generalissimo at Sian in 1936, in order to persuade him to stop fighting the Reds and unite with them against Japan. A truce was effected; then, after the the Japanese invaded North China, an agreement was reached which ended a decade of civil war. The Northern Red forces were recognized as part of the National Army. They dropped the Red flag and the Red star and accepted the designation "Eighth Route Army." Southeast of Shanghai other Red remnants were regrouped in 1938 as the "New Fourth Army."

But the Kungchantang (or Communist Party) continued to direct the reorganized Red forces, just as Chiang Kai-shek's Kuomintang (or Nationalist Party) maintained control of the other Chinese troops. Communists asserted that until the Kuomintang government legally recognized the rights of other political parties to exist they had no guarantee against a renewed attempt to exterminate them. They promised to surrender complete command of their forces to a constitutional, representative regime, as soon as the Kuomintang fulfilled its pledges to the people in that respect.

For Americans with little background on China the term "Communist" may here be misleading. The fact is real "Communism" was never established in China, even in the former Soviet areas, and Chinese Communists never claimed otherwise. There was a brief early period in Kiangsi when the youthful Red Army attempted collectivization and the abolition of all private ownership in the means of production; but experience brought many modifications. The Chinese Reds have always stated that their program was to lead China's "bourgeois-democratic revolution." In practice they have won their following by enforcing an immediate two-sided program of social, economic and political reforms (the overthrow of feudalism) and by leading the fight for national emancipation from foreign control. Socialism was and is an ultimate, but admittedly distant, goal.

Long before it became defunct the Comintern ceased to have much direct contact with the Chinese Communist Party, though it at times exerted a directive influence on it. The relative independence of this party was established when Mao Tsetung, today the acknowledged mentor of all Chinese Communists, broke away from the former leadership and was expelled (in 1927) for violating the party "line." In a subsequent struggle fought in a purely Chinese *milieu* he won out over Chen Tu-hsiu and later against Li Li-san, both at one time supported by the Comintern. Mao established the correctness of his own "line" through armed struggle. Moscow later on vindicated him, but the subsequent decade of civil war was fought with no significant material help from Russia or from the Comintern. In reality the party became a distinctly Chinese offspring of Marxism firmly rooted in the national problems of China's "semi-colonial" revolution.

Both the Kuomintang and the Kungchantang today claim to be the legitimate heirs of Dr. Sun Yat-sen, founder of the Chinese Republic. Both supported him in the early days of the revolution. Sun himself brought the Communists (the Kungchantang) into alliance with his Kuomintang party and it was only after his death, in 1925, that the counter-revolution, led by Chiang Kai-shek, tried to "annihilate" them. Even after the truce of 1936 there was no agreement over the practical application of Sun Yat-sen's political doctrine, known as the "Three Principles"—which are "nationalism, democracy and livelihood."

The Communists regard Sun as a social revolutionary and demand a radical interpretation of his principles. Briefly, they say they want a "thorough-going democratic revolution," with equalization of land ownership, universal suffrage, constitutional government establishing the people's power, and similar reforms that have accompanied the overthrow of feudalism elsewhere. The Kuomintang interprets the Three Principles much more conservatively. As the party draws its chief internal support from the landlord class it is naturally opposed to radical land reform. In general it wants to keep present economic and political relationships intact and to superimpose its dictatorship on the old Chinese semi-feudal structure. If it acknowledged the legality of other parties and their conflicting interpretations, especially if it conceded adult suffrage, that structure would almost certainly be overthrown.

But while such issues of democracy and livelihood remained still unsettled, the Communists and Nationalists at least agreed upon the principle of "nationalism" when Japan invaded the country. The Reds then took their military orders from the Generalissimo. In 1937 he sent them into the battle line in North China, where many Kuomintang leaders confidently expected them to be swallowed up in the Japanese drive. They did not disintegrate in that way, however, as some of the northern warlord armies did. They met the attack and were defeated in the cities, but instead of retreating or surrendering they withdrew to the villages and hills and continued fighting.

Infiltrating all the Northern provinces with experienced partisan leaders and political organizers, they soon enlisted valuable reinforcements from a thickening stream of refugees fleeing from the cities: students, workers, and various professional men and women including some intellectuals belonging to the non-Communist political parties, long suppressed by both the Chinese and Japanese regimes. Cut off from the rear, whole divisions of defeated Chinese troops came under their leadership. Their rifle power grew. By 1939 their stronghold had become so formidable that the Japanese were compelled to launch a full-dress offensive against them. They have been doing so semi-annually ever since.

The first partisan regime entirely inside occupied territory was set up in the mountains of Northeastern Shansi, east of the Yellow River, and now includes areas as far north as Jehol, or Inner Mongolia. Another regime, with its capital in Southeast Shansi, directs operations in recovered territory which stretches for over 300 miles across Southern Hopei and Shantung eastward to the Yellow Sea. There is a third border region centering in Northern Kiangsu, north of Shanghai, which is controlled by the New Fourth Army, with nearly 100,000 troops. A fourth regional government is established in the mountainous country north of the Yangtze River above Hankow, where the borders of Anhui and Hupeh enclose the southern extremity of Honan.

Political and military methods used to organize the people borrow heavily from the pattern developed in the only base *inside Free China* which the Communists now hold. That consists of the former Soviet districts of North China. The area lies west of the Yellow River, opposite Japanese fortifications, and includes Northern Shensi Province and small parts of Kansu and Ninghsia Provinces. The old Soviet government was abolished in 1937, and a "Shensi-Kansu-Ninghsia Border Area Government" took its place. This regime renounced class warfare, stopped redistributing the land, and legalized all anti-Japanese parties and organizations. Suffrage was extended to all citizens over the age of eighteen. Private enterprise was encouraged, and the economy was frankly described as "state-controlled capitalism."

The town of Yenan, the so-called "mother of the Chinese

partisans," is the capital of the Shensi-Kansu-Ninghsia Border Government. I have seen the Yenan area under the old regime and the new. My second visit* to Yenan was in 1939, after the present government was established. It remains, at this writing, the last trip made there by any foreign newspaper correspondent, for soon afterward the region was cut off by the military blockade.

In this area, formerly one of the poorest and most backward on earth, the Yenan government built up an intelligent and prosperous community life by a few years of energetic and honest administration. Free compulsory primary education was introduced, and middle schools, technical schools and colleges, including a College for Women, were established. Thousands of youths walked hundreds of miles across enemy-held territory to reach Yenan and study in its institutions. There was a public health service and several hospitals. There were many industrial co-operatives and also some state-owned industries, but private trade also flourished. Peasants in this "Shen-Kan-Ning" region opened up over 600,000 acres of new land and with government help tens of thousands of refugees from occupied China were settled here. Opium was extirpated. In the areas I saw prostitution and child slavery were effectively prohibited, and there were no beggars. The idle were put to work. Every village had its elected council and every country likewise. The regional government was elected by delegates chosen by popular vote, for the first time in Chinese history.

On the other side of the Yellow River, behind Japanese lines, the organization of the social, political and economic life was naturally more difficult than in Yenan, but in general the goals, if not always the degree of success achieved, were comparable. Although newspaper correspondents were not able to investigate the Shansi and Hopei areas, the various foreigners who escaped from the Japanese in Peking and made their way southward across the guerrilla territory have given fairly complete pictures of the system which prevails. Among these observers was Professor William Band, of the famous American missionary institution, Yenching University, whom I knew when I lectured there for a year myself. Another was Professor Michael Lindsay, also of Yenching, whose report was recently published in *Amerasia*.** The most comprehensive account of the partisan areas to

* Described in *The Battle for Asia*, N.Y., 1941.
** N.Y., March 31, April 14, 1944.

reach the outside world for some time, it was released for publication by the author's father, A. D. Lindsay, Master of Baliol College, Oxford.

According to Professor Lindsay, the partisan governments are elected from candidates nominated directly by the people and their organizations. Village and county councils carry on nearly everywhere. Villages are grouped into electoral districts for the *hsien*, or county, elections, which are preceded by meetings and debates. Voting is by secret ballot and there are rights of recall and referendum. Border or regional governments behind the lines are also elected directly, wherever possible.

Although in Kuomintang China members of non-Kuomintang parties are not permitted to hold office, in the partisan areas all the anti-Japanese parties of the Democratic Federation are recognized. Kuomintang party members have also been elected to office. In the Shansi-Chahar-Hopei Border Government both the chairman and vice-chairman are Kuomintang Party members.

The Chinese partisans aim to establish a united front of all groups and hence the Communist Party limits its own members to one-third of the total of any elected body. This peculiar policy is vigorously enforced, according to Lindsay. The purpose is to bring into the government both landowners (and even "landlords") and merchants, but above all to develop political leaders among the poor peasants and workers. It is "education in democracy by practicing democracy," according to the partisan leaders.

In the mass organizations there are no limitations on Communist leadership, however; and these organizations are the guerrillas' sinew and life. They include separate unions or associations for farmers, workers, youth, children and women, and membership in each runs into the millions. Most important of all such organizations are the self-defense corps, the militia, and the Youth Vanguards. These are crude but basic military organizations which locally support the 18th Group Army's main forces.

The hold of the Chinese Communists and the allied partisan leaders on all these organizations, and the extraordinary morale of the troops, traces to their disciplined and democratic personalities rather than to Marxist political propaganda. If I here cause lifted eyebrows among skeptical "Old China Hands," and particularly among newly arrived army officers in West China,

294

I cannot blame them. They have never seen the people I am talking about.

G. Martel Hall, former manager of the National City Bank in Peking, who was the last American to escape from the Japanese across the partisan areas, told me recently that there was simply no other way he could explain the success of the partisan leaders with the peasants, "except through their own incorruptibility and honesty, their energetic patriotism, their devotion to practical democracy, their faith in the common people and the continuous effort they made to arouse them to action and responsibility."

Take Mao Tse-tung, for example. He is now fifty years old and has been a "Red warlord" for twenty years. Financially it does not seem to have been very profitable. Mao still owns no property and is penniless. The army feeds and clothes him, as it does all partisan fighters. Colonel Evans Carlson describes General Chu Teh, Commander-in-Chief of the 18th Group Army, as a man who "has the kindliness of a Robert E. Lee, the tenacity of a Grant, and the humility of a Lincoln."* Chu was one of Dr. Sun Yat-sen's early disciples and once was a rich man, but he gave all his wealth to the army and today owns nothing but the pack he still carries—and he is over sixty—on his own back. Such stories are typical of many Chinese partisans whom I have known, eaten rice with, and slept side by side with for days.

Mao Tse-tung drew a salary the equivalent of less than three American dollars a month when I last saw him. Nobody in the 18th Group Army is making money out of the war: Commanders and enlisted men are paid only a few dollars a month for their personal needs. Officers and men live alike, eat the same food, wear the same kind of uniforms, and share their hardships in common with the peasants. It isn't asceticism such as Gandhi practices; they would all prefer the more abundant life. But the problem is to make every dollar and every bowl of rice go as far as possible, and to achieve self-sufficiency.

Mutual hatred of the Japanese provides the atmosphere in which these zealots exploit the people's patriotism, but side by side with political reforms have gone economic and social changes. In the case of women the enforcement of laws like monogamy, freedom of marriage at the age of consent, free education, and suffrage at the age of eighteen, has won a surprising response.

* Read Carlson's *Twin Stars of China*, N.Y., 1940, for an American military man's estimate of the 18th Group Army.

Lindsay says there are over 3,000,000 members of the women's organizations in the partisan areas. Many women have been elected to village and town councils and large numbers of young girls carry serious political and military responsibilities.

The primary school system operates widely in all the "permanent" guerrilla bases and education is free and compulsory. In some places as high as 80% of the younger children of school age are now literate. Space and time do not permit me here to offer a detailed description of the economic fabric which supports these areas; the basic reform is enforcement of a drastic reduction in land rent. Land of absentee landlords is tilled in common; the aim is to cultivate all cultivable land. Taxes are collected mainly in grain, and are kept at about 10% of those demanded by the Japanese. Consumers, marketing and industrial co-operatives are very widespread. Lindsay's report states that there are over 4,000 co-operatives in Shansi and 5,000 in Central Hopei alone.

Unimaginable hardships have accompanied partisan organization at every step. For a vivid and almost painfully realistic eyewitness account of these sufferings of growth in the midst of war read Agnes Smedley's powerful book, *Battle Hymn of China*.* While it is true the Japanese have failed to destroy the partisan forces, or to stop their increase, they have carried out literally thousands of large- and small-scale punitive expeditions against them. They have looted and burned thousands of villages, raped the womenfolk and slaughtered countless civilians, in a terror aimed to wipe out all thought of resistance. The guerrillas have always found ways to overcome the demoralizing effects of these tactics, but not without sacrifices as bitter as any endured in Russia. It is true the Japanese are now unable to control any village much beyond the range of their garrisons along North China's railways and roads. But it is also true that their fortified points have greatly increased and can now be seized only at a very heavy cost.

Partisan leaders were sometimes disparaged because they did not more often attack large fortified enemy strongholds. Such criticisms were usually based on ignorance of their circumstances. Lack of munitions industry was a basic weakness which ingenuity and improvisation could not wholly overcome. While the main forces of the Eighth Route and New Fourth armies,

* N.Y., 1943.

comprising perhaps twenty divisions, were relatively well equipped with machine guns and rifles, and some mortars, they were always short of artillery, ammunition, high explosives and transport. Consequently they had to select engagements which could be quickly terminated and promised the capture of more supplies than might be expended.

Judged on the basis of the millions they have mobilized, their combat efficiency may seem low; but contrasted with the inactivity of troops in China sitting in secure bases and receiving important Allied help, their performance is impressive. How long, the partisan leaders ask their critics, would Chiang Kai-shek have maintained belligerency against Japan if the Allies had blockaded him for five years in the way Chungking has denied all aid to them?

Lacking the favorable conditions enjoyed by troops in unoccupied China, the partisans nevertheless increased their sorties to average thirty-three *daily* clashes with Japanese troops throughout 1942 and 1943. "We are the fish and the people are the waters through which we swim," I was once told by the Field Commander of the 18th Group Army, General Peng Teh-huai. Only by the skilful use of their two main advantages, numbers and space, have his forces won their power. The millions behind them simply increase their mobility.

So much for background. How does all this affect our own plans to defeat Japan through China?

IV

American Dilemma

AFTER all, you saved the Kuomintang," a Chinese intellectual in Chungking said to me. "It is your baby now and you cannot avoid responsibility for its actions."

He meant simply that American money, arms and economic aid were given to the Kuomintang authorities, without conditions concerning policies pursued inside China. American government representatives several times made it clear to Chungking that we would disapprove of a renewal of civil strife during the joint war against Japan. But Americans did not go beyond that nor seek to have the blockade lifted against the partisan areas.

Chungking established its blockade against the 18th Group Army because Kuomintang Party leaders had become increasingly disturbed by the Communists' success in recovering areas behind the Japanese lines. The Generalissimo described their activity as "illegal occupation of the national territory." The Kuomintang's War Areas Political and Party Affairs Commission took the position that all the guerrilla administrations were "illegal" and should be abolished to await the re-establishment of the Kuomintang system.

In 1940 some Kuomintang troops engaged the rear echelon of the New Fourth Army while it was moving from its base south of the Yangtze River near Shanghai, to an area entirely behind the Japanese lines to which it was assigned by the Generalissimo. It was apparently a surprise attack and the partisans were reportedly outnumbered eight to one. The little detachment of about 4,000 was not a combat unit and it was easily encircled and annihilated. General Yeh Ting, the Commander of the New Fourth Army (who was himself not a Communist) was wounded and taken prisoner, and General Han Ying, the Field Commander, was killed, together with many of his staff, some doctors and nurses of the medical battalions, a number of convalescent wounded soldiers, some cadets, men and women students, and some industrial co-operative workers attached to the army.

The incident failed to liquidate the New Fourth Army, however, whose main forces were already north of the Yangtze River fighting Japanese troops there. But it did reopen all the old wounds of distrust. It drove a deep wedge between the Communist and the Nationalist parties which has never since been removed. Observers in China considered that the refusal of the Communists to retaliate at that time, combined with the sharply unfavorable reaction in foreign capitals, prevented a major recrudescence of civil war which would have greatly simplified Japan's political problem in China. The Generalissimo ruled that the incident was caused by the New Fourth's "insubordination" and henceforth withdrew all aid not only from that army but also from the Eighth Route.

For some months previous to the tragedy no part of the 18th Group Army had been paid. From this time on they not only received no pay nor ammunition but were blockaded by a ring of strong government forces from access to supplies in Free China, which they might have purchased or received as gifts from the people. Ironically enough the Kuomintang troops enforcing this blockade were largely equipped with Soviet Russian supplies. There were two group armies (the 37th and 38th) engaged exclusively in the blockading enterprise. It was suggested that they were needed in the campaign to recover Burma, but Chungking considered their "policing role" in the Northwest of greater importance and there they remained.

It was against this anomaly that Mme. Sun Yat-sen, the Generalissimo's sister-in-law, and revered widow of the founder of the Kuomintang, protested in a statement of extraordinary candor which was published abroad in February, 1944. "Reaction and fascism are strong in China," she warned. "This is proved by the diversion of part of our National Army to the blockading of the guerrilla areas, by the oppression of the peasantry, and by the absence of a true labor movement. . . . Some Chinese are preparing to destroy the guerrilla bases in North Shensi."

Foreign correspondents in Chungking, long irritated because they had been prohibited from visiting the fighting front in the North, and the blockaded areas, questioned a Chungking spokesman about Mme. Sun's statement. When he denied its charges ten correspondents sent a joint letter to Chiang Kai-shek asking for permission to visit Yenan to investigate for themselves. Back came Chiang's answer. Certainly they could go— "when the time comes."

All these facts are known to our army, to the State Department and to Americans in China, but probably few Americans at home realize that our Lend-Lease aid goes exclusively to the Kuomintang authorities. We maintain no consular representation in Yenan and no military liaison with the partisans. All our supplies flown over the Hump into China—modern bombers and fighters, artillery, transport and ammunition—support only the one party, of course. Financial aid sent to China by the C.I.O., A.F.L., and Railway Brotherhood also goes exclusively to Kuomintang groups—under which labor has virtually no freedom of press, speech, or organization.

What should be done about this admittedly internal affair of China? Our new treaty with China (1943) renounces extra-territoriality rights and restores full sovereignty to the Chinese government. Could we now tell the present government how to run its business without being branded neo-imperialists? But inevitably the war has already caused us to intervene in support of the Kuomintang, in terms of economic and military aid. Is it not merely playing ostrich to pretend that our future economic help to China does not carry implicit political responsibilities of the gravest kind?

Military necessity might yet cause us to insist upon an equitable distribution of supplies in China. Before long the question of relief goods must also arise. China has asked for half a billion dollars' worth of food and other materials from UNRRA, but as far as is known there is no plan to permit this aid to go to people in the partisan areas. Yet the good will of just those people may become more and more essential to us in the final phases of the war against Japan. North China bases will become important to us, and it would avail us little if we had to back the Kuomintang troops in a civil war against the Communists in order to secure access to them.

Could the Communists and the partisan troops united with them be destroyed by force? The Kuomintang spent ten fruitless years in the attempt, before 1937. Even with the use of American bombers and fighters on his side, the Generalissimo is not likely to secure greater success than the Japanese have had against these experienced guerrilla warriors. It is now a physical impossibility for the Chungking government to destroy this opposition in anything short of a long and bloody war, fully backed by Allied troops.

An interesting consciousness of immensely increased strength is evident in all recent declarations by Chinese Communist leaders, who now insist that their party and its troops must be treated "on a basis of equality" with the Kuomintang. Typical of this new firmness was the speech made by Chou En-lai, a veteran Red Army commander, after his return to Yenan from Chungking late in 1943. Here is a significant excerpt:

"Has the Chinese Communist Party lost its backing? It is true that during its birth and development the Chinese Communist Party received help from the Comintern. But the backbone of the party is not the Comintern but the Chinese people. Our party is a party of the masses. It has 800,000 members and 500,000 troops and it has united over 100 million people in blood and flesh through actual fighting.

"We are firmly supporting national unity. We are still prepared to talk with the Kuomintang, to discuss how to avoid the danger of civil war, how to solve existing problems. However, such negotiations must be sincere, equals meeting equals, mutually making concessions. It must not be negotiation on one hand, conflicts and clashes on the other; letters of liaison going back and forth on the one hand, massing of troops on the other. . . . We still hope that the authorities will correct their misguided internal policy and carry out Dr. Sun Yat-sen's People's Three Principles. We hope also to co-operate with all other anti-Japanese parties, groups and forces on a democratic basis in order to wage the war firmly and push on toward progress."

There is also the question of Soviet Russia and what her policy will be once she turns her eyes eastward. In an earlier chapter it was suggested that everything would depend on whether the European war ends with harmonious relations still effective among the Big Three. Russian participation in the war on China's side would obviously be incompatible with a Chungking policy of annihilating Chinese Communists. If we desire to have Russian co-operation and understanding in post-war Asia as well as post-war Europe, it would seem contradictory for us to finance and arm another anti-Communist crusade in China.

If, on the other hand, Chungking were to become reconciled to the idea of a representative government and re-establish co-operation with the Communist Party, we might quickly increase the tempo of warfare throughout North China and Manchuria. It is feasible to fly into the recovered areas large amounts of ammunition and explosives, air-borne troops to help the partisans wreck Japanese communications, and the means to force the enemy to double or treble his garrisons in China. Even with their present strength the partisans might hold airfields in Shantung and Kiangsu, where our bombers could refuel on shuttle flights to Japan.

It is not unnatural to suppose that such possibilities were discussed at the Cairo Conference. According to dispatches at the time "the conference took cognizance of the fact that internal differences between Chiang Kai-shek and the Chinese Communist army must be overcome before China could be opened as the primary base for direct attack against Japan itself."

The changing international picture seems unfavorable to those in China who want to have another try at annihilating the Communists. In the final analysis the Generalissimo is not likely to risk his international prestige by assuming responsibility for a major fratricidal conflict. Despite pressure from some of his generals, he has stated that he will solve the Communist-Kuomintang problem "purely by political means." At bottom a realist, the Generalissimo must also have taken careful note of Winston Churchill's declaration of support for Marshal Tito.

"The sanest and safest course for us to follow," said the Prime Minister early in 1944, "is to judge all parties and factions dispassionately by the test of their readiness and ability to fight the Germans and thus lighten the burden of Allied troops. This is not a time for ideological preferences for one side or the other."

Some think we should apply a similar test in China, with the change of only one word in the above text; that is, for Germans read Japanese. They think that as long as we do not, the combat efficiency of China's armies will be minimized and we shall remain cut off from millions of useful allies.

Another thing General Stilwell has to keep in mind is that Japan may yet occupy the whole of Southern and Western China. That she has the means to do so is hardly to be questioned. Japan has lost positions and equipment to us, but very little of the reserves of manpower and matériel she has been accumulating for many years. And no one who knows the true condition of Chiang Kai-shek's armies suggests that they would be able to defeat a large-scale Japanese offensive.

It would be entirely within the logic of Japan's past strategy to seek security by extending her flank in China, once Americans showed signs of building up bases there from which her "inner zone" in the northern provinces and Manchuria and in Japan itself could be invaded. The Hankow-Canton Railway, the railways of Kwangsi and Yunnan, and the roads of Fukien, Kiangsi and Kwangtung, would all be useful continental arteries of supply for the maintenance of Japanese troops in Southeast Asia, now that Japan's shipping situation grows extremely acute. It is quite conceivable Japan may consider the occupation of Southern China worth the cost—and it may not be high—for two other reasons: 1) loot, raw materials and food; 2) to prevent our setting

302

up a base around Hongkong and Canton, in co-operation with a Chinese attack from the west.

If such a campaign developed on a major scale, the bulk of the Generalissimo's forces would probably retire to Western Yunnan and Szechuan, and his government would assume the character of a regime-in-exile. The Communist forces have refrained from encroaching on any unoccupied territory. But in the event the Japanese made a new conquest there is little doubt that partisan warfare under the leadership of the 18th Group Army would quickly spread all over South China. The same institutions and system now prevailing in North China would be established in the villages behind the enemy lines. Thus the partisans, chiefly led by the Communists, would in fact take over the main tasks of resistance on a national scale.

The solution to the dilemma facing American policy in China thus became more urgent as a result of the startling successes of our fleet in the Central Pacific. They necessitated a reorientation not only in our own strategic thinking about the best approach to Japan—but a change in Japan's counter-strategy as well.

PART - III - THE ROAD AHEAD

I

Back to Burma

AMERICAN naval-*cum*-air victories in the Central Pacific in the winter and spring of 1944 demonstrated that complete superiority over the Japanese had been established in these two realms of power. After the attack on Truk it was evident that the approaches to Japan by sea—from the north, the east and the south —would be cleared long before the continental approach could be opened from the west.

The most important single factor in thus bringing about a spectacular reversal in Japan's position in the Pacific was the achievement of technical superiority by carrier-based American aircraft over Japan's land-based as well as carrier planes. We had to have ships to mother those planes and we had to have naval vessels ever ready to defend them in a major sea action; but without its superior air power the American fleet could not have ventured upon the bold and novel tactics enforced by Admiral Nimitz.

No longer protected by a naval fleet and aircraft capable of guarding and maintaining communication and supply lines to them, Japan's island possessions ceased to represent connected defense lines but in effect became mere isolated fortresses which could not seriously menace our operations beyond the range of their land batteries. Island-hopping was over. Wide outflanking operations, aimed to build up a series of bases along the shortest route to Japan, became the main strategy. In the south and west the path would lead through the Marshall Islands, Guam, the Philippines, the Ladrones and the Riu Kiu Islands. In the northwest it would lead across the Aleutians and down through the Kuriles toward the enemy's heart.

In this new perspective Southeast Asia became a long salient which it was important to remove in a diversionary campaign. In relation to the Pacific approach to Japan, it was somewhat as the African and Italian approaches were to the invasion of Germany. If it was more essential than that it was mainly because Southeast Asia provided Japan with many of the raw materials needed for her war effort. Greater than that, however, was its political importance, as we shall see.

America's vastly increased naval and air strength implied the possibility and the need for a movement out of India in coordination with our attacks on Japan's island possessions and a drive toward Hongkong and Canton from the sea. While landing operations in Western Europe naturally would absorb Allied attention during the spring, that would not draw upon forces available in India. Even at the end of 1943, the Allies already had far greater striking power in this region and much greater fire power, than the Japanese had used during the four months' blitzkrieg in which they overran roughly a million and a half square miles of territory.

Our superiority to the enemy was established in every branch, but was most strikingly demonstrated in the air. American planes roamed the skies of Burma meeting but negligible opposition. By the summer of 1943 it was evident that wherever we moved in Southeast Asia the Japanese would face such tremendous air superiority that they would, in effect, be obliged to fight without air cover.

Much the same thing applied to sea power in the Indian Ocean. As a result of acquisition of the Italian fleet, the conquest of the submarine menace, the launching of many hundreds of new fighting craft, and the heavy losses of the Japanese Navy, the Allies were in a position to attack Japan from both east and west.

The Burma-Malaya frontiers and beaches lay open to invasion across a distance of nearly 3,000 miles. The Allied Command could here choose, as in Europe, a point of main attack from a number of different alternatives. A logical plan of land campaign seemed to call for these moves:

1) An invasion of Upper Burma, via the Ledo Road, aiming to connect with the Burma Road and to reopen a land-line of supply to China, in co-ordination with

2) A second column invading along the Manipur Road, striking toward Central Burma, and a third column following the seaboard route through Chittagong and Akyab, thrusting toward Rangoon, supported by

3) An attack by Chiang Kai-shek's American-trained forces in China, which would hit at the Japs from Yunnan and aim to achieve a union with the American-led column on the Ledo Road.

Ideally, that campaign should be backed up by

1) A British-led amphibious operation in Southern Burma, with its object the recovery of Rangoon and control of Burma's main riparian communications, and by

2) Amphibious operations on the Malayan coast, aimed to cut Japan's Bangkok-Rangoon and Bangkok-Singapore supply lines; and

3) An attack on Singapore itself, affected by flank landings and the seizure of nearby bases and airfields in Sumatra.

Japan won all this southern territory by piece-meal tactics, going after Malaya first and then turning on Burma when Singapore was cinched. But Japan was operating from a strong continental base, with good interior lines of communication, and against an enemy unprepared in nearly every respect. She still had that base (Indo-China) and had immensely strengthened it. She had also heavily fortified new strategic bases in Burma and Malaya. And against her the Allies had to begin from distant bases, supplying invasion forces by sea and air, except for the Indo-Burmese roads and whatever forces could be used to attack from China.

By sea from Calcutta to Rangoon is 737 miles. From Colombo to Rangoon is 1,248 miles, and from Rangoon to Singapore is another 1,100 miles. Obviously a preliminary step to any amphibious operations would be the clearing out of the Japanese from the Bay of Bengal and islands which guard the approaches to Rangoon, and from the coasts of Tenasserim, Thailand and Malaya. Recovery of the Nicobar and Andaman Islands, which Japan seized in 1942 and made into strong points, would better than halve the distance between the mainland of the archipelago and our Indian bases.

But with all our sea and air supremacy, the battle for East Asia will be won or lost on the ground, where Allied superiority has been less well demonstrated. Do the British expect their Indian Army to provide the main forces of the offensive? If not, why have they built it up to a force of more than two million men? Much has been done to modernize that army since the days of the Burma debacle. A good part of it has been motorized, it has some excellent artillery, there is a tank force, and the best divisions have undergone an intensive re-training routine, supposed to fit them for jungle warfare. Yet when all is said about the Indian Army it still remains far from European standards; and no one can be quite sure what it will do against fellow Asiatics.

Indian troops are mostly illiterate infantrymen, with little political training, and they fight as mercenaries pure and simple. Indeed the British emphasize it as an asset that the average Indian soldier, whether Hindu or Moslem, is not inspired by patriotic motives or political slogans but by the traditions of his regiment, or tribe, or caste. That is why, the British say, the Army cannot be affected by political discontent of the Gandhian variety.

The British also believe—rather whimsically, it sometimes seems—that there is still a good deal of loyalty to the Crown in the Indian Army. This, as much as anything, lay behind the appointment of Lord Louis Mountbatten, a cousin of the King-Emperor, to the post of C-in-C of the East Asia Command. It was fully recognized that the prestige of the Crown had never been at such a discount and the British were determined to restore it fully. If they had their own way, they would doubtless prefer to wait till they could bring all Air Marshal Harris' RAF bombers out here and parade them across India.

But it was just here that Americans and Chinese found themselves in some disagreement with their allies. Whatever else the Cairo Conference decided it became clear that it had not completely reconciled conflicting political aims and strategic interests in this region nor brought about a complete co-ordination of effort between the China-Burma-India command of Lieutenant-General Joseph F. Stilwell and the East Asia Command under Lord Mountbatten.

It was America, not Britain, that had promised to supply the Chinese Army, and supply them Stilwell would, even if he had to fight a campaign all by himself up in his corner of the world where India meets Burma and China. Accordingly he started off, in the autumn of 1943, to make his way across the jungles ahead of American bulldozers building the Ledo Road. We have already seen that he had only his few American-trained Chinese divisions to begin the operation. The British did lend him some air-borne troops and he got a small detachment of American Rangers as reinforcements.

Still, the British did not move in the South except fitfully along the Bengal coast, with an operation aimed to recover the port of Akyab. Oddly enough they used mainly West African troops in that action. Was it true that the British were not anxious to see a supply line reopened to China before they had re-established control over colonial Asia? Was it possible that they realized the war against Japan would be decided in the Pacific and that the longer they waited here the less costly a destruction of Japanese power in Southeast Asia would be? Was it political strategy and not military considerations, that prevented them from entering into Stilwell's scheme with enthusiasm? Was it Mountbatten's fault—or Churchill's?

These questions cannot be answered here, but they were certainly being asked all over Southeast Asia. It was noted that this lack of support for the American-Chinese operations in upper Burma put General Stilwell out on an exposed salient which the Japs might outflank whenever they brought in sufficient forces to do so. The fact that Japan had kept but modest forces in the region to date signified little. She still had good communications along the China main and her manpower reserves were huge. She had been digging in here for more than two years. She had built good roads, leading to a deep, powerfully built defense system along the coasts and in the jungle. She could probably throw a million troops into Southern Asia if necessary and she might feed and supply them entirely from accumulated stores and local resources. Japan would not be dislodged in Burma by anything short of an all-out campaign.

As the dry season in Eastern India approached its end, and the East Asia Command showed no signs of large-scale action along the lines I have suggested, it became evident that Roosevelt and Churchill had not promised Chiang Kai-shek the recovery of Burma in 1944. It also became evident, when the Japanese themselves suddenly debouched from Burma into the Manipur Plain of India, that despite the overall advantages enjoyed by the Allies in this region, our own lack of cohesion and a plan of co-ordinated action could still cost us serious reverses and defeats.

The Japanese came into India across jungle trails and a road over which Americans had driven jeeps during our retreat from Burma. They struck at Imphal and toward the Assam-Bengal Railway, which fed Stilwell's main base in Assam at the western terminus of the Ledo Road. It was an obvious place to attack, for by breaking the railway and supply line they could cut off Stilwell's rear, and force him to retire from upper Burma. Furthermore, if the Japanese succeeded in getting astride the railway, they might raid far into famine-stricken Bengal and succeed in creating havoc in the main industrial base of India.

There was another factor, potentially very important, which Japan sought to activate by her invasion. That was the peculiar political weakness of the United Nations in this part of the world. Knowing the seething discontent in India, one might expect that extensive fifth columnism would aid the Japanese, particularly in Bengal, historically the center of Indian terrorism, and the home of Subhas Chandra Bose, the Indian nationalist leader turned fascist. Accompanying the Japanese as marshal of an "Indian National Army," Bose was relied upon to rally his followers to help make the expedition a success.

The battle emphasized the paradox which distinguishes the war in Asia from the war to liberate Europe. In Asia it is a fight

308

for control of subject peoples who did not have self-determination before their conquest by Japan and who are not promised it now. There is no doubt that as Japan utilized the nationalist ambitions of the colonial peoples during her periods of offensive so she will also exploit the same factor as her tide of Empire begins irretrievably to ebb.

II

Lands without Charters

RESTORING European rule in the Asiatic countries is not quite the same thing as liberating Nazi-held countries which were formerly free and are now guaranteed future independence by the Atlantic Charter. Mr. Churchill early perceived that and was quick to qualify Britain's acceptance of the Charter when he declared that it would in no way affect traditional policies of British rule in the colonial possessions—which contain more than four-fifths of the population of the British Empire.

Even a small power like the Netherlands, which could not hope for a revival of sovereignty at home except through a victory of Soviet Russia and the Anglo-Saxon powers, and could not keep it except with the protection of at least one of those nations, is apparently to be given full power over some seventy million Indonesians after the Japs have been driven out of the East Indies. It is true that Queen Wilhelmina has proclaimed a plan to put Java on an equal status with the Netherlands, but this means simply that the Dutch in Java will be allowed somewhat more freedom in ruling it. There is no indication that the Queen intends to offer the Javanese a plebiscite on such things as adult suffrage, or collaboration, and direct relations with their Eastern neighbors. Issues of self-determination or "independence" will not be allowed to arise at all.

The position of the French was equally curious. Like the Dutch, they had lost their sovereignty at home, but that did not suggest to them any parallel with the position of their colonials. The Atlantic Charter does not apply to the twenty million people in Indo-China.

This picture was not altered by the Cairo communiqué, except to point up the anomaly. The conference did recognize China's right to recover frontiers for which Chinese had been fighting for years before either ourselves or the British entered the war. It also pledged Korea's independence "in due course." But the communiqué naturally brought ironic comment from some Asiatics, who could not but note that it promised independence to a country which was formerly a suzerainty of China, but said nothing about the future status of nations Japan had taken from the European powers which conquered them during the last century.

On her part Japan announced plans to "emancipate" the Europeans' former colonies but remained mum on the subject of Korea. This omission did not greatly weaken her propaganda against "white domination" however. She actually set up "self-government" in several areas. It had to be anticipated that as her need for winning native support became more urgent she might give much wider authority to these quasi-independent regimes.

Such, at least, seemed true in the case of Burma. In the summer of 1943 the Japanese recognized the "independence" of the Burmese government under Dr. Ba Maw, who could not be so easily dismissed as a mere marionette. He had been legal premier under the old regime, but the British had put him in jail when he planked for complete independence and non-participation in the European war. Naturally this martyrdom made him something of a hero in his own country. Under the new "independent" government he united his own Sinyetha, or "Poor Man's Party" with the main nationalist organization, the Dobamma Aisyone Party, more commonly known as the Thakins. It was these same Thakins who helped drive the British out of Burma by guerrilla war, sabotage and arson.

The Japanese cautiously permitted the Thakins to maintain a "Burma Independence Army"—variously estimated at from 5,000 to 25,000 rifles. They had learned a lot about guerrilla war by now and doubtless realized that if the "free" Burma government and the Burma Army took themselves seriously, and enlisted the support of the native population, they could make life difficult for any invading forces. But the Japanese had also learned that the average Burman was no more pro-Japanese than he was pro-British, or pro-Chinese. This astonishing fellow was simply pro-Burman. Until he was a more thoroughly indoctrinated "co-prosperity-ite," or until the Japs were more hardpressed, they were not likely to arm him in large numbers.

In Indo-China the Japanese still nominally recognized French sovereignty, as represented by the Vichy crowd, but in practice collaboration was so broad that it had been unnecessary to liquidate the French entirely. At the same time the humiliation of France in the eyes of her subjects had been prolonged, so that it was doubtful if the Tricolor could very soon again command respect there. Japan was said to have won some measure of support from the Annamite Nationalists, to whom she also promised eventual independence. The Annamites are the most advanced of the Indo-Chinese races and form most of the French-officered army. Japanese plans included the fostering of an Independent Army of Annam, similar to the Burma Independence Army. They trained Annamite leaders in Japan—as they once trained, in Chamberlain's day, the leaders of the Burmese Thakins.

But the Japs would probably string along with the Vichyites until an Allied conquest of France.

In Java our busy little brown brothers made similar efforts to deflate the white man's prestige and mobilize native support for the slogan of Asia for Asiatics. The population was assiduously preached at, exhorted, and propagandized by radio, in the press, and in public meetings. A Javanese Cultural League was engaged full-time in spreading Japanese propaganda and poisoning the minds of millions of natives against their former Dutch rulers. Imprisoned nationalists were released, as in Indo-China and Burma. A Java Patriotic Movement was reorganized and allowed to promise eventual "independence" to the masses.

But of all the Asiatics enlisted on Japan's side perhaps none would prove of such direct military significance as Subhas Chandra Bose, who was head of a provisional "independent" government of India, as well as the Jap-appointed Marshal of the "Indian National Army."

The British did not underestimate Bose. As we have seen, it was his underground organization, the Forward Bloc, which was responsible for most of the arson, sabotage and murder carried out after the arrest of Gandhi and Nehru—though the latter officially got the blame. Indians who owned radios had for two years tuned

311

in regularly to hear him yelling over the ether—first from Japan, then Singapore, then Rangoon. Since he was the only one of the "Big Three" of the Indian Congress leaders who was not locked up, there was nobody in India to shout him down.

Possibly as many as 800,000 Indians were living under Japanese control, including roughly 60,000 captured Indian soldiers and officers. The Japanese usually treated them with marked consideration and reports indicated that their efforts were not wholly fruitless. Subhas Bose claimed that his Indian National Army would be "300,000 strong." Evidently he counted on many deserters he hoped to lure away from the British Indian Army. But even 30,000 Indians, trained to infiltrate and carry out sabotage and spread defeatist and revolutionary propaganda behind the lines, were able to create a grave problem for British officers trying to oppose the Japs with politically unindoctrinated Indian troops.

In the summer of 1943 the Japanese stage-managed their most ambitious political stunt when they convened a Greater East Asia Conference in Tokyo. Delegates were present from China (the Nanking government), Burma, Manchukuo, the Philippines, and Thailand—all now "independent"—and from Java, Malaya and Indo-China. This Conference issued some high-sounding declarations laying down foundations for the Co-Prosperity Sphere and future plans for a kind of Eastern League of Nations.

Had it been anything but a shadow play, useful chiefly for propaganda purposes, had it represented the will of even half of the 500 million men in territories under Japan's armed forces, then the Allies would really have had something to worry about. Fortunately for us the dream of the Tokyo Conference did not correspond to reality. Fortunately, Japan's own historic limitations made it impossible for her to carry out any true mission of liberation and prevented her from fully exploiting, for military victory, the political riches inherent in the situation she had brought about.

Owing to the semi-feudal basis of her own imperialism, Japan was quite unable to confer genuine independence on the colonies she seized and her rulers had no such thing in mind. Her industrial foundations and resources were inadequate to the prodigious military task, and she was compelled to adopt confiscatory economic policies which left no room for a true alliance with any legitimate native class interest in the colonies. Her backward political structure at home was inconsistent with the introduction

312

of progressive or revolutionary policies abroad. And this prevented her from carrying through the economic and political changes which would have enabled her to arm the peoples under her, train them to fight, and enlist all Asia in a struggle for equality and freedom from European domination.

By no stretch of the imagination could Japan be accused of spreading democratic ideas. All the natives she worked with supported the Axis—nominally, at least. In each country she tried to combine all factions into a single party amenable to her wishes. The masses and their problems figured little in her calculations, except for propaganda. Japan drew to her banner the opportunists and unemployed bureaucrats, to help run the countries: the riff-raff and gangsters for policemen and "soldiers," and the sultans and princes and *sawbwas* who had helped the previous rulers. But she could not reward her puppets as handsomely as the more mature British and Dutch systems were able to do. On the contrary, she had to squeeze them frightfully. As an indication, Japan's 1943-44 budget anticipated 3,300 million yen from Java alone—which obviously would be extracted in the form of raw materials and booty for which she could send little or nothing in return.

Honest nationalists among the pro-natives are doubtless by now disillusioned and fully aware of the contradictions between Japanese propaganda and Japanese performance. But some cling on, as in Burma, in the hope of acquiring more political power as Japan's position grows worse, or of securing arms. Some also support the Japs because they cannot see the alternative—the return of European imperialism—as offering any great advantages either.

The Allies can derive some comfort from such knowledge. Many of Japan's "converts," and all the bureaucrats, will turn coat as soon as it is safe to do so. The British also have Burmans and Malays working for them and so have the Dutch their Javanese agents. The Free French are planning to organize guerrillas in Indo-China if and when the Japs disband the French Army there. On the Burma border the anti-Burmese tribes people are on our side and they are proving to be useful allies. Our best friends in this area are probably the ten million Chinese scattered across Southeast Asia—valuable especially in Thailand. The Thai Army itself would probably revolt against Japan, given a good opportunity.

There is also a growing underground movement in all the Jap-occupied areas, organized by native Communists—in China,

Burma, Thailand and Malaya; and even in the Philippines, to some extent. In Thailand, Malaya and Java the leadership is chiefly Chinese; in Burma it is influenced by the Indian Communist Party. As in Europe, however, the Allies are reluctant to support Communist-led guerrillas. In Southeast Asia, as in China, we had no military liaison with them at all. They arm themselves only as the Chinese Communists do—by attacks on their enemies.

While the Japanese may fail to build up native nationalism as an ally of great military importance, it does not follow that we shall get much help from the populace, or find any Yugoslavs, Greeks, Czechs or Fighting French among them—except in the Philippines. It has to be admitted that there is little evidence to show that colonial peoples identify Europe's return to power with their own liberation. Allied strategy has not found any political means of enlisting broad native support.

Is it still possible that, after the end of the European war, some pronouncement of a Pacific Charter promising self-determination to all the colonial countries, might yet make a bid for such help?

III

Freedom for Asia?

IT IS clear that the war in the Pacific will end in a paradox for Japan. By wrecking her own empire, and not by expanding it, she may write the penultimate chapter of European imperialism in the East. In an effort to hold her conquests Japan may have to mobilize the native populations more thoroughly than has ever happened before, while in order to combat Japan's methods the Allied powers are obliged to arm and train large numbers of Asiatics—Chinese and Indians in particular.

Before they are finally driven from Burma, Malaya, Java and Indo-China the Japanese probably will go much farther in arming the natives, hoping to cause a maximum amount of trouble for

314

the returning Powers. No one should doubt that the Allies can disarm such native forces in Burma, Malaya, Java and elsewhere, but to disarm them militarily is not the same thing as disarming colonial nationalism as a political force. Post-war questions of native political power in all the colonies of Southeast Asia are bound to be posed in dramatic ways quite different from anything in the past.

Once the Japanese have left this part of the world, the contradictions in their teachings may be forgotten by men who will remember their slogans of "liberation from white imperialism." One thing is obvious: the former awe of the white man as master and lord of the machine has gone. In the past the commonest argument used by Europeans to justify their rule was that Asiatics were incompetent to manage machine-age society; they were incapable of governing and defending themselves; they were "just children." But these myths were blasted to bits when the white man failed at the essential tasks of government himself. Asiatics will not forget that an Oriental people in a few weeks defeated all the European colonial powers in Southeast Asia and Indonesia by the superior organization of machines and men. And no one will convince them that these powers could have returned again had it not been for the help of the United States and the victory of Soviet Russia.

China is now a great power only by courtesy of the Big Three; but she will quickly emerge (even if there is a brief interregnum of civil war) as a mighty, regenerative force in Asia. With her sovereignty fully restored for the first time in a century, she could become a graver menace to the whole European colonial system than Japan ever was. Two other Asiatic states have been guaranteed post-war independence: Korea and the Philippines. Thailand will doubtless find her Badoglio and successfully re-establish her sovereignty. Few peoples have acquired greater political experience out of the Far Eastern War than the Burmese, and the British will not easily satisfy these restless people with vague promises of Dominion Status—especially with a powerful and sympathetic China as their neighbor. India and Java will clamor all the louder for equality of treatment with other Asiatic states. And unless a socialist government comes to power in France, offering the possibility of planned colonial progress toward self-government, the Annamites may before long lead another revolt in Indo-China.

315

Nor is it realistic to imagine that the influence of Japan will be obliterated. Shorn of her empire and exploitative rule, her doctrines of "Asiatic co-prosperity" may find a much wider response. It is not to be supposed that the Chinese reject this idea fundamentally or will permanently refuse to co-operate regionally on a plane of true equality with a democratic or socialist Japan—which is the kind of state most likely to emerge from the shambles of the empire. All through Southern Asia the Chinese merchants and workers may in the future demand equality of rights with the Europeans. In Malaya, where Chinese are the majority in many places, they will sooner or later become the real political power of the State. In countries like Java they will eventually combine with native leadership to challenge the supremacy of the small Dutch minority.

Such are the implications which underlie the Allied return to the East. Whether recognition is made of them through pronouncement of a Pacific Charter now, or is deferred till later, whether it is declared that the Oriental world, as well as Europe, cannot remain "half slave and half free," to quote Mr. Sumner Welles, and that "the right of self-determination by peoples is not limited by divine warrant, nor by the Atlantic Charter, to the white race," will not change those facts.

These peoples will, not all at once and not all on the same level, but soon and inevitably and with increasing vigor and success against attempts to preserve antiquated empires in the East, these peoples will demand here the same freedoms and the same rights of self-determination which the master countries claim for themselves in Europe, and which no one will pretend they have enjoyed in the past.

"But they are not ready for self-government," the returning white men say of their subjects. When will they be ready? History's answer is that so far men have proved that "readiness" solely by armed struggle. Is that then to remain true in the future, is there no peaceful way to resolve class and racial antagonisms, is there no way to preserve the useful political framework of the old empires within former boundaries?

Yes, there is the way of planned social, economic, political and cultural progress for the colonial areas. All that is required is for a ruling group to start off with the idea of relinquishing power to the people, increasing the natives' wealth, and raising their cultural level, without reference to whether it pays immediate dividends to absentee foreign shareholders, or high profits to resident foreign business men and their ruling class. It is necessary to recognize that the only excuse for foreign rule now is to organize native society so as to enrich the lives of the producers and to recognize that exports and imports are desirable only as they help to increase the welfare of the producers, the mass of the people.

Once you established the paramountcy of such principles, development could go forward very rapidly. What is required is a plan for each colony which in broad outline would include these features: (1) an immediate declaration that the Four Freedoms apply here as much as in Europe; (2) a promise of self-determination, following completion of a definitely limited period—say, ten to fifteen years—of mass political training in democratic tradition and processes, in preparation for full self-government; (3) compulsory education for all, consisting of an integration of national culture and modern science, in a system designed speedily to secure from the younger generation the numbers of educators, engineers, technicians, scientists and other specialists needed for fulfillment of the national plan; (4) industrialization for the purpose of developing national resources and raw materials, and modernization of agriculture, in such a way as to lift the people from coolie-level existence to a decent standard of living, and to achieve a balanced economy reasonably free from dependence on foreign markets or foreign sources for the social, economic and political well-being of the nation.

That sounds simple enough, doesn't it? And so it would be, provided you had a ruling class which really believed in the ends indicated. It is also a kind of development which promises the richest future for American and European business men interested in the world market. It is pertinent for American capitalism in particular, for it is doubtful if any such plans could succeed without its wholehearted backing. One of the main causes of past depressions and unemployment under capitalism was the stagnation of big regions of the world market by a colonial system which embraced a billion people in backward undeveloped areas of Asia and Africa, where progress could not keep step with the scientific growth and technological expansion of production elsewhere.

Under the old *laissez-faire* imperialism those regions failed to develop their resources and failed to enlarge the world market. No one should have been surprised that a densely populated industrialized island nation like Japan aspired to expand into such large, underpopulated regions as neighboring Mindanao, Celebes, Borneo, New Guinea and Sumatra, for example, which could easily accommodate another one or two hundred million people if they were economically developed. They were a standing invitation to aggression simply because history is dynamic and abhors stagnation and vacuums.

The modernization of such countries, and other parts of the Philippines and East Indies, as well as of India, Burma, China, Thailand, Indo-China and Malaya, is essential to make the world safe for a democratic way of life. It is essential to the regeneration of the world market, without which capitalism eventually languishes and either gives way to socialism, fascism, or war. By planning of growth, and with the help of Anglo-American capital and technique on a large scale, the wealth and production of the whole colonial world could be increased from five to ten times in a decade or so and prosperity be assured for a long time to come.

But will such a reasonable solution be adopted now or at the close of the fracas? Will the interested powers be able to reconcile different class and national interests and enforce a planned development? The "colonial problem" can no longer be the exclusive concern of any one country whose early adventurers and conquerors happened to be the first to carry modern guns and machines to these areas and impose their will and domination. It is now a common problem of all nations, but particularly of those which carry the heaviest responsibilities for maintaining world security and livelihood. Will Britain and the United States in particular see the need for it and take the lead in organizing the forces to achieve it? That depends on whether we can have planned development, planned production and distribution at home. And it also depends on whether or not a world federation, or central council of nations, can be set up where ideas, needs, means and ends, can be reconciled in planning for the common growth of mankind.

318

INDEX

Chou En-lai, 300
Christian Science Monitor, 67
Chuikov, Lieutenant-General V. J., 121, 127-130, 135
Churchill, Winston, 16, 23, 24, 26, 27, 30, 47, 48, 49, 64, 191, 215, 243, 246, 247, 249, 250, 262, 266, 302, 307, 308, 309
Chu Teh, General, 286, 295
Clapper, Raymond, 6
Clark-Kerr, Sir Archibald, 43
Communist International, 209
Congress, Indian National, 11, 14, 21, 22, 24, 28, 29, 36, 41, 44, 45-53, 261
Coy, Wayne, 6
Cripps, Sir Stafford, 23, 24, 25, 26, 27, 29, 30, 41, 45
Curzon, Lord, 32, 248, 249, 250
Critique of China's Destiny, 281 *n.*

Daily Herald (London), 76
Daily Mirror (London), 170
Daniels, Lieutenant-General Adler von, 121
Davies, John, 27, 29, 32
Davis, Elmer, 238
Dimitriu, Brigadier-General Homilu, 121
Disney, Walt, 238
Dix, Dorothy, 49
Dohlpur, Maharajah of, 17, 18
Dorman-Smith, Sir Reginald, 33
Drebber, Major-General Moritz von, 121, 122, 123
Dreiser, Theodore, 238, 239
Dreyfus, Louis, 59
Duranty, Walter, 67
Dutt, R. Palme, 17 *n.*

Eisenhower, General Dwight, 252
Emeny, Guy, 46
Engels, Friedrich, 92, 218

Falkenhausen, General von, 207

Fawzia, Queen, 62
Faymonville, General Philip, 211
Fersman, 147
Ford, Henry, 93
Foundations of Modern India, 16 *n.*
Fuad, King, 7

Gagalbhoy, Mafatlal, 54
Galkinova, Vera, 184
Gandhi, Devadas, 28
Gandhi, Mahatma, 3, 11, 12, 13, 14, 21, 22, 23, 25, 27, 31, 41, 43, 44, 45, 46, 47, 48, 49, 50, 51, 52, 54, 56, 59, 151, 152, 261, 262, 263, 295, 311
Gandhi, Teroz, 14
Gegen-Khan, Bogdo, 196
George, Lloyd, 249, 250
Ghoram, Ahmed, 63
Gilmore, Eddy, 73, 74, 80
God Is My Co-Pilot, 38
Goebbels, Joseph, 100, 191, 249
Goering, Hermann, 191
Gogol, Nicolai, 92, 179
Grady, Henry, 33
Graebner, Walter, 173
Grant, Dr. John, 36
Grant, Ulysses S., 295
Gumbil, 154-155
Guriev, Major-General, 134, 135, 136, 202
Gurievitch, Sam, 75

Halder, General Franz, 192
Halifax, Lord, 16
Hall, G. Martel, 295
Hannibal, 120
Han Ying, General, 298
Harriman, Averell, 238
Harris, Air Marshal, 307
Haynes, Brigadier-General Caleb V., 39
Hedin, Sven, 63
Hemingway, Ernest, 238, 239

Merrill, Brigadier-General Frank, 267, 271
Mikhailovich, General, 286
Mikhailovna, Anna, 137, 138
Mikoyan, A. I., 235, 236
Mishakova, Olga, 150, 151, 182, 224 *n.*, 238
Mitchell, Kate L., 16 *n.*
Molotov, Premier V., 184, 207, 246, 250
Moltke, Helmuth von, 190
Morgan, J. P., 93
Moslem League, 28, 30, 41, 54, 261
Mother Russia, 158
Mountbatten, Lord Louis, 267, 306, 307
Mussolini, Benito, 171, 217, 269

Naidu, Sarojinu, 29, 36
Naidu, Mrs. Sarojinu, 46
Nawanagar, Jam Sahib of, 19
Nehru, Indra, 14
Nehru, Jawarhalal, 12, 13, 14, 22, 23, 25, 26, 29, 30, 31, 33, 39 *f.*, 43, 46, 47, 48, 50, 52, 56, 151, 261, 311
Nehru, Motilal, 14, 29
Nehru, Rajan, 19
Nehru, Ratan, 18
Nelson, Donald, 146
New Republic, The, 69 *n.*
News-Chronicle (London), 46
Nichol, Dave, 119, 125
Nicolai, Alexander, 102
Nimitz, Admiral, 286, 304

Ogoltsov, Sergei, 230
Osipov, Alexandrovich, 80

Pacific Ocean, The, 239
Pahlavi, Riza Shah, 60, 61, 63
Pares, Sir Bernard, 248 *n.*
Pasha, Nahas, 7
Patel, Sardar Vallahbhai, 31, 52, 54

Paulus, Marshal Frederick von, 119, 123, 124, 132, 133
Pavlichenko, Ludmilla, 182
Peng Teh-huai, 174, 297
Pétain, Marshal, 214, 248
Peter, King, 286
Petrov, Eugene, 240
Pettit, Sir Dinshaw, 55
PM, 6
Popov, Major-General N. C., 82, 83, 84
Popular Physics, 239
Prasad, Rajendra, 31
Pravda, 150, 161
Pregnesky, Georgi Alexandrovich, 145
Problem of India, The, 17 *n.*
Pushkin, Alexander, 92, 239
Pushnestikov, Babushka, 89-93
Pushnestikov, Guy, 89-93
Pushnestikov, Motka, 89-93, 127

Rajagopalacharia, Chakravarti, 28, 29, 54
Rajagopalacharia, Lakshmi, 28
Ram, Tulsi, 263, 264
Red Star Over China, 174
Reindhardt, 101
Reynolds, Quentin, 173
Ribbentrop, Joachim von, 77
Richardson, Major, 38
Rickenbacker, Eddie, 242, 273
Rigley, General, 63
Riza, Mohammed, 62
Robertson, Ben, 6, 7
Rodimstev, Major-General, 93, 130, 132
Rogov, Vladimir, 209, 210
Rokossovsky, Colonel-General K. K., 119, 120
Rommel, General Erwin, 100
Romero, Cesar, 62
Roosevelt, Franklin Delano, 4, 6, 48, 64, 93, 191, 238, 242, 246, 249, 266, 308